In Search of
the New Testament Church

The Baptist Story

Baptists
History, Literature, Theology, Hymns
General editor: *Walter B. Shurden*, Mercer University.

This series explores Baptists in all facets of Baptist life and thought. Open-ended and inclusive, this series seeks to publish works that advance understanding of where Baptists are and where they are tending. It will promote the exploration and investigation of Baptist history; publish classics of Baptist literature, including letters, diaries, and other writings; offer analyses of Baptist theologies; and examine the role of Baptists in societies and cultures both in the USA and around the world.

MERCER
UNIVERSITY PRESS

Endowed by
TOM WATSON BROWN
and
THE WATSON-BROWN FOUNDATION, INC.

In Search of
the New Testament Church

The Baptist Story

by
C. Douglas Weaver

Mercer University Press
Macon, Georgia USA
June 2008

ISBN 978-0-88146-106-0 MUP/H653 (casebound w/jacket)
ISBN 978-0-88146-105-3 MUP/P346 (perfectbound)

The paper used in this publication meets the minimum requirements
of American National Standard for Information Sciences—
Permanence of Paper for Printed Library Materials,
ANSI Z39.48–1984.

Library of Congress Cataloging-in-Publication Data

Weaver, C. Douglas.
    In search of the New Testament church : the Baptist story /
by C. Douglas Weaver. — 1st ed.
    p.   cm.
    Includes bibliographical references (p. 254) and index.
    ISBN-13: 978-0-88146-106-0 (hardback : alk. paper)
    ISBN-10: 0-88146-106-7 (hardback : alk. paper)
    ISBN-13: 978-0-88146-105-3 (pbk. : alk. paper)
    ISBN-10: 0-88146-105-9 (pbk. : alk. paper)
    1. Baptists—United States—History. 2. United States—Church history.
I. Title.
    BX6235.W43 2008
    286.0973--dc22

                                                    2008012724

Contents

Acknowledgments

Passion for the Baptist heritage is alive and well. Since 2002, I have participated in the annual Baptist Classics Seminar for Baptist Historians sponsored by the Center for Baptist Studies at Mercer University. Special thanks go to Walter B. Shurden for organizing these seminars. The readings and discussions with other historians have proved invaluable for me in reflecting upon and dialoguing about the Baptist story. Regular participants have included Sherri Adams, Wm. Loyd Allen, Rosalie Beck, Carolyn Blevins, Jimmy Byrd, Charles Deweese, Pamela Durso, Darlene Flaming, Bruce Gourley, Mel Hawkins, Carol Holcomb, Glenn Jonas, Sandy Martin, Rob Nash, Brent Walker, and Mark Wilson. Guests have included Bill Brackney, Wayne Flynt, Edwin Gaustad, and Bill Leonard. I never tire of talking and learning Baptist history with these colleagues. I am especially grateful to Dr. Shurden for his insights and for his gathering this community of scholars/friends.

Many persons have assisted my research and writing. The following persons read all or portions of the manuscript and made helpful comments: Pamela Durso, Nathan Finn, and Walter Shurden, as well as Baylor Ph.D. candidates in church history John Essick, Bracy Hill, and Michael Sciretti. Other graduate students assisted in other ways: Jesse Hoover, Alicia Myers, Keith Reich, Roy Millhouse, Marc Nicholas, Kyle Welty, and Brandon Frick. Paul Patterson, administrative associate in the Department of Religion, helped proofread and provided other assistance.

I am grateful for students at Baylor University and G. W. Truett Theological Seminary who have heard some of this material in their classes. Bill Bellinger, chair of the Department of Religion at Baylor University, and colleagues in the department have been supportive of my research. I am indebted to Marc Jolley, director of Mercer University Press, for his interest in publishing this book and for his interest in the Baptist heritage, which is demonstrated in the Press's commitment to the publication of works on Baptists.

I learned the historian's craft from Glenn Hinson, Bill Leonard, and "Buddy" Shurden. They are exceptional scholars and deeply committed to the ministry of the church. They taught a love for the Baptist heritage without losing sight of the formative influences of the larger Christian tradition. Through the years they have been there as mentors and friends, whether it be academic projects or life's journey.

Family members always deserve kudos for their love and support during the research and writing of a manuscript. To Pat, Aaron, Andrea, and Camden, I am forever grateful.

As biblical scholars will tell you, there never was *one* "New Testament church." Still, the Baptist story, in all its diversity, reveals a people who were committed to the sacredness of the individual conscience and a congregational community. Whatever else it meant, a New Testament church usually indicated a group of believers who insisted upon the freedom to practice the Christian faith voluntarily, according to the dictates of conscience and without coercion from any government or "established" church.

To anyone who believes the Baptist story—successes and embarrassments, depending upon your perspective—is worth learning, this book is dedicated.

Chapter 1

Early English Baptists: The Search for the New Testament Church Begins

Baptists have no recognizable founder like Martin Luther or John Calvin or John Wesley. Some Baptists have laid claim—to the neglect of historical accuracy—to John the Baptist of the New Testament as their founder. Baptists do have John Smyth and Thomas Helwys and roots in seventeenth-century English-Separatist Puritanism. The lack of well-known founders says something about how Baptists have treated history, but it also is ironically fitting. The earliest Baptist church was formed because the first Baptists believed that a fresh start was necessary. No human founder of a church had proved faithful. No succession from a church founder had produced a genuine body of Christ. All so-called Christian churches were corrupted because they did not follow the model for a true church outlined in the New Testament. The Puritans had claimed that they were purifying the church, but they had failed. When John Smyth organized the first Baptist church, the search for a pure church, a true church that embodied the New Testament blueprint, was the underlying motive for leaving Puritan Separatism. Smyth wanted to establish *the* New Testament church, and believer's baptism was the link to the New Testament model.

Other Christian groups, of course, have been created in search of the New Testament church. The Puritans themselves believed they were purifying the Church of England to complete the promise of the Protestant Reformation for an authentic biblical community of faith. Other examples of the search for genuine New Testament Christianity abound. For example, the Christian Church (nineteenth century) and Pentecostalism (twentieth century) were born as embodiments of the primitive faith of the earliest Christian believers.

To interpret Baptist history as a search for the New Testament church allows the reader to see the passion—some would say obsession—of Baptists for being faithful to, and in most cases, duplicating what they believed were the indispensable elements of, a biblical faith. A proper ecclesiology—Baptists maintained that the New Testament gave clear guidelines for how to be the "body of Christ"—was foundational to the pure witness of the gospel. Simply put, when Baptists justified the distinctives of the faith, they looked to the Bible, especially the New Testament, for answers. Baptists were biblicists. They believed that their motives were religious. Of course historians recognize that historical context—factors that include social, cultural, political, and other influences—is involved and thus key to understanding the Baptist (or any) story. People, whether they recognize it or not, usually read the Bible through the lenses of their culture, their political and economic situation, and so forth.

Consequently, this book contends that to get at the heart of the Baptist story/stories, the reader needs lenses that look for the ways Baptists have attempted to embody the New Testament church. A helpful way to read Baptist history, then, is to say, "Baptists did this because they believed the Bible or the New Testament church commanded it. Now let's also ask what else was going on that explains why they did what they did."

Historical Setting

The Baptist heritage is one of the ongoing stories of the Protestant Reformation. The Reformation in England was birthed when King Henry VIII broke from Roman Catholicism in 1534 and proclaimed himself to be head of the Church of England. Henry was essentially Catholic in doctrine and thus Protestant thought grew slowly. During the attempted reversion to Catholicism in the reign of Queen Mary ("Bloody Mary"), numerous Protestants were exiled. These "Marian exiles" returned during the reign of Queen Elizabeth I (1558–1603). Elizabeth's reign was a *via media* that demanded uniformity in worship through the required use of the *Book of Common Prayer* and in a broadly defined Protestant doctrinal consensus through required subscription to the *Thirty-Nine Articles* (1563). Protestants had hoped for more progress.

In reaction to the "Elizabethan settlement," Puritanism developed within the Church of England in an attempt to purify the faith of any remaining elements of "popery." Puritans were diverse in their goals. The earliest episcopal-styled Puritans affirmed Anglicanism's hierarchical structure of church officers (archbishop, bishop), but sought reform in external matters, especially in the liturgy. They opposed the use of a wedding ring, kneeling at the communion table, vestments worn by the clergy, and the celebration of Christmas, all because these elements were vestiges of the "bogus" system of sacraments in the "false" church of Catholicism.

Puritans after 1570 attacked the episcopal form of church government as unbiblical. Following the teachings of the reformer John Calvin, these were presbyterian-styled Puritans who asserted that presbyterian church government was the divine pattern for congregations. Independent Puritans felt that the church was not responsive to reform, but they still considered the Church of England a true church and felt no need to separate from it.

The most radical group of Puritans was the Separatists. Robert Browne is acknowledged as the "father" of the Separatist movement with his rallying cry, "Reformation without tarrying for anie!" (1582). These Puritans separated from the Church of England because they felt it was corrupted and no longer capable of being reformed. Most Separatists emphasized the necessity of a conscious conversion experience (personal confession of faith) and thus a "regenerate church membership." The church was to be a body of believers committed to God and each other in covenant relationships. Most Separatists also touted congregational church governance. The local church made its own decisions without interference from external bodies like a presbytery or an episcopal hierarchy.

English kings often persecuted the Puritans. King James I asserted the divine right of kings, enforced conformity to Anglicanism and its *Book of Common Prayer* in worship, and irritated Puritans when he—to their way of thinking—defied the Ten Commandments with the promotion of sports on Sunday. Persecution of dissenters was intense during the reign of King James's son, King Charles I. Charles's archbishop of Canturbury, William Laud, aggressively sought to stifle Puritans. During several years of persecution, especially in the early seventeenth century, many Puritans left England for Holland and/or America.

Puritans attained some power and influence during the era of "English Civil War" in the 1640s. Presbyterianism was given support by the "protectorate" of Oliver Cromwell. The Westminster Assembly put together the Westminster Confession of 1646, a summary of faith that adhered to the theology of the Protestant reformer, John Calvin. Baptists and other dissenters supported Cromwell and fought in his army. Other sects also achieved some freedom to worship during the Cromwellian era.

A final wave of intense persecution against Baptists and other "nonconformists" occurred when England restored its monarchy, and King Charles II assumed the throne in 1660. The repressive Clarendon Code required a return to Anglicanism which meant forced conformity to worship according to the *Book of Common Prayer*. Unlicensed preaching and "illegal" worship services were tickets to government retaliation. For example, the Baptist John Bunyan was imprisoned for illegal preaching. Despite having four young children (one was blind), he refused to promise that he would stop preaching. Consequently, he served twelve years in jail (1660–1672). His commitment became legendary, and after he was released 3,000 persons flocked to hear him preach at Bedford each Sunday. In his later devotional classic, *Pilgrim's Progress* (1678), Bunyan spoke of the martyred character, "Faithful," and revealed something of the psyche of the dissenter:

> When faithless ones with all their vain delights
> Are crying out under their hellish plights,
> Sing, Faithful, sing, and let thy name survive,
> For though they killed thee, thou art yet alive.

The Act of Toleration in 1689 did not provide full religious liberty for Baptists and other English dissenters, but a new day had dawned. They had survived.

General Baptists

Baptist beginnings produced a variety of Baptist groups. The most prominent and influential were the General Baptists and the Particular Baptists. John Smyth's spiritual journey was all across the map, but he slowed down enough to become a Baptist and form the first-ever Baptist congregation.

John Smyth. The Christian journey of John Smyth revealed a constant and restless search for the New Testament church. He was an Anglican, then a Puritan within the Anglican Church, then a Separatist-Puritan, then a Baptist, and finally sought membership in a Mennonite church. Smyth was educated at Cambridge and later ordained in the Church of England (1594). His Puritan sympathies evidently began during his student years at Christ's College, the hotbed of Puritan sympathy at Cambridge. Subsequently, he served as a lecturer in Lincoln but was dismissed for "personal preaching." At this time he was a Puritan in theology: he affirmed Calvinism and criticized Separatists for opposing the practice of formal worship. However, Smyth's search for a true church soon carried him into Separatism.

In 1606, Smyth joined a Separatist congregation at Gainsborough and was soon invited to become the pastor. Many Separatists, in an environment of harassment and persecution from King James, fled to Holland. In 1608, Smyth's congregation went to Amsterdam and worshipped at a Mennonite bakehouse. Another congregation, led by John Robinson, left Gainsborough and settled in Amsterdam briefly before leaving for America. They are now known as the Pilgrims.

While a Separatist, Smyth had conflict with another Separatist leader, Francis Johnson, leader of the "Ancient Church" and Smyth's former teacher at Cambridge. Smyth had adopted congregational church governance with a twofold church-office structure (pastor, deacons) as opposed to the use of elders by Johnson. As a typical Separatist, Smyth emphasized the idea of the "gathered church," a body of professing believers that was bound together in a voluntary covenant of faith and obedience. Governing authority within the church belonged to the members of the congregation because they were participants in the covenant. The test of a regenerate church membership was a visible faith. Smyth (and other Separatists) wanted a regenerate church to model itself after the New Testament church.

Smyth's congregation adopted several practices to avoid limiting the movement of the Holy Spirit as Smyth felt Johnson's version of the New Testament church was doing. Smyth refused offerings from the unconverted and the reading of the English Bible in worship. (The reading of Scripture in the original languages was allowed to prepare for worship.) Preaching and prayer were to be spontaneous, at the direction of the Spirit. However, Smyth soon decided that his church did not yet model a New Testament congregation.

The issue was infant baptism. Traditionally, Separatists had discussed the validity of baptism in the "false" Church of England, but had not abandoned their infant baptism, in part because they did not want be associated with the "rebaptism" of the Anabaptists, the most maligned group of the Reformation. However, Smyth's search for the true church led him to the conclusion that there was no biblical basis for infant baptism. Baptism of believers—those old enough to profess their faith voluntarily— rather than a covenant, was the New Testament method of constituting a church. The sacrament of baptism was the initiation rite—commanded by Jesus—into a New Testament church.

Having concluded that no genuine New Testament church existed, Smyth disbanded his own congregation of about forty persons, baptized himself by pouring (effusion), and then baptized his fellow believers into a new church—what is acknowledged as the first "Baptist" church in history. (Thus Smyth earned the moniker "Se-Baptist," that is, self-baptizer, one who baptizes himself. Smyth's followers are even occasionally called "Se-Baptists.") Smyth's Separatist colleagues were shocked, but Smyth affirmed that no rebaptism had occurred since infant baptism was not real baptism.

In the *Character of the Beast* (1609), Smyth used the typically harsh rhetoric of polemics to criticize Separatists and defend his Baptist position. According to Smyth, Separatists possessed the "mark of the beast"—infant baptism—which meant that their churches were illegitimate. As a result, Separatists were "a harlot" like their grandmother, Rome, and their mother, the Church of England. Smyth also attacked the Separatist idea that infant baptism was the seal of the New Testament covenant that corresponded to circumcision as the seal of the Old Testament covenant. God had made two covenants with Abraham, Smyth asserted. Circumcision was the seal of the covenant for Abraham's "carnal seed," but the covenant with his "spiritual seed" was based on faith.

The New Testament did not link circumcision with infant baptism, according to Smyth. Baptism was an outward profession of the inward conversion that God had already effected upon a believer's heart. It followed the sealing of the Spirit, was the basis for church membership, and served as a voluntary demonstration of belief. For the church to be pure—regenerate—infants must be excluded from membership because they were incapable of expressing faith and repentance, the conditions of obedience in God's spiritual covenant with the church.

In 1610, Smyth published *A Short Confession*, and two years later (after Smyth's death), his followers produced another confession (of 100+ articles) that reflected his views. In earlier phases of his ministry, Smyth had relied on the Calvinistic understanding that a civil magistrate should help keep the church pure by punishing heretics with the sword of the state. It was a type of union of church and state in which the church provided society with a common faith, and infant baptism was entrance into both church and society. In the 1612 confession, a strong affirmation of religious liberty (the first by an Englishman) was advocated. Magistrates were to handle civil affairs and should "leave the Christian religion free, to every man his conscience."

Beginning with the Baptist phase of his life, Smyth also rejected the doctrines of Calvinism for Arminian beliefs. He rejected original sin, irresistible grace, and double predestination, and affirmed the possibility of a believer losing his or her salvation. Smyth's rejection of limited atonement in favor of a general atonement—Christ died for all persons and thus salvation was available to all—was the reason these earliest Baptists were eventually called General Baptists.

Thomas Helwys. The Baptist story started with John Smyth, but it quickly shifted to Thomas Helwys. Helwys was a wealthy layperson in Smyth's congregation who most likely funded the group's journey from England to Amsterdam. Helwys led a split of ten persons from Smyth's congregation after Smyth pushed the larger congregation to affiliate with the Mennonites. Smyth had decided that baptizing himself was a mistake after learning more about the Mennonites. They appeared to be a true "believer's church" formed on the basis of believer's baptism. Smyth thus opted for the principle of "succession," that is, if a genuine church existed, then baptism should be received from that church. Helwys strongly opposed the necessity of succession. Helwys pointed to the example of the unbaptized John the Baptist who preached the necessity of New Testament baptism for repentance, and he cautioned the Mennonites to distance themselves from Smyth. (The Smyth congregation, after his death in 1612, eventually joined the Mennonites, probably in 1615.) According to Helwys, the need for ministerial succession was "Jewish and ceremonial," an Old Testament practice not binding upon New Testament believers. The creation of a New Testament church was dependent only upon faithfulness to biblical instructions.

In 1612, Helwys and his small group returned to England and established the first Baptist church on English soil at Spitalsfield outside London. They wanted to return home and did not want their children to be Dutch. Furthermore, the English needed the true gospel. The group recognized the risks of returning: during their time in Holland, Helwys's wife, Joan, had been imprisoned in England for her faith. In England, the young congregation emphasized many features that have for four centuries continued to describe a Baptist identity for most Baptists. In *A Declaration of English People Remaining at Amsterdam* (1610), Helwys advocated

- regenerate church membership based on personal conversion and believer's baptism (the method of the "primitive institution")
- the independence of each local church ("as one congregacion has Christ, so hath all . . . no church ought to challenge anie prerogative over anie other")
- congregational church governance
- support for complete religious liberty
- each church should select its own ministers; pastors and deacons were the biblical church officers

Women were "deacons" in Helwys's congregation ("deaconesses" in Smyth's), but this facet of ministry soon became controversial in Baptist life.

In clear contrast to the Mennonites, Helwys believed that a Christian could be a magistrate, take oaths, and support "just war" rather than pacifism. The congregation at Spitalsfield also promoted Arminian theology and thus initiated the General Baptist tradition in England. Some scholars have suggested that both Smyth and Helwys, in reaction to the coercion of conscience, accepted the view of a general atonement which gave some role to free will to respond to God's initiative of grace. John Murton, a colleague of Smyth and Helwys in Holland, and Helwys' successor at Spitalsfield, articulated a strong Arminian view of free will and he affirmed that the Spirit of God was given to each individual to understand and interpret the Scriptures.

In 1611/1612, Helwys wrote *A Short Declaration on the Mistery of Iniquity*. He utilized a fascination with apocalyptic "end-times" imagery to describe persons who claimed to be Christian, but did not affirm believer's baptism. He called Catholicism the "mistery of iniquity" and the beast of the Book of Revelation. The Church of England was the image of the beast. Puritans had a false profession and were "unreformed" for their failure to leave the Church of England. Congregationalism, not the Presbyterianism of the Puritans, was the New Testament method of church government. Separatism, Helwys' most recent affiliation before becoming Baptist, was also a "false profession" of a "false Christ." Bluntly, Helwys said that the Separatists' adherence to infant baptism meant that they were "infidels and unbelievers."

The *Mistery of Iniquity* is best known as the first treatise in England that called for complete religious liberty. Helwys directly challenged the role of the state in the affairs of the church. He berated the state Anglican Church for demanding conformity in worship. He also found it contradictory that the church's "Lord Bishops" allowed common people to have access to the Scriptures yet demanded conformity in interpreting them. According to Helwys, believers must be free to read and understand the Bible for themselves. Some scholars have noted that Helwys's constant derisive use of the titles of the state church officers ("Lords Spiritual," "Reverend Fathers") reflected his belief that they were attempting to deny the sovereignty and glory of God in the church.

Writing with the flair of a biblical prophet, Helwys challenged King James. In an inscription (intended for the king) on the inside of the cover of one copy of his treatise, Helwys daringly wrote: "The King is a mortal man and not God therefore hath no power over the immortal souls of his subjects, to make laws and ordinances for them, and to set spiritual lords over them." In the text, Helwys acknowledged the divine right of civil government (according to Romans 13), but said that the king had nothing to do with "God's spiritual kingdom" and "does not have power over subjects' consciences." The King was "but dust and ashes: like every other human being."

Helwys's view of religious freedom was radical for his day: the king dealt with the material sphere but not the spiritual sphere of life. Bluntly stated, every person must be free to follow God according to his or her conscience.

> For men's religion to God is between God and themselves. The king shall not answer for it. Neither may the king be judge between God and man. Let them be heretics, Jews, Turks, or whatever, it pertains not to the earthly power to punish them in the least measure.

For Helwys and early Baptists, individual freedom of conscience was indispensable. Individual believers must have the right to choose their religious beliefs "seeing they only must stand before the judgment seat of God to answer for themselves." This focus on conscience was not a rabid individualism run amok, but was at the heart of what it meant to have genuine faith and be an authentic believer's church. Dissent was tied to fidelity to God. Helwys evidently learned about the lack of religious freedom and the cost of dissent firsthand. In 1612, soon after *The Mistery of Iniquity* appeared, he was imprisoned in London and evidently died there.

Early Baptists wrote more on the subject of religious liberty than any other topic as they confronted persecution. In 1614, Leonard Busher wrote *Religion's Peace: A Plea for Liberty of Conscience*, the first Baptist work dedicated exclusively to the topic of religious liberty. Busher compared forced religion to spiritual rape, an image later popularized in the American colonies by Roger Williams. In 1615, John Murton wrote from prison a work eventually titled *Persecution for Religion Judg'd and Condemn'd*. Murton's treatise was reportedly written on paper smuggled from outside the prison as a milk bottle "stopper." Murton exhorted that the parable of wheat and tares (Matthew 13)—again popularized in the American context by Roger Williams—meant that no attempt should be made to separate genuine and "false" Christians this side of heaven. Persecution, by the state and its established church, of people they considered to be heretical was unbiblical and a usurpation of God's prerogative.

Not every early Baptist writer affirmed the radical notion of absolute religious liberty. For example, in the 1640s, John Toombs allowed a role for a Christian magistrate to deal punitively with polytheists and atheists. Nevertheless, in the midst of persecution, Baptists realized that the separation of church and state was needed to obtain full religious freedom—which would allow them to be faithful to their reading of Scripture and thus able to implement a New Testament church.

Particular Baptists

In the 1630s a second and extremely influential Baptist tradition developed separately and independently of General Baptists. The Particular Baptists were known for their adherence to Calvinism and its doctrine of limited (particular) atonement: salvation through Christ's death on the cross was limited to a particular number of people, the elect that God had chosen without the involvement of human choice before the foundation of the world. Particular Baptists traced their origins to the "Jacob-Lathrop-Jessey" (JLC) Church, a church in London named for its pastors: Henry Jacob, John Lathrop, and Henry Jessey (or Jacie). It was a nonseparating or "semi-separate," independent, congregationalist church that developed during the Puritan movement. Unlike Smyth and Helwys and their followers, the JLC Church was not fiercely opposed to the Church of England.

The JLJ church experienced a series of separations that ultimately culminated in the formation of a Baptist church. The first two separations dealt with the validity of baptism in the Church of England. In 1630, a group, led by a Mr. Dupper, protested the church's nonseparating stance toward the Church of England. They were not opposed to infant baptism, but they did oppose its administration by a member of the Anglican clergy. Consequently, they left the JLC church and formed a Separatist congregation. Further discussion in the JLC Church about baptism administered in a "false" church led to another separation in 1633. A new congregation of about nineteen persons included Samuel Eaton, Mark Luker (who later appeared in the story of Baptists in America), and Richard Blunt. Church records indicated that Eaton and some others received a "further baptism." Most likely they received believer's baptism by pouring. It is uncertain whether they rejected the validity of infant baptism or just baptism administered by a minister from a "false" church.

Discussions about baptism moved from the question of the proper administrator of baptism to the proper recipient of baptism. In 1638, a group of six separated from the JLC church, rejecting infant baptism in favor of believer's baptism. They joined with John Spilsbury, who had become pastor of the Eaton separatist congregation (some historians suggest that the Eaton and Spilsbury groups initially were separate), and affirmed believer's baptism as the basis of a genuine New Testament church. This Spilsbury congregation is acknowledged as the first *Particular* Baptist church.

The traditional reading of Baptist history has attributed the initial adoption of believer's baptism by immersion to the Particular Baptist tradition. The standard interpretation is based on material found in the famous "Kiffin manuscript," which was part of the church records of the JLC congregation. In 1640, the JLC church had separated into two groups, one led by Henry Jessey and one by Praise God Barebone/Barbon. Some members of the Jessey group had decided that New Testament baptism was by "dipping" or immersion. They concluded that the practice of immersion was necessary to recover the biblical meaning of baptism—a sign of the death and resurrection of Jesus. Consequently, Richard Blunt, a member of the Jessey group, went to Holland to learn about immersion since they had no knowledge of it being practiced in England.

Evidently Blunt was baptized by the "Collegiants" (so-called because they called their communities "colleges," but also known as "Waterlander" Mennonites, after the North Holland district of Waterland) or at least received instructions about baptism from them. In 1641, upon his return to England, Blunt baptized a "Mr. Blacklocke" and then the two of them baptized others—about fifty-three persons—from the Jessey and Barebone groups "that ware so minded." Other Calvinistic Baptists did not pursue baptism from an already existing church like the Collegiants. John Spilsbury, pastor of the first Particular Baptist church, adopted immersion, but asserted that reliance upon an existing church was unnecessary. In *God's Ordinance, the Saints Priviledge* (1646), Spilsbury said that Scripture was the only authority necessary to restore immersion as the New Testament practice of baptism. While most Particular Baptists implemented believer's baptism by immersion, a few did not. In 1645, Henry Jacob of the JLC church became a Baptist and practiced open membership: believer's baptism was not demanded for church membership.

Revisions to Early English Baptist History?

Recent scholarship has questioned the traditional reading of Baptist origins that believer's baptism by immersion began in 1641 with the Particular Baptists. An alternate reading is that Edward Barber of London was the first to adopt immersion in 1640 and then Thomas Lambe and his Bell Alley congregation did the same in 1641. After analyzing two calendars used during this era, this revisionist perspective has suggested that the introduction of immersion to the JLJ church by Richard Blunt and Samuel Blacklocke did not occur in 1641 but in January 1642.

The traditional idea that the General Baptists and Particular Baptists were two distinct groups from the outset of their existence—because of their differences regarding the theology of the atonement—also has been challenged. According to revisionists, no direct linkage between the General Baptists of the 1640s back to Smyth and Helwys has been documented adequately. Early Baptist interchurch alignments were more theologically flexible. Thomas Lambe, usually identified as a General Baptist leader of the 1640s, had contact and evidently cooperated with members of the Calvinistic church of John Spilsbury. In 1641, for example, Lambe and some members of Spilsbury's church were arrested together at Whitechapel. In 1642, Lambe wrote *A Treatise of Particular Predestination* which argued for the unique combination of a general atonement and election of particular persons. However, members of his church did not have to affirm a belief in a general atonement. To muddy the waters a bit further, Edward Barber, another identifiable General Baptist of the mid-1640s, was originally a Calvinist.

Recent scholarship has suggested that an identifiable division between Particular Baptists and General Baptists occurred after the publication of the London Confession of 1644 by seven Calvinistic churches in London. Before that time, churches were distinct, not on the basis of theology, but on the basis of the proper method of forming a church. The Blunt and Barber groups both favored the position that John Smyth took regarding baptism when he applied to join the Mennonites: the necessity of ministerial succession was affirmed. In contrast, John Spilsbury and Thomas Lambe— like Thomas Helwys—argued against the necessity of succession. The church as a covenant community had the right to start baptism anew without any connection to a previous church.

Baptist Growth and Baptist Diversity

Whatever the case regarding Baptist divisions along theological lines, after 1644 identifiable Baptist groups—Particular Baptists and General Baptists—existed in England. They both objected to their identification with Anabaptists, and often they were unwilling to cooperate with each other. Scholars have counted forty-seven General Baptist congregations by 1650 and 146 congregations in 1715. The development of a larger denominational identity was evident when they met in their first national assembly in 1654. Particular Baptists had seven congregations in London in 1644. At the time of their first national assembly in 1689, they numbered 197 churches.

In addition to the diversity found in the General and Particular Baptists, other smaller groups impacted Baptist life. Some Baptists were attracted to the heightened "end-time" speculation of radical sectarians during the era of the English Civil War (1642–1651). Some Baptists became "Levellers." Others, including Particular Baptist leader Hanserd Knollys, became involved in the anti-Cromwellian "Fifth Monarchy." This religious-political movement, named after apocalyptic passages in the biblical book of Daniel, sought to usher in the "end-time" kingdom of God—the culmination of the New Testament church—with the violence of the sword. Knollys and others were arrested and the movement dissipated.

Many Seventh Day Baptists were involved in the Fifth Monarchy movement and gained some popularity in the 1650s–1660s. The question of sabbatarianism—the biblical day for worship—had been discussed in religious circles in England since the end of the sixteenth century. Sabbatarians did not believe that the New Testament had ever abrogated the Sabbath worship commanded in the Old Testament in favor of Sunday services.

Some sabbatarians became Baptists, perhaps because they were attracted to the limited atonement emphasis of Particular Baptists. Some Baptists, like the Particular Baptist Henry Jessey, held sabbatarian views but remained in their churches, revealing the possibility of interaction between Seventh Day Baptists and the larger Baptist groups. Biblicism, the literal application of biblical practices, went a step further for sabbatarians than for most Baptists in embodying the New Testament church. An Old Testament practice found in the New Testament needed to be duplicated.

Church Life for Seventeenth-Century English Baptists

Baptism. In Puritan-Separatist thought the church was a covenanted community of believers and their children. The Separatist "A True Confession" (1596) said that infant baptism was one of the "signes and seales of Gods euerlasting couenant" [*sic*], that is, it signified the infants' election through birth in the elect covenant community. John Smyth and the earliest Baptists asserted that infant baptism was incompatible with the doctrine of a regenerate church. In his "A Short Confession of Faith" (1610), Smyth said that the proper subjects for baptism were those "which hear, believe, and with penitent heart receive the doctrines of the Holy Gospel . . . and no unspeaking children." Baptism was to be received only after a profession of faith and repentance.

The earliest Baptists developed an extensive theology of baptism. Proper ecclesiology was inextricably tied to believer's baptism. The regenerate church was a body of believers who freely submitted to baptism. Infant baptism was by necessity excluded because infants were incapable of having a conscious conversion experience. General Baptists especially emphasized that believer's baptism was the initiatory rite into church membership. Beginning with the Particular Baptist "First London Confession of Faith" (1644), both Particular Baptist and General Baptist confessions asserted that the proper New Testament method of believer's baptism was by immersion ("dipping or plunging the whole body under water"). Early Baptists like John Smyth called baptism a sacrament, but a shift to the idea of ordinance (to be baptized because Christ commanded—"ordered" or "ordained"—it) appeared with the First London Confession. Perhaps not surprisingly, given Thomas Helwys's rejection of the necessity of ministerial succession for proper baptism, early Baptists did not insist that only ordained clergy perform baptism. Not a single General Baptist confession discussed the question of the "baptizer" until the "Orthodox Creed" of 1678, but even it said that a "minister or administrator" should baptize. The "Second London Confession" of the Particular Baptists (1677) said that the "qualified" and "called" are the appropriate administrators of baptism. Gradually, baptism was tied to the office of the pastor.

Early Baptists were criticized for their insistence upon believer's baptism by immersion. In 1646, Anglican Daniel Featley ridiculed Baptists for "dipping" and "plunging over head and ears." The name of Baptists was given to the earliest Baptists as a derisive nickname for a people that unnecessarily rebaptized Christians.

Lord's Supper. English Baptists, General and Particular, generally regarded the Lord's Supper as a memorial observance of Jesus' Last Supper. However, the relationship between baptism and the Lord's Supper—the two primary worship rituals for Baptists and other Protestants—was a vexing question. Most early Baptist churches practiced closed communion: the reception of the Lord's Supper was reserved for persons who had submitted to believer's baptism. Controversy arose among Particular Baptists, however, by the latter half of the seventeenth century. While influential leaders like William Kiffin and Hanserd Knollys held to the majority and traditional view of closed communion, Henry Jessey and John Bunyan advocated an open communion policy: believer's baptism was not a prerequisite for participation in the Lord's Supper.

The author of eighty works, John Bunyan was the most prolific Baptist author of the seventeenth century. His *Pilgrim's Progress*, still considered a classic of Christian devotion, sold an amazing 100,000 copies and went through twelve editions in its first decade (1678–1688). In a lesser known work, *Differences in Judgment concerning Water Baptism No Bar to Communion* (1673), Bunyan addressed the issue of baptism and the Lord's Supper. He affirmed believer's baptism, but said that the sacraments were "shadowish or figurative ordinances" and were not the fundamentals of Christianity like faith and holiness. He suggested that his opponents exalted baptism too highly. It was possible, he retorted, to commit idolatry even with God's own appointments. Should the church reject someone that God has not?, Bunyan asked. Consequently, practicing Christians should not be barred from participation in communion. Bunyan's perspective was also personal: he had an infant sprinkled because of his "grieving wife."

William Kiffin, an influential London pastor, countered that baptism was one of the marks of the holy life and the initiation rite into the church. The meaning of Scripture was clear: communion followed believer's baptism and had to be followed exactly. To share the Lord's Supper with persons not scripturally baptized was to compromise biblical truth. In other words, Kiffin tied closed communion to the literal restoration of the New Testament church.

Given the diversity of perspectives in Particular Baptist life, the Second London Confession of 1677 was silent regarding the relationship between baptism and the Lord's Supper. An appendix noted that the silence was an effort to keep peace among the Particular Baptists. Historians have suggested that the insistence on closed communion had become impractical in the midst of persecution of Baptists by government authorities. Still, closed communion remained the dominant perspective regarding Baptist ordinances until the twentieth century.

Other Elements of Worship: Footwashing, Laying on of Hands, and Singing. When the literal restoration of a New Testament church was at stake, practically every element of worship had the potential for conflict. What in the New Testament had to be duplicated to faithfully model the primitive pattern? Since Jesus practiced footwashing on his disciples, John Smyth and subsequent General Baptists practiced it as an ordinance of the church before it finally lapsed among most General Baptists after the eighteenth century. (Some Free Will Baptists and of course most Primitive Baptists still practice foot washing.)

While controversial, many Baptists—most General Baptists and some Particular Baptists—added the laying on of hands to the baptismal ceremony. Based on the six "principles" set down in Hebrews 6:1-2, some Baptists—often referred to as "Six-Principle Baptists"—argued that the reception of the Holy Spirit occurred in a believer's life at the time of laying on of hands after baptism. In 1655, General Baptist John Griffiths wrote *God's Oracle and Christ's Doctrine* in which he asserted that a love for Christ's truth required the repetition of biblical practices. The influential General Baptist "Standard Confession" of 1660 also emphasized that "hands" was a "doctrine of Christ." The most influential General Baptist in the latter half of the seventeenth century, Thomas Grantham, argued in *Christianismus Primitivus* (1674) that "hands" was the primitive biblical ordinance designed to signify the filling of the Holy Spirit in the life of the believer. Consequently, Baptists who insisted on connecting believer's baptism and the "laying on of hands" demonstrated the need to restore the exact method of initiation into a New Testament church.

Singing in church was a contentious issue for both General and Particular Baptists. In describing the primitive New Testament church, General Baptist Thomas Grantham opposed "manmade hymns" as extrabiblical. Only Psalms—the words of God—sung solo by males were permissible since the New Testament only allowed for silent participation by women in worship. Prewritten hymns were reminiscent of prewritten prayers, Grantham lamented, bearing close resemblance to the lifeless formality found in the Anglicans' *Book of Common Prayer*. Consequently, General Baptists strongly opposed congregational singing at their national assembly in 1689.

Most Particular Baptists also were initially opposed to congregational singing. Katherine Sutton did publish a hymn collection in 1663. However,

Benjamin Keach, a former General Baptist, was mainly responsible for successfully introducing hymn singing to English Baptist life. In 1675, at his church at Goat Street, Horsleydown, Keach inserted a hymn at the conclusion of the observance of the Lord's Supper. He contended that this followed the primitive pattern found in the New Testament (Matt. 26:30). In 1690, Keach pushed the issue again when he added the singing of a hymn to the end of each week's service. To ward off critics, he noted that the congregational hymn was a voluntary activity after the official service.

Church member Isaac Marlow led the opposition against Keach's innovations. Using arguments similar to Grantham, Marlow opposed "promiscuous singing"—singing by an audience that included believers and nonbelievers—and he complained that congregational singing permitted women to speak in church. Musical instruments were "unneeded frivolities"; indeed, singing in the Scriptures had been a supernatural gift for the early church but had ceased this side of heaven.

In *The Breach Repaired in God's Worship* (1691), Keach defended congregational singing. Prewritten hymns were not analogous to the prewritten prayers of Anglicanism; they were more like sermons written under God's leadership. Keach found no restrictions against musical instruments in the New Testament. Furthermore, the New Testament church sang. While several members of Keach's church left for a church that did not sing, singing won the day. A flurry of books appeared on the issue and the Particular Baptist national assembly of 1692 had to confront it. Delegates asked churches to refrain from un-Christlike behavior in dealing with the issue. Not having rejected congregational singing, the debate ceased by 1698. Singing was gradually seen as vital to the practice of New Testament Christianity.

Ministry: Messengers. Early English Baptist churches had pastors and deacons. Some Calvinistic Baptists added ruling elders. Both Particular and General Baptists (especially the latter) employed the office of messenger. General Baptist Thomas Grantham was a messenger who wrote a defense of the office (1674). In light of the Baptist aversion of the episcopal government of the state Anglican Church, Grantham was careful not to call the messenger a bishop. Nevertheless, the itinerant messenger was to evangelize, help start churches, ordain ministers, especially in remote areas, as well as correct deficient theology and solve disciplinary problems. The messenger, seen in the example of the Apostle Paul's evangelists, Timothy and Titus, was a divinely instituted office of the New Testament church. However, the tendency toward excessive centralized organization hampered the concept of the messenger: it bore too many similarities to an office of a bishop and lost its effectiveness.

Interdependence of Churches: Associations. Baptist life has accented the independence of the local church more than the interdependence of churches. At the same time, Baptists from their earliest decades of existence sought to practice cooperative work with other Baptist churches in associations. Churches met for fellowship and mutual encouragement and sought doctrinal unity with like-minded churches. "Circular letters" were submitted by local congregations to share information about themselves with other churches. Congregations often sought advice from associations about disciplining members.

Associational gatherings characterized both General and Particular Baptists. In the early 1620s the first General Baptist church at Spitalsfield and four other General Baptist congregations around London had at least informal contact with each other. In 1651, General Baptists organized their first formal association in the region of the Midlands. In 1644, seven Particular Baptist churches of London together published a confession of faith, the so-called "(First) London Baptist Confession of Faith."

General Baptists were more "connectional" than Particular Baptists. They were more willing to focus beyond the local church to a larger General Baptist Church. Thus, they celebrated the Lord's Supper at associational meetings. On the other hand, Particular Baptists believed that communion was reserved for the local church and would speak of Particular Baptist churches rather than a collective Particular Baptist Church.

Confessions of Faith. The spread of Baptist beliefs encountered stiff opposition. Baptists were accused of being theologically unorthodox, politically subversive, and morally impure (doing "unseemly acts" during baptism). One of the most damaging charges was their identification as anarchic "Anabaptists" who denied the concept of a Christian magistrate and who accepted Pelagianism (that is, that a person can take the first step toward God and help save himself via free will). In order to defend themselves against these and other accusations that they considered slanderous, Baptists of the seventeenth century composed numerous confessions of faith. John Smyth, Thomas Helwys, and others wrote personal confessions. Baptist assemblies and associations also developed confessions to represent the views of cooperating churches in a specific region.

Confessions developed statements covering basic Christian doctrines. In doing so, they revealed another purpose of the confessions: to gain acceptance in the larger Christian community by emphasizing Baptist agreement with the accepted orthodoxy that prevailed among Protestant dissenters. For example, the General Baptist "An Orthodox Creed" of 1678 (the only confession to use the word "creed" in the title) went further than other confessions in describing the desire to find unity with other Protestants. It actually called itself a "Protestant Confession of Faith" (the subtitle) and affirmed several historic Christian confessions, such as the Apostles' Creed, and the Nicene and Athanasian Creeds. The inclusion of these ancient statements helped to affirm a belief in the Trinity, a classic belief that was being questioned among some General Baptists.

Confessions also supported the Baptist plea for religious liberty and freedom of conscience. In article 46, the Orthodox Creed enunciated a clear call for religious liberty:

> The Lord Jesus Christ . . . is the only Lord of Conscience . . . he would not have the consciences of men in bondage to or imposed upon by any usurpation, tyranny, or command whatsoever, contrary to his revealed will in his word, which is the only rule he hath left. . . . And the requiring of an implicit faith, and an absolute blind obedience, destroys liberty of conscience. . . .

Two confessions developed by Particular Baptists in London revealed the nature of Baptist confessions and their influence. The First London Confession of 1644, representing seven churches, was the first Particular Baptist confession. In this confession, these early Baptists affirmed that a civil magistracy was an ordinance of God and thus they strongly denied that they were Anabaptist. They also declared that a delineation of their beliefs was needed to vindicate the "truth of Christ." The confession evidently drew upon an earlier document, the Separatist "A True Confession" of 1596 (some scholars also suggest the influence of the theological writings of Menno Simons), but also articulated some Baptist distinctives. It was the first Baptist "group" statement to affirm believer's baptism by immersion— called a representation of the death, burial, and resurrection of Jesus—as the proper mode for New Testament baptism. The confession also affirmed the Baptist distinctive of religious liberty, moving beyond the True Confession of 1596 which admonished the government "to suppress and root out by their authoritie all false ministeries, voluntarie Religions and counterfeyt worship of God."

Another Particular Baptist confession, the Second London Confession of 1677, articulated a stronger Calvinism than previous Baptist confessions.

It reflected the Presbyterian 1646 "Westminster Confession" except in areas of Baptist ecclesiology such as believer's baptism by immersion, which demonstrated the Baptist desire to identity with the orthodoxy of other English dissenters. The standard Calvinistic doctrines in the confession included:

- total depravity and original sin passed down from Adam
- the complete inability of a sinner to approach God in any way at any time or to do anything good unless God's grace preceded the act
- a substitutionary atonement (though the phrase in not used)
- the sovereignty of God that declares nothing at all happens without God's decreed assent, or in the confession's language, "whatever befalls the elect is his appointment"
- the inability of natural revelation to lead to God
- predestination of the elect, including angels

The confession also used the word "infallible" to describe the Scriptures as the "rule of all saving knowledge, faith, and obedience." Typical Protestant anti-Catholicism was expressed: the pope was called the antichrist and the Catholic practice of the Eucharist was "repugnant."

Given the biblicism common among Baptists, it is surprising that Baptist writers used resources other than the Bible and confessions of faith. First-generation writers—who had been university trained—actually cited the church fathers of the Catholic church from Greek and Latin texts. Scripture texts were always cited first, but the church fathers were used to buttress apologetic arguments that persecuted Baptists were doctrinally orthodox. Ironically, church fathers were also cited to highlight that Baptist distinctives were ancient (for example, freedom of conscience and congregationalism) and more biblical than the received traditions of the Catholic and Anglican churches. Second- and third-generation Baptists were less educated and the use of the church fathers declined in frequency and quality. When the laws changed so that dissenters enjoyed toleration, seventeenth-century Baptists ceased to make use of the church fathers.

Church Discipline, Role of Women. English-Baptist women usually followed the traditional pattern of submissiveness to males at home and in church life. They believed the primitive plan of the New Testament demanded it. When it came to church discipline (discussed further in the American context, below), Baptist men pointed to the women as the chief culprits of sin. Women were more often excommunicated—by male disciplinary structures—from church life than men. General Baptist men were admonished to marry only General Baptist women, ·but disciplinary cases involving "mixed marriages" often appeared in minutes of church business sessions.

Some early Baptists, primarily General Baptists, believed the New Testament church had women deacons (or deaconesses) or women preachers. Following 1 Timothy 5, deacons/deaconesses were often widows sixty and older who ministered to other women and were supported by the church. While not ordained, some women preached.

One "she-preacher," as women preachers were called, was Dorothy Hazzard of Bristol. For several years, she maintained a rented house just outside the boundaries of the Anglican parish and stayed there on Sundays to avoid the required church attendance at parish services. On weekdays, Hazzard made the house available as a home for dissenter women so that they could give birth outside the parish and escape the required infant baptism.

Hazzard was also a church planter. A group of dissenters met in her home for Bible study and worship. Occasionally, the group traveled to other places to hear dissenting preachers. It was a daring act to leave the parish minister to hear another minister, especially for Hazzard since the minister was her husband. Hazzard led the group of dissenters to accept believer's baptism, and they organized the Broadmead Baptist Church of Bristol, an important church in subsequent English-Baptist history. She was a pillar of the church for thirty-four years, preaching, leading Bible studies, and practicing personal evangelism.

Women preachers were controversial among Baptists, and their presence was one reason upper-class Anglicans and Presbyterians were scandalized by the activities of Baptists and other lower-class sectarians. For example, in 1646, Presbyterian Thomas Edwards published *Gangraena* and criticized Baptist women preachers as a sign of the spiritual gangrene that radical sectarians brought to family life and social (class) order. A Mrs. Attaway was a Baptist preacher who had left organized religion and had become a "seeker," and who was, in Edwards's view, evidence of sectarian chaos. As Baptist churches became less sectarian, women's opportunities for leadership were usually limited to ministries that involved only women or children.

Baptists and Anabaptists

Historians have given special attention to the influence of Anabaptists upon the earliest Baptists. Opinions vary greatly and are still disputed. Both Baptist and Anabaptist distinctives include believer's baptism, regenerate church membership, and religious liberty. Some historians see extensive Anabaptist influence; others acknowledge little if any direct influence.

Much discussion centers on the story of John Smyth and Thomas Helwys. Most likely Smyth had heard of Mennonite believer's baptism before he baptized himself, but did not seek baptism from them because he felt that they were theologically suspect in other matters. Consequently, he was not significantly influenced by the Mennonites until after his baptism when he began to accept the wider Mennonite theological system. At the same time, Thomas Helwys rejected Mennonite influence in his move from Holland back to England. His theological views also differed: the concept of ministerial succession was rejected, but the taking of oaths was affirmed, as was the right of a civil magistrate to be a church member.

General Baptists in England had some contact with Dutch Mennonites in the era before the English Civil War and Oliver Cromwell. The church of Elias Tookey of London was one example of friendly correspondence. Again, the amount of contact between General Baptists and the Anabaptists is disputed. Some contend that the Tookey congregation was the only example of significant cooperation. However, some later General Baptists were pacifists and refused to take oaths. Yet some scholars do see significant influence of Mennonite "founding father" Menno Simons upon the (First) London Baptist Confession of Faith (1644).

The amount of interplay between the Particular Baptist and Mennonite traditions is also disputed. The traditional story of Particular origins—the story of Richard Blunt traveling to Holland to learn about immersion and perhaps be baptized—suggests at least some influence. However, recent scholarship that rejects the claim that Blunt's baptism was the recovery of immersion in England complicates the story. Questions have also been raised regarding whether Blunt actually received instruction from the Collegiants. An alternative reading of the sources is that Blunt did not receive instruction from John Batten and his Mennonite church; rather, Blunt had contact with a General Baptist living in Holland named Timothy Batte—the abbreviations for John and Timothy were similar—who practiced immersion in England in the 1640s.

Early Baptists claimed over and over again that they were not Anabaptists. Mennonite distinctives—pacifism, and the denial of church membership to a civil magistrate—never found a home in the fledgling Baptist movement. Some Anabaptist-Baptist influence was apparent, but a direct connection between English Separatism and the first Baptists—both

General and Particular Baptists—seems the best way to explain the historical evidence.

Conclusion

Baptist origins were rooted in the Separatist wing of English Puritanism. Baptists were a Reformation people: they were biblicists who read the Bible and sought to restore its practices. They attempted to purify the Puritans who had failed to purify the Church of England. They sought to recover the New Testament church, most fundamentally in their insistence upon a *believer's* church which meant believer's baptism, immersion, regenerate church membership, and local-church independence. Some Baptists went further and insisted upon the duplication of laying on of hands, foot-washing, apostolic-type "messengers," "biblical" singing, and Sabbath worship. At the foundation of early English Baptist beliefs was the sacred importance of the freedom of the individual conscience. Freedom to worship God without state intervention was a persistent call from Baptist voices in an era when the English crown rarely looked kindly at dissenters.

Baptists were diverse. Both Arminian and Calvinist strains developed early. Other smaller groups like the Seventh Day Baptists were a reminder that freedom to follow the Bible brought multiplicity. The Particular Baptist tradition became the strongest Baptist witness. But the General Baptist tradition, through the ideas of founders John Smyth and Thomas Helwys, implanted Baptist ideas that still characterize the Baptist identity in the twenty-first century.

Baptist Origins in America: The Search for the New Testament Church Begins Again

Colonial New England Puritanism provided the context for early Baptist life in America. The earliest Baptists—for example, Roger Williams, John Clarke, Obadiah Holmes, and others—came out of the English Puritan tradition. A few colonial Baptists had been Baptists in England before arriving in the colonies. Most colonial Baptists became Baptists in a fashion similar to English Baptists: they were Puritans who rejected infant baptism for believer's baptism on account of their reading of the New Testament.

Colonial Puritans attempted to create a meticulously detailed Bible-based society. Only Christians—persons who testified of a conscious religious experience—could vote. Puritans believed they were the "redeemer nation," God's chosen people on an "errand into the wilderness." In the words of John Winthrop, the first governor of the Massachusetts Bay Colony, the Puritans were "a city on a hill."

New England Puritans were Calvinists and sought to form a "Holy Commonwealth." They sought to duplicate the covenant theology of the Old Testament theocracy. For this community, infant baptism was the ritual entrance into the covenant relationship. Consequently, the "New England Way" had one official voice. Only the ministers of the established state-supported church were to interpret the Scriptures. Theological dissent or public grievances were anathema. In good Calvinistic fashion, individuals were taught that they could not earn salvation; however, they could find evidence of personal election in their conformity to the laws of the "Holy Commonwealth." Puritans sought religious freedom for themselves, but did not extend it to rabble-rousers. Persons who dared to defy the stated orthodoxy—for example, visionary female preachers like Anne Hutchinson, Quakers like Mary Dyer who spoke of an "inner light" that enabled direct communication with God, Roger Williams who opposed the concept of a "Holy Commonwealth" in favor of an unfettered conscience, and Baptists who defied the laws regarding infant baptism—were heretics who had to be banished from the Massachusetts colony, or worse.

Baptists in Rhode Island

Roger Williams. Roger Williams is best known for his many significant contributions to the formation of American society. In early 1639, he founded the first Baptist church in America in Providence, Rhode Island. He was a pioneer in establishing friendly relations with Native Americans by intentionally treating them with respect and dignity, an attitude uncharacteristic of most colonial Americans. Perhaps he is most famous for founding the colony of Rhode Island on the principles of democracy and complete religious liberty for both believers and nonbelievers.

When Williams left England for America in 1630, he was already committed to the Separatist left wing of Puritanism. He had totally spurned any attachment to the Church of England, and he had left his native land to avoid inevitable imprisonment for religious dissent. His first years in America were tumultuous because of his unwillingness to compromise his principles and because of his evolving understanding of Christianity. Williams refused to "climb the ladder" of success. He rejected a teaching position at the Congregational church in Boston because the Bostonians had not completely separated themselves from the Church of England. His tenure as the minister of a church in Salem was cut short after three months because of pressure from leaders in Boston. A two-year ministry (1631–1633) in Plymouth was initially less contentious. He developed relationships with local Native Americans and learned native languages. In 1633, Williams left Plymouth and returned to Salem to the dismay of Boston leaders who were anxious about his teachings. William Brewster of the Plymouth church worried that Williams' preaching had begun to sound like "Anabaptistry."

By 1635, Puritan leaders decided Williams's religious dissent must cease and desist. They found four of his assertions particularly dangerous. First, Williams had declared that Native Americans were the legitimate owners of the land of the colony. The colonists were stealing the land when they acquired it by English patent. Second, Williams said that a government should not require a "wicked person" to swear or pray. He objected to a political oath that used religious language because he believed it was a form of government-required prayer. Third, Williams's uncompromising separatism offended the colony's authorities. He had exhorted colonists to avoid hearing any of the ministers of the parish assemblies of England. Williams believed that the semiseparate stance of the Boston leaders was a hypocritical "middle walking." The fourth charge against Williams attacked his belief "that the Civill Magistrates power extends only to the Bodies and Goods, and outward State of men." As early as 1631, Williams had taught that the biblical Ten Commandments had two sections. The "first table," the laws regulating a person's relationship with God, could not be governed by the state. Civil authorities could only enforce the "second table," which dealt with social relationships (that is, civil laws). This fourth accusation was the most volatile and demonstrated the real threat that Williams posed to the colony. Colonial authorities feared that if Williams's two-spheres approach was left unchecked, it would undercut and destroy the Puritan concept of a "Holy Commonwealth," and its theocratic union of church and state.

In October 1635, Williams was banished from the Massachusetts Bay Colony. Showing mercy because Williams's wife, Mary, had recently had a second child, the Boston court allowed him to remain within the colony on the condition that he refrain from teaching his "heresy." The gadfly Williams did not comply with the court's order. After being secretly warned by Governor Winthrop of his impending arrest, Williams fled for the "howling wilderness." He found refuge during the difficult winter season with the Native American Narraganset tribe. In June 1636, Williams and several supporters, who had followed after him in the spring, settled in a new home. They purchased land from the Narragansets, who then deeded to them a safer area further from Massachusetts authorities. The infant settlement was named Providence to acknowledge God's care through the wintry ordeal. The colony quickly became a home for "persons distressed of conscience," although Puritan leaders called it a "cesspool." In 1644, Williams received a charter from England recognizing the settlement and consequently, he is called the founder of Rhode Island. Williams is honored for establishing the colony upon the principles of political democracy, the separation of church and state, and complete religious freedom for all people.

Soon after creating an atmosphere of freedom in Rhode Island, Williams helped to start the first Baptist church in America (later called the First Baptist Church of Providence). While the exact date is unknown, the church clearly was established by March 1639. Governor Winthrop of Massachusetts wrote that Williams had become a Baptist, and attributed the conversion to Catherine Scott, the sister of New England's other infamous dissenter, Anne Hutchinson. The Hutchinson family had fled to Rhode Island after Anne was accused of preaching and having visions which she attributed to the Holy Spirit. Most likely Williams had already been exposed to Baptist tenets when he lived in England.

Although the baptismal mode is uncertain (most likely pouring), records show that Ezekiel Holliman baptized Williams who then baptized about twenty other believers to constitute the Providence church as Baptist. The congregation was theologically mixed; most were Calvinist like Williams, but by 1652 a theological shift had occurred and Arminianism became predominant. Following this shift, a Calvinist minority left the church to form another congregation.

Williams's adoption of believer's baptism was a move to restore a New Testament church, but such restorationist desires prompted him to leave not only the fledgling Baptist community, but all institutional religion after about four months. Williams concluded that baptism needed apostolic authority and such authority clearly had been lost in the church's apostate history. No true church was possible until the second coming of Christ restored an apostolic ministry. While Williams became a "seeker," his views on religious liberty helped fuel the Baptist commitment to the separation of church and state to this day.

In the 1640s, Williams published several works that called for complete religious liberty, not simply toleration (which assumes the state has the power to grant permission to worship). In 1644, Williams published what is now his most famous work, *The Bloudy Tenent of Persecution, for Cause of Conscience*. In the book he included a tract on religious freedom by English Baptist John Murton, as well as his own views which were immersed in biblical explanations. Williams repeated himself constantly— as if he knew his readers would not comprehend his message—and used vivid, sometimes violent imagery to drive home his points.

Williams attacked the "Holy Commonwealth" at its very foundation— its reading of Scripture. Puritans like John Cotton, pastor of the Congregational Church in Boston, read the Old Testament literally and applied it literally to his day. The covenant theology of Israel should be duplicated in God's new land, America, the "New Israel." In contrast, Williams's biblicism was strongly eschatological, employed typology (Old Testament events/persons foreshadow more important New Testament realities), and thus fiercely criticized the idea or possibility of a Christian nation. Israel was no longer a pattern for nations to follow; rather, Israel had been fulfilled in the antitype of the church. Williams said that it was tragically ironic that the English Parliament went to great lengths to make Bibles accessible to "the poorest English houses" and to urge the "simplest man or woman" to study the Scriptures. Why worry about whether the people read their Bibles when they must believe the official interpretations of the state church?

Throughout the church's history, Williams asserted, churches supported by the state had consistently spilled oceans of the blood of dissenters whose nonconformity was based on conscience. "Christendom," a despicable legacy from the fourth-century Roman Emperor Constantine, was a disastrous polluted mixture of religion and politics. Williams rejected the divine right of kings; civil magistrates were not competent to judge what only God could judge—the individual conscience. "It is rare to find a king, prince or governor like Christ Jesus," wrote Williams, who also noted that neither Jesus nor Paul nor New Testament churches ever relied on the power of the magistrate to support them.

Williams also separated the purposes and methods of the civil and spiritual realms. Jesus had refused to be an earthly king and "thus refused to give a precedent to any king, prince, or ruler to manage both swords." Similarly, the church had stepped beyond God's order by using the sword of the state ("carnal weapons"). Contrary to the historical claims of the church, Williams argued that the only appropriate sword in matters of faith was the sword of the Spirit and its methods of persuasion and love. When will the church wake up, Williams bemoaned, to the fact that "the sword may make a whole nation hypocrites, but it cannot bring one single soul in genuine conversion to Christ."

A Holy Commonwealth demanded religious uniformity, and dissent was categorized as blasphemy and social anarchy. The punishment of heretics was not persecution, John Cotton preached, because these "damnable persons" were sinning against their conscience. Williams, however, recognized that for faith to be genuine, it had to be completely voluntary. A person must be free to worship according to the dictates of his or her conscience. Coercive faith was an oxymoron. Arguing in the same fashion as Thomas Helwys, Williams radically declared that "it is the will and command of God that (since the coming of his Son the Lord Jesus) a permission of the most paganish, Jewish, Turkish, or antichristian consciences and worships, be granted to all men in all nations and countries." The state had no business determining the identity of God's elect. A "hedge or wall of Separation between the Garden of the Church and the Wilderness of the World" was needed to preserve the purity of the New Testament church and the freedom and integrity of the individual conscience.

Williams's insistence on complete religious freedom was not the later modern idea that persons should demonstrate absolute tolerance toward other faiths. He said that Catholics were "whores" (a typical Protestant reading of the Book of Revelation seen earlier in the writings of John Smyth); the English Anglican and Puritan establishments were daughters of the whore; the Quakers were deluded; Arminianism was a "popish doctrine." At the same time, Williams warned against the deceptive effects of the self-righteousness of spiritual finality. Rhode Island was open to all types of religious views because fallible persons must be free to disagree this side of heaven.

The same year *The Bloody Tenent* was published, Williams also addressed the English Parliament with a series of questions entitled *Queries of the Highest Consideration*. In a preface, Williams set the tone for his attack. Liberty of conscience was impossible in a state church, he wrote, since people in power "seldom hear any other musick but what is known will please them." Williams again attacked the idea of a national church which had Parliament overseeing a "spiritual court," and bluntly asked, "Are you Moses' or Christ's followers?" The only way to have conformity of belief was to commit "spiritual rape" against the conscience.

In 1645, Williams's *Christenings Make Not Christians or a Brief Discourse concerning That Name Heathen, Commonly Given to the Indians* was published. He refused to call Native Americans "heathen," and instead applied the word to all non-Christians. So-called Christian nations were actually more guilty of sin because they had been more exposed to the light of the gospel. Williams extended his views against coercive conformity to the subject of the conversion of Native Americans. Why force Native Americans to leave one false worship for another? They should not be compelled to submit to something they do not understand. Reiterating his characteristic vivid imagery, Williams concluded, "[Jesus] abhors, as all men, yea, the very Indians, an unwilling spouse to enter into a forced bed."

The English Parliament ordered Williams's *The Bloody Tenent* to be burned, but copies flourished and Williams safely returned to Rhode Island. His American opponents likewise thought he was crazy and theologically dangerous. Cotton Mather (d. 1728) later articulated the Puritan perspective: "There was a whole country in America like to be set on fire by the rapid motion of a windmill in the head of one particular man." Williams's call for complete religious liberty would one day set the tone for the American doctrine of the separation of church and state. While he did not remain a Baptist, his stand for religious liberty helped to define for later generations what it meant to be Baptist. In Williams's own day, John Clarke and Obadiah Holmes preached a strong separation of church and state. Subsequently, Isaac Backus (eighteenth century) and Francis Wayland (nineteenth century) reclaimed Williams in their writings and made him a Baptist hero.

John Clarke. While Roger Williams is better known to modern readers, John Clarke was the most recognized Baptist of the mid-seventeenth century and he is regarded by some as the "father of American Baptists." Broadly talented, with training in medicine, law, and theology, Clarke was the founder of the Baptist church at Newport, Rhode Island, the second Baptist congregation established in the colonies.

John Clarke arrived in Boston in 1637 but left the next year because he was uncomfortable with the doctrinal rigidity there. He served briefly as pastor of a Separatist church in Portsmouth (Rhode Island), then helped found a settlement and a church at Newport the following year. The date on which the church in Newport became Baptist is disputed. Some historians opt for 1641 because Robert Lenthall, who had opposed infant baptism by 1638, was a teacher at the church that year. Other historians suggest that by 1644 the congregation was a believer's church, that is, believer's baptism was affirmed. The fifteen-member Newport church was the second Baptist church in America, but, evidently, the first Baptist church to practice believer's baptism *by immersion.* The church apparently espoused baptism by immersion by 1648 when Mark Lukar, who had affirmed immersion as a Particular Baptist in England, settled in Newport and most likely helped to persuade Clarke to adopt the practice.

Theological diversity was evident in the "baptized Church of Christ of Newport." (Early Baptist churches were not originally called "Baptist" churches.) Both Arminians and Calvinists were church members. Clarke, based on friendships he made in the 1650s in England, appeared to be more Calvinistic. The church practiced "closed communion," that is, they excluded non-Baptists from "partaking" the Lord's Supper. Consistent with his democratic political perspective, Clarke advocated a spiritual egalitarianism that allowed the laity to "prophesy."

The year 1644 was a decisive year for the Baptist movement. In the same year that Roger Williams' published *The Bloody Tenent* and Clarke's Newport congregation became a "believer's church," the Massachusetts Bay Colony passed a statute that outlawed "Anabaptistry." Baptists were called "incendiaries of the commonwealth," obstinate "troublers of churches in all places where they have been," and heretics for their attack upon infant baptism. Another law was passed in 1646 that forbade any further criticism of the baptism of infants. These laws were further efforts to squelch dissent in the Puritan "Holy Commonwealth." In 1643 a widow, Lady Deborah Moody, had already been forced out of Salem when she refused to recant her Baptist beliefs.

Consequently, much of Clarke's career was spent in pursuit of religious freedom for Baptists and other dissenters. In 1647, Clarke prepared a "General Code of Laws" for Rhode Island. The preamble, which Clarke possibly wrote, stated that the government was to be "democratical." In 1651, when the colony needed a new charter, both Roger Williams and Clarke went to England.

In 1652, soon after his arrival in London, Clarke published *Ill Newes from New England*. He wanted to pressure the English Parliament—hopefully capitalizing on the more tolerant atmosphere of the reign of Oliver Cromwell—to grant freedom of conscience back home in New England. Clarke sounded some of the same themes Roger Williams had voiced earlier: the church's use of government coercion only produced hypocrites; the parable of the wheat and tares called for protection rather than persecution of conscience; civil magistrates (or any "servant of Jesus") had no divine authority to force faith on others. In an oft-repeated emphasis of colonial Baptists, Clarke argued for freedom of the individual conscience from the belief that each person, without the aid of others, will appear before the sovereign God at the Day of Judgment and "give account of himself." Consequently, at the communal level, in spiritual matters the church must submit only to the Lordship of Christ "who never made use of kings of the earth to make him disciples, or call for their sword to constrain them or others to the worship of God." Clarke also defended the Baptist insistence upon believer's baptism as the only authentic biblical baptism and the duty of every believer to share the faith—both clearly subversive tenets in a Puritan society that allowed no dissent.

One of the most compelling stories in the fight for religious liberty in the American colonies was the basis for Clarke's "*Ill News from New England*." In 1651, Clarke, along with fellow minister Obadiah Holmes and layperson John Randall, paid a ministerial visit to an elderly, almost blind man named William Witter, a resident of Lynn, Massachusetts and possibly a member of Clarke's church (as there was no Baptist church in Massachusetts for him to attend). Witter was well known to local authorities for being persistently defiant about his Baptist beliefs. He once told the Salem court that "they who stayed while a child is baptized do worship the devil."

When Clarke preached at Witter's home, the three men were arrested. They were escorted to a service of the established state church, but in a defiant act, they refused to take off their hats during worship and Clarke read a book. Knowing beforehand that a preaching mission into Massachusetts was illegal revealed that Baptist dissenters were willing to provoke a confrontation to practice their faith and affirm freedom of conscience. As they later declared, they were obeying God rather than men (Acts 5:29).

The three Baptist dissenters were sentenced without a trial for conducting private worship, seducing others into heresy, and for rebaptism. Imprisoned for ten days, Clarke and Randall escaped bodily harm. An unknown benefactor paid Clarke's fine, and Randall was released after posting his own bail. Holmes received a larger fine (thirty pounds) because he had already been excommunicated from the Puritan church at Rehoboth, and he then refused an anonymous donor's offer to pay his fine. After spending several weeks in jail, Holmes was whipped in the Boston Commons—thirty lashes across his bare back. (The Puritans claimed biblical precedent—Deuteronomy 25:2-3—for a maximum whipping of "not more" than forty lashes.) Before the whipping, Holmes said he would not dull the effects of the punishment by any strong drink; rather, he would rely on the strength of the Holy Spirit. While being whipped, Holmes preached to the crowd, and when the beating was finished, he told the civil authorities, "You have struck me as with roses." In an (embellished?) account of the beating published years later (1746), Holmes's injuries were described as so severe that for weeks the only way he could rest was to be crouched on his elbows and knees. The "roses" reportedly left their imprints on Holmes's back for the rest of his life.

Clarke's publication of *Ill Newes* successfully brought some attention to the oppression of dissenters in the colonies. Massachusetts authorities were alarmed enough by Clarke's story that they provided a rebuttal. Puritan leader John Cotton, however, was unfazed by the suggestion that colonial Puritans were hypocritically persecuting dissenters when the Puritans themselves had come to America to flee persecution:

> We believe there is a vast difference between men's inventions and God's institutions. We fled from men's inventions to which we else should have been compelled; we compel none to men's inventions.

Justice was light years away in Massachusetts (for example, Benanual Bowers of Cambridge was jailed six times and whipped on three occasions between 1655 and 1682 for turning his back on baptismal services held in the established church), but after a thirteen-year stay in England, Clark returned to Rhode Island with the charter of 1663. He had procured for the colony a provision of complete religious liberty—its first legal sanction in America—and a democratic government. The charter served as the foundation for the government of Rhode Island for 179 years and has been cited as one of the sources used by Thomas Jefferson when he wrote the Declaration of Independence at the birth of the United States.

Obadiah Holmes and Newport Baptists. While modern-day Baptists quickly anoint Obadiah Holmes a Baptist "hero" for the public whipping he received in 1651, his influence was actually much broader, and more contested, in the fledgling Baptist movement. After arriving in Massachusetts in 1638 as part of the "Great Migration" of Puritans, Holmes had his children baptized as a member of the Salem church. By 1650, however, he had accepted Baptist views and was excommunicated from the church at Rehoboth. He then moved to Rhode Island and joined the Baptist church at Newport. His wife, however, did not join the church, revealing the family tension that dissent sometimes entailed.

With the departure of John Clarke to England, Holmes became the pastor of the Newport church in 1652 and served the church for thirty years. (Both Clarke and Holmes refrained from identifying themselves as a pastor in their writings because of their shared disdain for a paid ministry with its connection to a state-supported church). As Baptists continued to practice religious freedom, conflict resulted in the Newport church, first over the laying on of hands, and then over the proper day for worship.

Six-Principle Baptists. Early Baptists were constantly attempting to follow the Bible literally but often disagreed about what that meant. In 1652, the Baptists of Providence were wracked by disagreement over the "laying on of hands," and the issue remained a contentious one for more than a century. At Newport, the ceremony threatened the survival of the church during Obadiah Holmes's ministry.

Like some early English Baptists, colonial Baptists who advocated the "laying on of hands" pointed to its inclusion in the "six principles" the writer of Hebrews considered Christian basics (Hebrews 6:1-2). New converts could receive "hands" after their baptism as a symbol of the reception of the Holy Spirit for a life of Christian service, that is, a symbol of the priesthood of all believers. During the first four years of Holmes's ministry, the "hands" ceremony was considered optional. In 1656, conflict erupted when a group demanded that the "laying on of hands" become a mandatory ordinance for every church member. The pattern of the New

Testament church clearly described in Scripture had to be followed completely. Holmes refused. Much like John Bunyan of England, Holmes believed external ordinances, while biblical, could be idolized. Since the Christian faith was rooted in the experience of Christ, Holmes contended, "my soul's consolation and rest is not in them but in the Lord himself."

Consequently, the group that demanded "laying on of hands," twenty-one of the approximately fifty members, left and formed a second Baptist congregation in Newport. Called "Six-Principle Baptists," they (there were exceptions) gravitated toward Arminianism instead of the Calvinism of Holmes and other "Five Principle Baptists"—that is, those rejecting the "hands" principle.

Seventh Day Baptists. A second church split occurred during Obadiah Holmes's ministry over the proper application of the fourth of the "Ten Commandments," that is, worship and rest on the Sabbath day. Sabbatarians insisted upon a literal application of the biblical Saturday Sabbath worship. In 1665, the English Baptist Sabbatarian movement spread to the colonies when Bell Lane Seventh Day Baptist Church of London sent Stephen Mumford to Newport. He immediately won some converts, the first being Tacey Hubbard and the second her husband, Samuel. Mumford also angered people in Newport for plowing his fields on Sunday. In 1667, Holmes rebuked the seventh-day converts but soon resigned as pastor, most likely in response to criticism he had received from John Clarke about how he had handled the potential conflict.

In 1670, Mumford's converts began aggressively defending their beliefs. Four converts had committed "apostasy" and returned to full communion with the church majority. (The seventh-day advocates were abstaining from communion.) English Seventh Day Baptists, who were experiencing persecution, encouraged their American counterparts to separate from "unbelievers."

The conflict came to a head when Holmes returned as pastor in 1671. He did not avoid personal attacks and accused the "sabbatarians" of deserting Christ for Moses. William Hiscox, the spokesperson for the "seventh day," retorted that Holmes and the church were denying the scriptural authority of the Ten Commandments. They treated the command-ments as "a stink in their nostrils."

A schism occurred in December 1671, and the first Seventh Day Baptist Church in America was established with five members. Led by Hiscox, the members believed that they were persecuted on behalf of faithfulness to

Scripture and the preservation of the worship practices of the New Testament church.

The Seventh Day Baptist General Conference was formed in 1801 and continues into the twenty-first century. They are strongly against any union of church and state, especially in their vigilance about worship rights and the Sabbath.

Rogerenes. Some Christians believed that the surest path to embodying the New Testament Church was to stifle tradition and rely directly on the Holy Spirit. The Rogerenes (also known as "Rogerens Quakers") were a proponent of such a theology. Their existence also revealed the tendency of sects to produce other sects that claimed to be a more perfect model of the New Testament church.

John Rogers, the founder of the Rogerenes, became a Seventh Day Baptist in Newport, Rhode Island, in 1674. By 1677, however, Rogers had created his own church at New London, Connecticut. Like other Baptists, the Rogerenes were opposed to government interference in religion. Rogers was arrested frequently for his religious practices—seven times with combined penalties of fifteen years in prison. The Rogerenes originally observed the "seventh day" Sabbath, but after shifting to Sunday worship, they still worked on Sunday, even bringing their jobs (knitting, whittling) to church. Influenced by the Quakers, the Rogerenes were pacifists, and their spirit-led worship meant that they denounced rituals such as spoken prayers. They did practice the ordinances of believer's baptism and the Lord's Supper. Unique for Baptists, the Rogerenes opposed the use of medicine. The small sect had three churches by 1770, but disappeared by 1900.

Obadiah Holmes's Last Will and Testimony. In 1675, Obadiah Holmes wrote his "last will and testimony." In retrospect, the writing provides the most detailed testimony of conversion and spirituality by a seventeenth-century Baptist in America. Holmes was a Calvinist: "I believe that none has power to choose salvation or to believe in Christ, for life is the gift only of God." Insisting upon the necessity of a "born-again" conversion, Holmes declared that civility was not the same thing as Christian faith. His picture of a "respectable sinner" was most likely a slap at the New England establishment. In contrast, Holmes considered the gospel to be powerfully "plain"—a term he used repeatedly in his testimony.

Not educated like Clarke, Holmes embodied the oft-cited portrait of colonial Baptists as uneducated persons of lowly means. (Only one-half of New England was literate at the time). But as Clarke had said in *Ill Newes*, Baptists believed God had chosen "not many wise . . . , not many mighty, not many noble" (a reference to 1 Corinthians 1:26ff.). Consequently, Holmes, like Clarke earlier, had promoted a type of spiritual egalitarianism that said each church member could "prophesy."

The elder Holmes admonished fellow Christians to lean on the sole sufficiency of Scripture, and to avoid relying on the counsel of men for spiritual guidance since they often pursued vain honor. Reminiscent of his battle for the individual conscience in his younger days, Holmes told readers to rely on the Holy Spirit to understand the Scriptures and "preach your own experiences rather than other men's words."

Baptists in Boston

Boston was not only the site of persecution against Baptist ideas; eventually it became a center of Baptist strength. The church there gave birth to numerous other churches in New England. The first Baptist church of Boston was established by Thomas Goold in 1665. Goold, however, had been influenced, at least in part, by Henry Dunster, the most prominent Puritan to "fall from grace" over the issue of infant baptism.

Considered an excellent preacher and biblical scholar, Henry Dunster left England for the Massachusetts Bay Colony in 1640. Upon his arrival, he was elected, almost by acclamation, the first president of Harvard College, established in 1638 as the first college in America. Dunster's success and reputation led some English families to send their sons to attend Harvard. By 1651, Dunster had concluded that infant baptism was not biblical, but he realized going public with his views would cripple his career. After learning of the arrest of John Clarke and the whipping of Obadiah Holmes, however, Dunster went public and debated the subject of baptism. In 1653, he refused to have his newborn son baptized, openly defying the Puritan establishment; consequently, he was forced to resign from Harvard. Temporarily, he lived with a friend, Thomas Goold. Although Dunster never explicitly became a Baptist, his situation was evidently a factor in Goold's spiritual journey.

Thomas Goold. In 1655, Goold and his wife were censured by the Con-gregational Church in Charlestown for refusing to baptize their infant daughter. Goold did not separate from the church, however, even though he was barred from participation in communion. In 1663, a group of Baptist sympathizers began having worship services in his home. This group of nine (seven men and two women), which included some Baptists who had recently fled the harsh Clarenden Code in England, became the first Baptist church in Boston in 1665 with Goold as pastor.

Upon its organization, the church adopted a brief confession of faith, most likely the first Baptist confession of a local church written in America, and still used by the congregation today. Consistent with other early Baptists, the confession advocated believer's baptism as the basis for a "Church of Christ." Perhaps to distinguish themselves from the Anabaptists, the confession acknowledged the legitimacy of the office of the magistrate as an "ordinance of God." At the same time, the role of conscience was not forgotten.

Debate of 1668. As might be expected, Goold's dissent from the state church met continued persecution. In 1666, he and other church members were arrested as "schismatics." Two years later, there was another arrest. A jury trial precipitated a decision to hold a public debate at First Congregational Church, Boston, in April, 1668. The Puritan ministers accused the Baptists of the sin of division and "separation from the people of God."

The Baptists who participated in the debate actually revealed the diversity in Baptist life on the relation of Baptist dissent to the established church. Not all Baptists were as radical as Roger Williams or John Clarke. In addition to the insistence upon complete religious liberty and the breakdown of the Puritan establishment (a view not emphasized in the debate), two other Baptist views prevailed in Boston. One view recognized that Puritans participated in genuine churches, but different understandings of Scripture necessitated separation on account of conscience. Church member William Turner asked, "Is it not a reasonable thing that every man have his particular judgment in matters of faith seeing we must all appear before the judgment seat of Christ?"

A third perspective was held by Goold and others: separation was not always necessary. Goold had been willing to stay a member of the established church. He asserted, "I did not *go* away from you until I was *put* away from you." Unwilling to compromise on the issue of baptism, however, Goold was willing to separate and suffer the consequences. The Baptist individualistic spirit of Goold also riled the Puritan debaters. When he was told that he should not have separated from the Charlestown Church because it was "God's temple," Goold answered, "Christ dwelleth in no temple, but in the heart of the believer." The Puritans loathed such individualistic talk. After the debate, one Baptist returned to Congregationalism and Turner and Goold lived in "semi-banishment" on an island in the Boston harbor. Obadiah Holmes visited Boston Baptists during Goold's imprisonment. In 1674, Goold returned to Boston when a new colonial governor proved to be more tolerant.

First Baptist Church, Boston. During the last half of the seventeenth century, the Puritans struggled and ultimately failed to maintain their "Holy Commonwealth." Implementation of the "Halfway Covenant" of 1662 was an irreparable crack. This compromise, which allowed parents who had not had a conscious experience of grace to baptize their infants, weakened covenant theology which said children entered into the church through the faith of their parents. Ironically, the ranks of dissenters increased due to dissatisfaction with the Halfway Covenant. Stoddardeanism, the theology of Solomon Stoddard that advocated giving the Lord's Supper to children as a "converting ordinance," also served to undermine the foundation of Christian experience that was required in early Puritanism. To make matters worse for the establishment, dissenters simply were not going away.

The Baptist goal of toleration and fair treatment continued to meet obstacles even as it was gradually attained. The year 1679 brought renewed conflict for Baptists in Massachusetts. On one occasion the church in Boston was boarded up in order to stop worship. A leading Congregationalist, Increase Mather, published a diatribe against the Baptists entitled *The Divine Right of Infant Baptism*. A few months later a "Reforming Synod" made Baptists a scapegoat for the decline and corruption in New England society. One of the judgments of God against the Puritans, the synod declared, was the development of the Baptist movement.

In 1681, John Russell, then pastor of the Baptist church in Boston, responded to the attacks against the Baptists with the publication of *A Brief Narrative*. In this history of the Boston church, Russell painstakingly discussed the Puritan charges leveled against the Baptists: "Schismatical, Scandalous Persons, Disorderly Disturbers of the Peace; Underminers of the Churches, Neglecters of the Public Worship of God on the Lord's Day, Idolaters, Enemies to Civil Government, &c." Like the debate of 1668, Russell revealed that many colonial Baptists were willing to cooperate with the Congregational church. He recounted the story of Thomas Goold to demonstrate that not all Baptists left the Congregational church—instead, they were "shut out" because they would not compromise on the biblical doctrine of baptism.

Similar to the 1677 London Confession—which served the English Particular Baptists as a device to demonstrate their similarity to English Puritans and the Puritan *Westminster Confession* rather than to the reviled Anabaptists—Russell's history revealed the desire of a young struggling group for toleration and acceptance by society. Surely in the midst of the increased tolerance of the "Halfway Covenant" culture, he pondered,

Baptists could be tolerated. They were not enemies of the government. In contrast to Roger Williams's positive attitude toward Native Americans, Russell reminded his audience that Baptists had willingly fought in the recent King Phillips's War against the Indians, those "barbarous heathens." Russell also claimed that the lack of Baptist deaths during the recent outbreak of smallpox was even more evidence that Baptists had received God's favor, and thus Puritans should accept them. Russell believed that peaceful coexistence could occur if Cotton Mather and other Congregationalists would cease their practice of transferring guilt by association. Don't call us Anabaptists, Russell said, and we won't call you murderers for the massacres committed by infant baptizers throughout Christian history.

Despite the conciliatory tone, Russell insisted that proper ecclesiology was not founded upon infant baptism, but upon baptism for professing believers. Baptists, Russell contended, were acting on the "tenderness of conscience" in order to be as close to the New Testament church as possible. They were not disorderly, but simply trying to obverse "the ordinances of Christ with more purity and according to Gospel-institution."

Congregationalist Thomas Cobbet, pastor of the first church in Ipswich, Massachusetts, understood the potential revolutionary church-state implications of the dissent of voluntary individuals and congregations to the concept of a "Holy Commonwealth," and responded to Russell. At the moment, however, John Russell and most Bostonian Baptists seemed to have tolerant coexistence on their minds. Puritan society, itself struggling to survive, begrudgingly began to tolerate dissenters. Complete religious freedom was another matter. The more radical words of Roger Williams and John Clarke were rediscovered in the eighteenth century and used to disestablish a state supported church.

Other Baptist Beginnings

New England. The first Baptist church in New England was organized in 1663 at Rehoboth, Massachusetts, but in 1667 moved to Swansea, just across the state line from Providence, Rhode Island. The pastor, John Myles, was a Welsh Baptist and he and most of the congregation had previously been members of the first Baptist church in Wales, at Ilston (near old Swansea), which Myles and others also had founded (ca. 1649). Myles, a Calvinist, advocated tolerance on issues not related to salvation, and thus practiced "open communion" toward Congregationalists. Moreover, he was more like the Congregationalists than other Baptists in his views on religious liberty. In his role as the leading minister in the township, he rejected the admission of persons into the community (for example, Quakers) whom he believed held heretical views on fundamental doctrines like the Trinity or the Lord's Supper.

Some American colonies had pockets of individual Baptists but no organized Baptist churches. The first known Baptist in Connecticut was Mrs. Theolphilus Eaton, the spouse of the colony's first governor. Eaton became Baptist by 1644, but Connecticut had no Baptist congregation until 1677. The first known Baptist in New Hampshire was also a woman, Rachel Thurber Scammon (1720), but no church was established in that colony until 1755. Some Baptists in Maine were members of the Baptist church at Boston before forming their own congregation. William Screven, an English Baptist pastor, left the oppressive environment of England's Clarendon Code and migrated to Maine in 1668. He was baptized in the Baptist church in Boston—evidently this rebaptism of an English Baptist was deemed necessary because of the difficulty of verifying church membership claims—and in 1682 established a church in Kittery, Maine. The Kittery church adopted a church covenant, likely the earliest one in American Baptist history. The church was also Calvinistic; they adopted the 1689 Second London Confession of Faith.

With congregational Puritanism functioning as the established church in New England, dissenting churches grew slowly. By 1700, there were ten Baptist churches in the region, most of which were "Six-Principle" Baptists.

Middle Colonies. A greater degree of toleration was found in the Middle Colonies where an early type of religious pluralism prevailed. In Pennsylvania, the Quakers, under the leadership of William Penn, offered an environment of freedom to dissenters, second only to Rhode Island. No individual church in the Middle Colonies was strong enough to be the dominant church establishment, and economic conditions (for example, trade priorities in New York) nurtured tolerance. In 1684, the first Baptist church in Pennsylvania was formed near Philadelphia. The oldest surviving and mother church of Pennsylvania Baptists was the Pennepek (now Lower Dublin Baptist Church) church, organized in 1688 under the leadership of Elias Keach. Son of well-known English Baptist, Benjamin Keach, Elias was not a Christian upon arriving in America in 1687. Baptists around Philadelphia assumed Elias was a believer and invited him to preach. During his remarks, Elias was burdened with guilt and began to tremble. The audience thought he was ill, but Keach admitted his hypocrisy and begged for forgiveness. Converted by his own preaching, Keach became the minister at Pennepek and then extended his preaching into New Jersey. New converts to the Baptist message worshipped in their own locales, but were members of the Pennepek church. They all met on a quarterly basis in one location for worship before gradually becoming separate churches. The Pennepek "extended churches" became the basis for the Philadelphia Baptist Association which was organized in 1707 as the first permanent Baptist association in America.

Baptists in the South. Colonial Baptist growth was slowest in the South. The Church of England was the government-supported church in the southern colonies. Dissenters were constantly harassed. Virginia, the strongest southern colony, did not have a Baptist church until 1714, although some Baptists were residents before 1699. The First Baptist Church of Charleston, South Carolina, is acknowledged as the first Baptist body in the South. The "Charles Towne" settlement was organized in 1680; individual Baptists evidently lived there in the 1680s. Between 1694 and 1696, William Screven and his Kittery congregation left Maine and settled in Charles Towne. The move was most likely for economic reasons; Screven was a shipbuilder and timber was plentiful in the area. The Baptist church of Charleston constructed its own church building in 1701 and Screven remained the pastor until 1708 when he returned to Maine. While General Baptists were members of the congregation, Screven's leadership bequeathed a Calvinistic legacy to the church.

English Baptists

British Baptists provided support to colonial American Baptists in a variety of ways. English Baptists such as Mark Lukar, William Screven, and John Myles (of Wales) all became leaders in American congregations. Intercontinental Baptist correspondence was ongoing. Obadiah Holmes kept in contact with English Particular Baptists. London Baptists wrote a preface to John Russell's 1680 history of Boston Baptists. Seventh Day Baptists contacted British "seventh-day" adherents for support and advice. American Baptists were not simply transplanted English Baptists, however. Some English Baptists continued their Baptist faith in America, but most colonial Baptists migrated into Baptist life out of congregational Puritanism in the same fashion that Roger Williams, John Clarke, and Thomas Goold did.

Conclusion

Like Baptists in England, colonial American Baptists of the seventeenth century were confronted with persecution, from the Puritans in New England to the Anglicans in the South. Boston Baptists revealed the diversity of opinion regarding attitudes toward relating to the Puritan establishment and questions of religious liberty. Still, these early Baptists "drew the line" on what it meant to be a believer's church: believer's baptism (by immersion) was nonnegotiable for New Testament Christianity. Colonial Baptists of the seventeenth century also left a legacy of strong radical voices—Roger Williams, John Clarke, and Obadiah Holmes—for complete religious liberty and the necessity of freedom for the individual conscience before God. The search for the pure church was driven by individual conscience in the context of the coercion of the "Holy Commonwealth."

Baptist diversity over New Testament practices was also apparent on the American scene. Six-Principle Baptists, Rogerenes, Seventh Day Baptists, General Baptists, and Particular Baptists all dotted the colonial map with their emphases on what it meant to be a New Testament church. Amidst persecution, Baptists survived, but grew slowly in seventeenth-century colonial America. The eighteenth century was another story.

Baptists in America during the Eighteenth Century: The Quest for New Testament Faith through Revivalism and Religious Liberty

In the eighteenth century, struggling colonies slowly developed an American identity. Continued immigration brought population increases. In New England, for example, the population rose from 90,000 to 360,000 the first half of the century. In the South, the figure jumped from 100,000 to 500,000. Churches experienced growth and reported renewal in a series of local revivals that were felt throughout the colonies. The First Great Awakening focused on the need for personal conversion. This emphasis easily merged with the philosophy of the Enlightenment which valued the inalienable rights of individuals. America did by no means, however, become a "Christian nation" united in some evangelical consensus. Church membership at the time of the American Revolution was no more than six percent of the population.

Colonial America in the eighteenth century is known for the American Revolution and the creation of the United States of America. The process of becoming America ultimately hinged on the belief in freedom and independence. Colonists rallied around a declaration of independence to be free from tyranny and oppression. For many of those who were Christian, the battle cry for freedom meant an attack against tyranny in both government and spiritual realms. King George of England as well as ecclesiastical elites, who denied dissenters their freedom because of the union of church and state, became objects of scorn in the developing American psyche. For Baptists constantly in search of the New Testament church, "inalienable rights"—which included the rights of the individual conscience in matters of religious faith—found a hearing. The country's new democratic ideals seemed a perfect fit with an already existent egalitarian Baptist polity.

Baptists before Revivalism

Baptists began the eighteenth century few in number—only about ten churches in New England and twenty churches in all the colonies. But by the end of the century, they had almost 1,000 churches and were one of the fasting growing denominations in America. Before the First Great Awakening, there were actually more Six-Principle Baptists in New England, especially in the cradle of early Baptist life, Rhode Island. Most, but not all, Six-Principle Baptists affirmed Arminian theology. After 1750 and the First Great Awakening, the majority of Baptists were "Five-Principle," Calvinistic, and practiced "closed communion."

Due to the scattered nature of Baptist churches, some congregations had both Calvinistic and Arminian members. Occasionally they coexisted without great trouble, but church schisms over theology were not atypical. Splits already had occurred at Providence in 1652 and at Newport in 1665.

The ministry of John Comer revealed the interplay and tensions between Baptists of different theological persuasions. Converted in 1721, Comer served as an elder in First Baptist Church, Boston, before becoming the pastor of First Baptist Church, Newport. As a Six-Principle Baptist, Comer insisted upon the "sixth principle" of laying on of hands after baptism. Some members in the church resisted the practice, however, and Comer lost his pastorate. He then became the regular "supply preacher" of Second Baptist Church, Newport. The church was Six-Principle and Arminian. Unlike most Six-Principle Baptists, Comer was a Calvinist. While the congregation relied on Comer to fill their pulpit, he left the church after two years (1731) because he was uncomfortable with their Arminian belief in the general atonement. Comer then became the pastor of the Calvinistic church at Rehoboth, Massachusetts. Even though he preferred a Calvinistic church, Comer's diary revealed that he visited with and corresponded with Paul Palmer, the General (Arminian) Baptist pioneer who founded the first Baptist churches in Maryland and North Carolina. Despite theological tension, small, struggling, and scattered Baptist congregations sometimes cooperated by necessity.

Regular Baptists: The Philadelphia Baptist Tradition

The legacy of the Particular Baptist tradition of England ultimately came to be known as the "Regular" Baptist tradition in America. Regular Baptist life in the eighteenth century is often viewed through the lenses of the Philadelphia Baptist Association. Organized in 1707, the association was the first permanent interchurch body in American Baptist life. Scholars call it the most important Baptist entity of the century and thus refer to its influence as the "Philadelphia tradition."

Not having participated directly in the evangelistic growth of the First Great Awakening, at mid-century Regular Baptists were still a small struggling group dealing with survival issues. By 1761, nineteen of twenty-eight churches still had less than fifty members. Consequently, the association attempted to assist churches in their internal problems (doctrinal conflicts) or the ever-difficult task of securing a pastor in an age where churches were more numerous than available ministers. Annual minutes of the association reveal the practice of "queries": churches posed questions to the association leaders who subsequently answered with advice. For example, in 1730 a church was told to "disown" a member who had joined the Seventh Day Baptists; in 1748 a church was told that it should not accept for membership a "man who hath two wives living."

Doctrine and Discipline. Baptists in the Philadelphia Baptist Association affirmed the final authority of the Bible in religious matters. Nevertheless, they used a confession of faith as a doctrinal guideline and standard for orthodoxy. Doctrinal agreement was a condition for associational membership. In their struggle to survive, these Baptists wanted to define themselves as orthodox as their Protestant neighbors and even more biblical on Baptist distinctives such as believer's baptism. As early as 1724, a query was answered by referring to a confession "owned" by the association. In 1742, the association officially adopted this confession—the Second London Confession of 1689 produced by the Particular Baptists of England—and the reprint became known as the Philadelphia Confession of Faith. The Philadelphia document was distinguished from the English confession by two exceptions that were derived from the 1697 personal confession of English Baptist Benjamin Keach: articles that approved the singing of hymns in worship and the laying on of hands after baptism. The strong Calvinism of the Philadelphia Confession made that theological persuasion dominant in much of American Baptist theology during the eighteenth and nineteenth centuries.

In 1743, Benjamin Griffith wrote a tract for the Philadelphia Baptist Association entitled, *A Short Treatise of Church Discipline* (which was published with the Philadelphia Confession of Faith). Just as the association adopted a confession in the attempt to standardize their ministry, they also wished to present a united front on matters of church polity. To embody a congregational pattern rather than the nonbiblical national church model, Griffith said that persons should attend the Baptist church nearest their home for "disciplined oversight and intimate fellowship." Discipline was tied to doctrine and moral purity. To emulate the apostolic church of "primitive times," a church should be "orthodox in the fundamental articles of the Christian Religion." Candidates for membership should even be asked doctrinal questions (for example, their understanding of "original sin"). At the same time, doctrinal strictness was functionally pragmatic. The church was not to discourage the "weak"; those with the "least degree of saving grace" were not to be rejected for membership. With its 1742 confession and its 1743 tract on church discipline, the Philadelphia association provided common standards for churches to affirm and thus developed a common identity.

Associational Authority. In 1749, Benjamin Griffith wrote another essay at the request of the Philadelphia Baptist Association entitled "The Authority and Power of Associations." To calm any fears that a Baptist association was a clone in the mold of an established church hierarchy, Griffith asserted that the association was "not a superior judicature" that could usurp the authority and independence of the local church. Each church had authority directly from Jesus Christ to administer baptism and the Lord's Supper, to determine and discipline its membership (admission and exclusion), and to ordain its ministers.

Independent churches, however, should voluntarily join together in associations for "mutual strength" and "counsel." Associational membership should be based on doctrinal agreement. Like churches, associations were independent and self-governing. They could exclude a member church which they believed became wayward in the faith. Qualifying this power was the recognition that a local church was still a church regardless of its connection to a larger group of believers. An association had no power to "de-church" a congregation, that is, "deliver a defective or disorderly church to Satan."

Nevertheless, according to Griffith, associations were biblical because of the precedent found in the apostolic "Jerusalem Council" that was convened to discuss the Apostle Paul's ministry to the Gentiles (Acts 15). An association could function in an advisory capacity to churches. When the association decided that one of its participating churches had a matter to be addressed, "a delegation of able men" could be sent to advise and assist the congregation and hopefully reach a biblical resolution. Sometimes a member congregation might be censured; still, the association could only recommend, not dictate, action to churches.

Griffith's essay revealed that Baptists were struggling to find a proper role for a developing associational life. Griffith found much value in inter-church cooperation, but was not interested in granting an association any power that would undermine the freedom of self-government embodied in the independence of a local congregation. (The Shaftsbury Association in Vermont also published a circular letter in 1791 to protect the independence of local churches by emphasizing the advisory nature of associational authority.) A growing denominational identity was nurtured as additional associations dotted the Baptist landscape in the eighteenth century. Voluntary participation in associational life provided some order to Baptist life without imposing a hierarchical top-down structure of authority that Baptists loathed in a state-supported established religion.

Education. In the latter half of the eighteenth century, the Philadelphia tradition broadened its focus and helped to develop a Baptist identity around ministerial education, religious liberty, and missions. In 1756, financial support was initiated for a Latin grammar preparatory school. Isaac Eaton, pastor at Hopewell, New Jersey, led this "Hopewell Academy," the first Baptist educational institution in America. The Philadelphia Baptist tradition's belief in ministerial education was evident in a 1754 ordination sermon that Eaton preached for John Gano. Eaton presented an ideal that pointed toward the professionalization of ministry and yearning for respectability that characterized urban-educated Baptists of the early nineteenth century. He argued for training in the original biblical languages, rhetoric, moral philosophy, and logic. While he acknowledged that education was not "absolutely necessary" for a God-called minister, Baptists should not be accused of backwater ignorance.

Baptist educational ventures extended to the collegiate level in 1764 with the establishment of Rhode Island College. Its primary purpose was to train Baptist ministers. The idea for a college came from Morgan Edwards of First Baptist Church, Philadelphia, and its initial support came from the Philadelphia Baptist Association. An alumnus of Hopewell Academy and the College of New Jersey, James Manning, became the school's first president. The school opened with one student; in 1769 the first graduating class had seven students. The college relocated from Warren, Rhode Island, to Providence in 1770. The Charleston Baptist Association (South Carolina) and the Warren Baptist Association also played important supporting roles in the college's life throughout the eighteenth century. In 1804, the college changed its name to Brown University.

Influence in the South. While a new group known as the Separate Baptists was heir to the evangelistic growth of the First Great Awakening, Regular Baptists also expanded after mid-century. Northward, the Warren Baptist Association was formed in 1767. Southward, some General Baptist churches—the original type of Baptists in Virginia and North Carolina—joined the Philadelphia Baptist Association before eventually becoming part of distinct Southern Regular Baptist associations. These Southern associations were usually direct outgrowths of the work of the Philadelphia tradition. The creation of the Charleston Baptist Association in 1751, the first in the South, was led by Oliver Hart, who had become pastor of First Baptist Church, Charleston, in 1749, after serving as a young leader in the Philadelphia Baptist Association. In essence, the various manifestations of the Philadelphia association's influence in the South foreshadowed the developement of a larger national Baptist identity.

Itinerant Evangelists. An important reason the Philadelphia Baptist Association expanded its influence was its decision to commission evangelists to travel through the southern colonies. (The influence of Great Awakening-styled preaching had spread.) The earliest evangelist of the Philadelphia tradition, and considered one of the most successful, was John Gano. Gano made several trips that extended from Virginia to South Carolina. In his *Memoirs*, Gano revealed a spirituality of individual conversion that came to typify eighteenth-century Baptist religious experience. He described a Calvinistic understanding of human nature: in his unconverted state he was a "wretched sinner" and "worshipper of Satan." According to Gano, he spoke to a Presbyterian evangelist about his developing concerns regarding infant baptism, but then decided to follow the Bible alone as the supreme religious authority and opted to affirm believer's baptism. His father, a Presbyterian, told him to follow his conscience. When Gano first traveled to Virginia in 1752 as an agent of the Philadelphia Baptist Association, he was not yet ordained. Consequently, he was rebuked for preaching and reprimanded for "disorder." Yet, Gano wrote, his "conscience acquitted him."

Gano eventually held a twenty-six-year pastorate in New York, but during those years he continued itinerant evangelistic work. In the stereotyped language of his day, Gano's preaching style elicited the comment, "You make a good Negroe preacher." Scholars suggest that Gano's *Memoirs*, replete with accounts of his travels, indicate a change in spiritual autobiographies. While "diaries" of the seventeenth century emphasized the struggles and growth of the Christian life, Gano's concern was primarily with evangelistic proficiency. Identifying spirituality with evangelistic witnessing would provide an enthusiasm for missions that blossomed at the turn of the nineteenth century.

David Thomas, educated by Isaac Eaton at Hopewell Academy and then at Rhode Island College, was for many years the preeminent Regular Baptist in colonial Virginia. Many of the Regular ministers regarded him as their spiritual father. Active in the Philadelphia Baptist Association, Thomas relocated to northern Virginia in 1760 as a "self-appointed missionary." He helped organize and assumed the pastoral duties of the Broad Run Church in Fauquier County after submitting a certificate of his ordination from the Philadelphia association. (Only recently had the association begun issuing certificates; typically ministers were reordained whenever they changed churches.) In 1766, Thomas helped organize the Ketoctin Baptist Association, the first in Virginia. Due primarily to his evangelistic efforts, the association increased from four to twelve churches in a decade. Early nineteenth-century historian David Benedict remarked that the fame of Thomas's preaching brought listeners from sixty miles away. Virginia Regular Baptists continued the Calvinistic heritage of the Philadelphia tradition. In 1774, Thomas published *The Virginian Baptist*, the first printed presentation of Baptist faith and order in the influential colony, which contained his own edited version of the Philadelphia Confession as an apology for the Baptist cause in Virginia.

Associational leaders still pressed doctrinal concerns in the late eighteenth century. Beginning in 1774, the Philadelphia Baptist Association produced an annual "circular letter" that provided an exposition of one of the articles of their confession. The projected series was abandoned in 1798 with twenty-two of the thirty-four articles completed. At the end of the eighteenth century, both John Gano and David Thomas were elderly ministers on the Kentucky frontier. The Philadelphia Baptist tradition continued to expand.

Calvinism. The continued strength of Calvinism in the Philadelphia Baptist Association was seen in the ministry of Samuel Jones. He was educated at Isaac Eaton's academy at Hopewell and attracted to the strict Calvinism of the prominent English Baptist theologian John Gill. Like Benjamin Griffith and Morgan Edwards of First Baptist Church, Philadelphia, Jones was a native of Wales and revealed the strength of the Welsh Baptist tradition on early American Baptists. (Welsh immigrants started seven of the early Baptist churches in the Philadelphia Association.) Jones, pastor of the Southampton and Pennepek churches, then exclusively of the Pennepek church, led the Philadelphia association to abandon its commitment to the ordinance of laying on of hands. He decided that the ordinance was due more to Welsh tradition than to apostolic practice.

Jones also published for the association a *Treatise of Church Discipline* (1797/1798). The tract continued the Calvinistic emphasis on sound doctrine but revealed that the use of "ruling elders," which Benjamin Griffith affirmed in the 1740s, was becoming controversial (that is, Calvin's threefold ministerial organization of teaching elders (pastors), ruling elders, and deacons). Jones exhorted: "Let the churches judge for themselves, and practice as they see fit." Gradually, most Baptists concluded that the officers of a New Testament pattern were only pastors and deacons.

Universalism. While Baptist leaders generally advocated historic Protestant orthodoxy, the doctrine of universalism—that all persons will go to heaven—surprisingly made noticeable inroads into Baptist life in the latter part of the eighteenth century. The most prominent Baptist convert to universalism was Elhanan Winchester who in 1780 became pastor of First Baptist Church, Philadelphia, after five years at the Welsh Neck church in South Carolina. First an Arminian, then a Calvinist indebted to the teachings John Gill, Winchester became a universalist shortly after accepting the Philadelphia pastorate. Controversy soon erupted at the church. A majority of the church's members supported Winchester—he was once called a "loquacious and flaming preacher" by Ezra Stiles, the president of Yale University—but his opponents appealed to the 1781 associational annual meeting for assistance. The association sided with the opposition party who had affirmed the Philadelphia Confession of Faith and recommended that Winchester's supporters be excommunicated. Samuel Jones wrote a circular letter to all the churches of the association denouncing universalism. The association also wrote letters to Baptists in Virginia and Rhode Island warning them of Winchester's heresy. Subsequently, Winchester and his supporters left First Baptist Church and formed the Society of Universal Baptists. He did not, however, cease communication with other Baptists. In 1783, prominent religious-liberty advocate John Leland traveled with Winchester which led to some suspicion of Leland's own ministry.

Baptist universalism was never a large movement, yet six of seven ministers at a universalist convention in 1790 were Baptist. In the early nineteenth century, a leading apologist for universalism and the moral-example theory of Christ's atonement—which some scholars say helped push the movement toward Unitarianism and the denial of the divinity of Jesus—was former Baptist, Hosea Ballou. However, the focus on "universal restoration" was more than most Baptists could fathom, despite their own desires to restore the New Testament. Nevertheless, evangelistic "universal Baptists" were one manifestation of the growing challenges Calvinism faced in Baptist circles at the turn of the nineteenth century.

English Baptists. English Baptists continued to influence American Baptists in a variety of ways. This was especially true in the Philadelphia Baptist Association. In addition to the Association's adoption of the Second London Confession, the books of English leaders John Gill and Andrew Fuller were recommended to pastors for reading. Letters were exchanged with English churches. English influence extended beyond Philadelphia. For example, James Manning of the Warren Association consulted with English Baptist John Ryland, Jr. about the propriety of having a lottery to raise funds for Baptist higher education. Ryland said no, and Manning listened. After the American Revolution, London pastor John Rippon told Manning that the majority of English Baptists were glad that the fight for independence had been successful.

National Body. Throughout the eighteenth century, the Philadelphia Baptist Association functioned as a national body for Regular Baptists in colonial America. In 1770, the Philadelphia Baptist Association, led by Morgan Edwards, pastor of First Baptist Church, Philadelphia, discussed a plan to unite Baptists nationally in some formal fashion. Edwards wanted Baptists "in every province" to form associations and be "knit together" by a central body, the Philadelphia Association. The work had already begun, he noted, with the harmonious separation of churches from the Philadelphia body into an association in the North (Warren in Rhode Island) and in the South (Ketoctin in Virginia). The basis of the union would be Baptists' "denominating article," believer's baptism.

Between 1775 and 1815, 104 Baptist associations were formed. While Edward's plan was too centralized in a context where dissenters still felt the shadows of state-establishment religion, the Philadelphia Baptist Association subsequently issued additional calls for national cooperation (1799 and 1800). The 1800 resolution suggested the idea of Baptists nationwide creating a home missionary society to minister to Native Americans. By 1802, the Association formed a committee to facilitate contact with other associations. In 1814, Baptists organized a national body to support foreign missions. Baptists' "denominating article" was believer's baptism, but voluntary cooperation to support missions soon became an equal sign of modeling the New Testament church.

First Great Awakening

Historians have debated the impact of the First Great Awakening (1720s–1740s) upon American life in the eighteenth century. Traditionally, it has been called the first major revival in American history. The awakening was "great" because it was widespread—from New England to Georgia—and it involved multiple groups. Leaders included Theodore Frelinghuysen (Dutch Reformed), Gilbert Tennent (Presbyterian), and especially Jonathan Edwards (Congregationalist) and English itinerant George Whitefield. Their focus on individual conversion facilitated among supporters a common "national" identity. The revival was a precursor to the focus on individual liberty and a common "national" identity in the battle against England in the American Revolution. Some recent historians have questioned whether the First Great Awakening was as cohesive and influential as the traditional interpretation suggests. Whatever its impact on a "common" identity, the revival spurred religious growth in the colonies.

The relationship of Baptists to the First Great Awakening revealed some of the ironies and unintended effects of history. Baptists were generally opposed to the revival. The Arminian churches in New England disliked the Calvinism of the revival leaders. Many Baptists were wary of the episodes of wild emotionalism that characterized some of the conversions. Most of the conversions were among Congregationalists: persons who practiced infant baptism and who represented the legacy of the established church "standing order" that had persecuted dissenters like Baptists. Boston Baptists, under the leadership of Jeremiah Condy, were against the revival. During Condy's twenty-six year pastorate at Boston's First Baptist Church, only forty-three new members were added. During the height of the revival (1742), the church closed its weekly lecture because of poor participation. The church eventually split over Arminianism and lack of evangelistic fervor. However, a few Baptists in Newport, Rhode Island did directly benefit from the revival.

Separate Baptists

The First Great Awakening ironically was a major factor in Baptist growth. Baptists benefited from splits in the ranks of Congregationalists. Many "New Lights"—those who advocated revival methods—left the Congregationalist fold after abandoning their commitment to infant baptism in favor of believer's baptism. Regarding "Separates" becoming Baptists, the leading evangelist of the awakening, George Whitefield, reportedly said, "My chickens have turned to ducks." Important Baptist leaders like Shubal Stearns and Isaac Backus were Congregationalist converts of the awakening. In the decade between 1740 and 1750, forty-one Baptist churches were organized, five more than the total of the previous four decades. The majority of Baptists in New England shifted to Calvinistic theology; cooperation and contact with the developing Calvinistic Philadelphia tradition also was a stimulus to growth. Few Calvinistic Baptist churches existed before the First Great Awakening in New England. At the end of the eighteenth century, Calvinistic Baptists, known as Regular Baptists, dominated the 300-plus churches in the New England region. Baptist growth in the South was also primarily the result of Separate Baptist evangelism.

Isaac Backus. Historians often use Isaac Backus as a prominent example of the journey numerous adherents of the New England state-church system took to become Baptists, which led to the despised minority group ultimately becoming a major player in religious America. In 1741, at the age of seventeen, Isaac Backus became a "New Light" Congregationalist in his native colony of Connecticut. Four years later, as the revival fires spread in the First Great Awakening, he joined a Separate church (a congregation, considered illegal by the government, whose members had experienced the "new birth" of conversion and left the state-supported parish church). Backus began preaching about 1745 and was ordained in 1748 when he became the pastor of a new Separate church at Titicut, Massachusetts.

Then in 1751, after a period of much wavering, Backus adopted believer's baptism by immersion. A baptismal controversy brewed in the Titicut church. Initially, Backus did not insist upon believer's baptism for all members, and practiced open communion. But in 1756, Backus and the adult baptized believers in the church left and formed a Baptist church at Middleborough, where he was pastor for the rest of his life, and where closed communion became the norm. Backus's ministry also included itinerant evangelism and writing history. His preaching tours averaged more than 1,200 miles a year throughout his ministry. He also published the earliest history of Baptists in America, a three-volume *A History of New England with Particular Reference to the Denomination of Christians Called Baptists* (1777, 1784, 1796). Backus's history of course included an agenda of revealing the plight of dissenters under an oppressive, established, state church.

Shubal Stearns. Separate Baptists extended their influence to the South under the leadership of Shubal Stearns. Stearns was converted under the preaching of George Whitefield, and became the first farmer-preacher of a new Separate congregationalist church in rural Connecticut. Stearns became a Baptist, moved to Virginia and ultimately settled at Sandy Creek, North Carolina, where, in 1755, he organized the first Separate Baptist church in the South. Joined by his sister and brother-in-law, Martha and Daniel Marshall, who had become Baptists, Stearns became the undisputed leader of the Separate Baptist movement in the colonial South. Separate Baptist revivalism flourished and the Sandy Creek Church grew from sixteen to 606 members. The Regular Baptist Morgan Edwards, who toured and wrote about Baptists in the South, reported that in seventeen years the Sandy Creek Baptist Association, which was formed in 1758, became "mother, grand-mother, and great-grandmother to 42 churches from which sprang 125 ministers."

The movement was especially strong in Virginia. While Presbyterians initiated the Virginia phase of the First Great Awakening in the 1750s, Separate Baptists continued and defined its growth. For example, in 1769 Separate Baptists had seven churches in Virginia; five years later they had fifty-four churches. Daniel Marshall and Martha Stearns Marshall— Virginia Baptist historian Robert Semple called Martha Daniel's "Priscilla" and more eloquent than her husband—also expanded the Sandy Creek tradition's influence by doing pioneering work in South Carolina and Georgia. By the time of the American Revolution, Separate Baptists were the largest dissenting group in the South.

Contemporaries said that Shubal Stearns had a spellbinding preaching style and "penetrating" eyes. Other Separate Baptist ministers imitated him "in tones of voice and actions of body." Stearns preached extemporaneously ("Spirit-led") and utilized a "holy whine," a shouting preaching style that evidently modulated between singing, chanting, and normal speech. The practice, rooted in George Whitefield's dramatic style, has led some scholars to contend that Stearns was the "father" of Appalachian mountain religion.

Stearns became known as the "Reverend Old Father" in the Sandy Creek Association. He asserted autocratic authority at times. On occasion, ministers and churches who disagreed with the association were "disfellow-shipped." Associational gatherings focused on preaching and, according to some scholars, were evangelistic "camp meetings" thirty-years before the nineteenth-century Second Great Awakening popularized camp meetings on the frontier. In 1770, the Sandy Creek Association split into three associations, a move which limited Stearns's controlling influence.

John Leland. A third prominent Separate Baptist was John Leland of Virginia and later Connecticut. Better known as the most radical exponent of religious liberty among eighteenth-century Baptists, Leland was at heart an evangelist, a preacher of conversion. When asked what should be put on his tombstone at his death, Leland wanted it to read that he had worked for religious liberty and had strived to "promote piety." Leland's personal faith story reflected the Separate Baptist pietistic emphasis on the "conversion experience." At the outset of his spiritual journey, he struggled with how conversion should be experienced, believing that "if ever I was converted, I should know it was distinctly as if a surgeon should cut open my breast with his knife."

Leland also reflected the Separate Baptist softened attitudes toward Calvinism. When he was baptized, the minister asked him if he believed in "the Calvinistic doctrine?" Leland remarked, "I did not know what it was, but I believed in free grace." During his ministry, Leland grappled with the proper method of addressing sinners with the gospel. He concluded that no theological system, including the strong Calvinism of John Gill, the modified "evangelical" Calvinism of Andrew Fuller, or the Arminianism of John Wesley satisfied him. Nineteenth-century Baptist historian David Benedict described Leland's influential approach as "two grains of Arminianism, with three of Calvinism, he [Leland] thought, would make a tolerably good compound."

Leland, like other Separate Baptist preachers, was a biblicist. Whenever he preached from a text in the Old Testament, he "preached a New Testament sermon." His motto was: "just keep within the lids of the Bible." Because preaching was a calling from God, Leland preached a year before he was officially licensed by a Baptist church. Throughout Leland's biographical memoirs, constant references were made to the number of sermons he preached and the number of baptisms he performed during his itinerant ministry in colonial Virginia. Toward the end of his life, Leland declared that he had preached more than 8,000 sermons, baptized more than 1,500 converts and spoken to crowds as small as five and as large as 10,000 hearers. Contemporaries acknowledged Leland to be the most popular preacher of his day in Virginia, although educated observers lamented that his genuine warmth was often conveyed through eccentric, irreverent humor. He was the best show in town.

Leland left Virginia for Connecticut in 1792. Five years earlier, he had participated in the creation of the United Baptists. Leland's ministry evidently was a small part of the larger tensions among Virginia Baptists.

He had been ordained without the traditional ceremony of laying on of hands. Consequently, some Baptists refused to acknowledge the legitimacy of his ministry. When he agreed to a second ordination with the ceremony in 1787, Leland suggested that the action was a small link in the union of Regular and Separate Baptists in Virginia.

Union of Regular and Separate Baptists

Early nineteenth-century Virginia Baptist historian Robert Semple said that differences between Regular and Separate Baptists were never great and that jealously played a significant role in the tensions between them. Separates and Regulars gradually united in the North without any formal mergers. Isaac Backus's ministry in the Warren Baptist Association, which was an outgrowth of the Philadelphia Baptist tradition, symbolized the gradual melding of a Baptist witness. In the South, Regulars and Separates maintained different identities until a merger in Virginia in 1787. The perspectives and practices of both groups revealed the continued diversity in colonial Baptist life.

Regular Baptists of the South—often called the Charleston tradition— were heirs of the Philadelphia Baptist tradition and used the Philadelphia Baptist Confession of Faith (1742). Separate Baptists disliked confessions and believed that creedal statements led to formality and spiritual stagnation and diverted believers from the authority of the Scriptures. Both Baptist groups were Calvinistic, but the revivalistic practices of the Separate Baptists modified their theology in the Arminian direction of the general atonement, both in substance and aggressive evangelistic style.

Calvinistic Baptists gave themselves the name, "Regular," which obviously implied the irregularity of other Baptists. One of the Regulars' main discomforts concerning the Separates was the Separates' style of preaching and the effects it produced. John Leland described the Regulars as "solemn and rational," but the Separates were "the most zealous" and "very noisy." Both groups preached personal conversion and believer's baptism—New Testament necessities—but, in the opinion of Regular Baptist David Thomas, the excessive emotionalism of the Separates produced unbiblical "horrid vociferations and obstreperous commotions." Virginian William Fristoe criticized emotionalism at the end of a preaching service. Some preachers, he bemoaned, walked through the crowd and sang a song which manipulated the emotions of hearers so that they fell down and begged for prayer on their behalf. Such practices have led some historians to contend that the Separate Baptists were key forerunners of modern revivalism, utilizing these "prayers of faith" before Charles Finney, in the nineteenth century, popularized zealous "invitations." Whereas Regular Baptists focused on order, Separate Baptists emphasized the charisma of zeal.

Many Separate Baptists felt that the emotion generated in their revivals was biblical and the Regulars' lack of emotion was a sign of spiritual lethargy. Isaac Backus, the most influential Separate Baptist in New England, did claim to be embarrassed by the excessive emotion in revivalism. At the same time, he utilized a victim defense to account for it. People who were oppressed sometimes acted in "mad" ways. Who could really blame them?, Backus queried. Prominent Separate Baptist pastor, Philip Mulkey, reported that he literally saw the Devil during his conversion experience. However, such explicit demonology was claimed only among a minority of Southern evangelicals.

Regular Baptists clearly preferred orderly worship and an educated ministry. For the Separates, a divine call made a person competent to preach. Two prominent Separate Baptist preachers, Elijah Craig and Lewis Craig, were converted by Regular Baptist David Thomas, but when they began preaching at the encouragement of Separate Baptist leader Samuel Harris, Thomas opposed it. Both Regular and Separate Baptists claimed that their constituents were of the "poorer sort," but in addition to education, another sign of social differences was attitudes toward dress. Separates criticized Regulars for allowing "superfluity of apparel."

While both Baptist groups attempted to model the New Testament church, Separates were even more restorationist than the Regulars. Some Separates practiced the "nine rites": baptism, Lord's Supper, love feast, laying on of hands, foot washing, anointing the sick, right hand of fellowship, kiss of charity, and child dedication (labeled "dry christening" by their opponents). The duplication of these literal biblical practices was too physical for opponents. The Separates' willingness to have female exhorters was another barrier to cooperation with Regulars. Separates in Virginia even ordained an "apostle," but soon realized the office did not sit well with the insistence upon local church independence.

As early as 1764, Regulars approached Separates about uniting but were rebuffed. Gradually, the Separates modified their aversion toward confessions. They were willing to accept the Regulars' confession with the stipulation that it was not a binding statement of faith on anyone's conscience. Despite differences in style and doctrine, the two groups were drawn together by revivalism. In Georgia, for example, Separate Baptist

Daniel Marshall worked with Regular Baptist Edmund Botsford. Marshall performed baptisms for Botsford before he was ordained. In Virginia, David Thomas corresponded with Separate Baptist James (Jamie) Ireland when the latter was imprisoned at Culpeper for preaching. The quest for religious liberty was the climactic push towards union. In 1787, Regulars and Separates united and renamed themselves the United Baptist Churches of Christ in Virginia. In other Southern states (Georgia and South Carolina, for example), no formal action was taken but Regulars and Separates united. Separate Baptists had joined Regular Baptists on the road to respectability.

Richard Furman. The ministry of Richard Furman revealed the uniting of Regular and Separate Baptist perspectives. In 1771, Furman was converted under Separate Baptist preaching. At age sixteen, the "boy evangelist" began preaching and was pastor of the Separate Baptist High Hills of Santee Church in South Carolina. He immediately began cooperating with Regular Baptists: Oliver Hart of Charleston, for example, preached in his revival services. In 1778, Furman's church joined the Regulars' Charleston Baptist Association and in 1787, Furman assumed the pastorate of First Baptist Church, Charleston. Furman, like his predecessor Hart, wore a robe while he preached in the Charleston pulpit. Furman also built upon Hart's earlier effort—the creation in 1755 of an education fund by the Charleston Baptist Association; and in 1790, he led the association to form an education committee. Furman directed the work for thirty-four years, acknowledging that a divine call was indispensable for preaching but adding that ministerial education was worthy as a "handmaiden to grace." His vision of a centralized work of missions and education was a vision for the future, and was later implemented by the South Carolina Baptist Convention (Furman was its first president) and the Southern Baptist Convention. On a more human level, Furman and his wife of fourteen years had two children. After she died, Furman married fifteen-year-old Dorothea Maria Burn who gave birth to thirteen children in twenty-six years.

Baptist Ministry and Distinctives

The views of Isaac Backus on ministry and principles—now called "Baptist distinctives"—help illuminate the understanding of Baptist identity in the eighteenth century. Backus voiced his ideas in a tract (*A Fish Caught in His Own Net*, 1768), against Joseph Fish, a scathing indictment of the ministry of the Standing Order, the established church of colonial Massachusetts. Whenever there is a decline in religious fervor, Backus declared, just look toward the elitist, college-trained ministers. They read dull sermons and preach for money: the "worldly sum turned the scale," as they chose a parish. These clergy opposed the need for personal conversion—many were probably not converted themselves—and they failed to require verbal confession of faith from their parishioners. Backus queried, "How is a regenerate church to be maintained?"

The state-supported Standing Order, according to Backus, had abandoned the congregationalism of the Puritan founding fathers. Backus believed that dissenters who emphasized the necessity of experiential faith (conversion) were the genuine legacy of the Puritans. He eagerly praised the "excellent Mr. [Jonathan] Edwards" for his insistence upon "saving grace." However, the Congregationalists had apostasized from the founding Puritan fathers with their creation of a national church and a hierarchy of ministers. Echoing John Locke's enlightenment concept of churches as voluntary societies, Backus affirmed that the church was a local voluntary society of converted individuals baptized as believers and in covenant together. There were to be no "pressed soldiers" in the church.

Backus's strong congregationalism was evident in his insistence that the church's government rested in the people. He attacked the Standing Order for approving the ordination of ministers rather than giving the power to the local church where it belonged, according to the New Testament. Revealing a strong "doctrine of the laity," Backus said that the common people, not a group of elitist ministers, were the best judges of the daily walk of a minister. Backus cited 1 Peter 2 on the priesthood of believers and noted that the New Testament spoke of lay people, not ministers, as priests. The common folk should follow teachers only if their teaching is correct. According to Backus, deferring to veteran experience was good in some areas of life, but not in religious matters. The common people were not owned by the clergy.

Successful congregational government of the independent local church was based on a healthy pietistic individualism. Backus said that the Standing Order had modeled itself after the state; they developed a hierarchical leadership and let one leader speak for the whole. In contrast, Backus contended, each regenerate individual in the local church had the Spirit-led ability to judge. This belief was rooted in the Protestant Reformation.

Backus cited the ministry of Hezekiah Smith to illustrate freedom of individual conscience. Smith was a popular itinerant Baptist preacher who was told by the Standing Order not to speak publicly about his beliefs against infant baptism. But Smith could not remain silent and be "denied liberty," reported Backus, because believers do not stand before the judgment as a group, they stand individually before God.

Backus's argument for the freedom of individual conscience had a corollary: the church should use spiritual weapons and must not use coercive power or carnal weapons. The worst mistake of the founding Puritan fathers, Backus declared, was the "confounding" of church and state. The Standing Order, while they claimed to be biblical, had a secular head rather than a high priest.

In his writings, Backus cited Enlightenment thinkers like John Locke, but also relied on Baptist ideals that preceded the Enlightenment. Enlightenment ideas were read through pious eyes. Backus always attempted to defend his positions by using Scripture. When Backus was considering whether to adopt believer's baptism, he said that he saw some "bad tempers" among the Baptists. Finally, however, one question was most important: What say the Scriptures? Since the New Testament advocated believer's baptism, Backus had to adopt the "divine pattern" of the New Testament church.

Backus's focus on individual religious experience was also rooted in his understanding of the Bible.

> And all the saints know that when they received Christ they had no creature to see for them, but each soul acted as singly towards God as if there had not been another person in the world. . . . Now if each saint is complete in him which is the Head of all wisdom and power, then they have no need of philosophers to see for them, nor of princes to give them power to act for God, but they freely confess with their mouths what they believe in their hearts, and so their hearts are comforted, being knit together in love.

Isaac Backus said that each individual must have a personal conversion because he/she stood alone before God in the judgment. God accepted no proxies. Freedom for the individual, according to Backus, was biblical. At the same time, the individual was a part of a local congregation. Individuals were "knit together in love," and as a congregation, they followed not a secular head, but Jesus, the Head of the Body of Christ.

Religious and Political Liberty

American Revolution. Baptists overtly siding with the British crown during the American Revolution were rare. In 1774, Morgan Edwards, influential pastor of the First Baptist Church of Philadelphia, declared that he supported the British (this contributed to his dismissal from the church roll when he was charged with drunkenness in 1785; he was allowed to become a member again three years later). Prominent Congregationalist Ezra Stiles also pointed fingers at other Baptist ministers, including James Manning, the Baptist president of Rhode Island College. Support of the patriot cause was mild among some rural Baptists. Some sense of allegiance to the British crown was possible because it had on occasion responded to dissenter cries for relief from persecution by the Congregationalist establishment in New England. Moreover, aligning with the patriot cause did not stop mistreatment of dissenters. In 1778, an unruly crowd disrupted a river baptismal service in Pepperell, Massachusetts. When Isaac Backus promised to press the matter in court, the mob's leader, Henry A. Woods, declared "I'll wring his nose and kick his arse." Because of their dissenting ways and their status as poor social outsiders, class prejudice against Baptists often died hard.

Baptists did rally around the war effort. Baptist preachers supported the war effort with Scripture and some actively recruited for the patriot's cause. South Carolinians Oliver Hart of First Baptist Church, Charleston, and Richard Furman of High Hills of Santee, both worked to garner patriot support in the backcountry frontier of South Carolina where Tory sentiment was strong. Similar to Massachusetts, Tory sentiment had social overtones; it was strong among rural folk. Some dissenters, including Hart and Furman, left the colony for safety reasons. Baptist hagiography later popularized the story that the famous English General Charles Cornwallis had placed a $1,000 price on Furman's head because he was more afraid of Furman's prayers than he was of the patriot forces led by Generals Francis Marion and Thomas Sumter.

Some Baptists served as chaplains during the war. These included Virginians Elijah Craig and Lewis Craig as well as John Gano of New York and one of Gano's converts who became an influential evangelist, Hezekiah Smith of Massachusetts. Gano wrote of his experiences in his memoirs. He noted that in one battle he found himself at the front of the regiment. He did not retreat, however, because he did not want to be accused of being a coward by the soldiers. Some soldiers occasionally skipped the preaching services that were held. Their punishment, Gano wryly noted, was "digging up of stumps, which, in some instances, had a good effect." Later Baptist hagiography popularized the legend that Gano baptized (by immersion) George Washington during the war. While Gano may indeed have been Washington's chaplain, no evidence exists to substantiate the baptism story, which obviously was used to make Baptists more respectable in the public's eye.

Baptist support for the American Revolution usually tied religious freedom to political freedom. This is clearly seen in the work of Isaac Backus and the Warren Baptist Association.

The Massachusetts Story. The Baptist quest for religious liberty in revolutionary America is most clearly seen in the work of Separate Baptists. Persecution in New England by the Congregationalist Standing Order and in Virginia by the Anglican Church pushed Baptists from asking for the right to exist ("toleration") to an insistence upon full religious liberty and the separation of church and state.

Laws and harassing prejudice—religious and social—were mountainous barriers for dissenters to overcome. In 1728, Baptists obtained exemption in Massachusetts from paying taxes to support the Congregational church. Taxes collected were to be refunded, but restrictions often jettisoned the process. Church members had to live within five miles of their church and many did not. These congregations had to acquire from three other churches certification that they were in good standing within their group. (Regular Baptists churches were not always willing to affirm Separate Baptists.) Exemption laws frequently lapsed and dissenters were forced to pay the religious tax until new laws were in place. On numerous occasions, the Standing Order imprisoned dissenters and confiscated dissenters' property when they refused to comply with the restrictions. When one Separate Baptist was informed that his swine would be taken by civil authorities until the religious tax was paid, he responded with sarcastic biblical imagery: "Your claim to that animal may be good for I have understood that your master took possession of that species of animals in the land of the Gadarenes many years ago" (Mark 5).

Isaac Backus. Isaac Backus became the face of the Baptist battle for religious liberty in colonial New England through the work of the Warren (Rhode Island) Baptist Association. Not atypically, Backus did not originally join the association (1767) because he feared its infringement upon local church independence. In 1772, however, he began a twelve-year tenure as the agent of the association's "Grievance Committee," what has been called the earliest religious lobby in American history. Backus understood persecution firsthand. In 1756, his mother had been imprisoned for failure to pay the religious tax. Consequently, Backus defended persecuted Baptists with petitions seeking redress in the courts and pressured government bodies to stop coercive compulsory religion in favor of the separation of church and state.

Backus tied the quest for religious liberty to the cause of political liberty. He utilized the popular revolutionary language of "no taxation without representation" to do so: "Many who are filling the nation with the cry of LIBERTY . . . are at the same time themselves violating that dearest of all rights, LIBERTY of CONSCIENCE." They denounce "being taxed without their consent . . . [but] force large sums from [their neighbors] to uphold a worship which they conscientiously dissent from." Backus seized upon the colonial disgruntlement over the now-infamous tea tax in Boston by noting that the tax could be escaped by not drinking tea, but the tax on dissenters could not be avoided without going to prison or denying conscience. In essence, Backus contended that full political freedom was not really possible without religious freedom.

As the revolutionary spirit heated up, Backus and the Warren Baptist Association elevated their opposition to state-sponsored religion. Many refused to apply for exemptions from the religious taxes and thus willingly practiced civil disobedience to avoid violating their consciences. In 1774, Backus, James Manning, and Chileab Smith attended the First Continental Congress to argue for religious liberty. Political leaders denigrated their concerns. Thomas Paine suggested the Baptist complaints were more about money than violations of conscience. John Adams lumped the Baptists with Quakers—suggesting they were really opposed to the unification of the colonies—and declared that Baptists "might expect a change in the solar system as to expect the people of Massachusetts to give up their establishment."

Backus continued to battle Massachusetts authorities after the Revolutionary War began. In 1780, he argued (unsuccessfully) against a new state constitution that provided tax support for the majority religious leader of each town—obviously the Congregationalists. Backus's response echoed his earlier calls for the freedom of the individual conscience: "As religion must always be a matter between God and individuals, so no man can be made a member of a truly religious society by force or without his own consent." The church should govern itself; the secular government should govern itself. Since coercion was wrong, Backus argued, the gospel should be advanced freely and voluntarily like it was in the New Testament and in the earliest centuries of Christianity before the advent of a state church.

In an 1804 abridged edition of his history of Baptists, Backus reflected upon the scriptural errors of the union of church and state. Like Roger

Williams, Backus believed that Jesus' parable of the wheat and tares (Matthew 13:24-30) indicated that while the "wheat and tares" may grow together in the world, the church is to be pure. The Standing Order, according to Backus, misread Scripture when they contended that the wheat and tares grow together in the church and thus the world and the church are essentially one and the same. This union of church and state had produced the tragic consequences of persecution: "While they were for having the tares grow in the church, they would not let the children of God grow peaceably in the world, but took up and imprisoned many of them." Despite the efforts of Backus and like-minded dissenters, it was not until 1833 that the state of Massachusetts finally disestablished the Congregational Standing Order in favor of the separation of church and state.

Historians offer different evaluations of the radical nature of Backus's views on religious liberty. In modern terms, some call him an "accommodationist" rather than a "strict separationist." On the one hand, Backus clearly emphasized the sacredness of the individual conscience before God. He helped rediscover and popularize Roger Williams and viewed himself as a part of the Williams legacy. In his 1804 abridged church history, Backus commended Thomas Jefferson's "An Act for Establishing Religious Freedom" which was pivotal to the achievement of full religious freedom in Virginia.

At the same time, Backus seemed primarily interested in battling coercive established religion rather than advocating a completely neutral separation. He did not take issue with religious oaths that were required to participate in the government of Massachusetts. Neither did he object to "blue laws" (Sabbath closings) or state-supported chaplains. (Some other Massachusetts Baptists had no problem with the government mandating Sunday church attendance.) Because Christianity would provide the indispensable underpinnings of successful civil democracy, Backus desired a "sweet harmony" between church and state. Advocating a postmillennial vision for the new country (typical in American Protestantism in the nineteenth century), Backus believed that a Christian America that voluntarily obeyed the Bible was God's chosen vessel to usher in the future end-time golden age.

The Virginia Story. In the eighteenth-century struggle for religious liberty, Virginia Baptists were frequently persecuted by the Anglicans, the established group in the colony. The English Toleration Act of 1689 permitted Protestant dissenters to conduct their own worship services. Similar to Massachusetts, this usually meant that a limited number of dissenting meetinghouses were government approved. Other restrictions on dissenter religion included the requirements that a preacher must receive a license from the government to preach and must restrain from preaching at certain times. Individuals who allowed ministers to preach on their property were also subject to fines. Regular Baptists generally complied with the laws and respectfully obtained preaching certificates. Separate Baptists often did not, believing that they had a divine call and only God could tell them when and where to preach. Their aggressive evangelistic efforts brought scorn and ridicule. An Anglican opponent once referred to them as gnats because they had the disposition and ability of "those little insignificant animals to tease, to sting, and to torment." Another said, "They cannot meet a man on the road . . . [but have to] ram a text of Scripture down his throat."

Consequently, during the 1760s and 1770s, at least thirty Virginia Baptist ministers were beaten or spent time in prison. Most of these were Separate Baptists, although the leading Regular Baptist, David Thomas, was also persecuted. Lewis Craig, the first Baptist preacher to be arrested, told the court,

> I thank you, gentlemen of the grand jury, for the honour you have done me. While I was wicked and injurious, you took no notice of me; but since I have altered my course of life, and endeavored to reform my neighbors, you concern yourselves much about me.

John Leland. Along with Isaac Backus, during the eighteenth century John Leland was Baptists' most ardent advocate for religious liberty. These leaders, especially Leland, continued the Baptist plea for the separation of church and state already seen in Thomas Helwys, Roger Williams, and John Clarke. Leland wrote in the context of the Enlightenment in colonial Virginia and thus echoed freely from the thought of James Madison and especially Thomas Jefferson. During his later Connecticut years, Leland became known as the "Mammoth Priest" after he presented a large block of cheese to President Jefferson in Washington to demonstrate his political support.

Leland's most influential pamphlet on religious liberty was *Rights of Conscience Inalienable* (1791). He attacked the idea of religious establishments in favor of the sacredness of the unhindered individual conscience. Echoing a longstanding Baptist theme, Leland declared that conscience cannot be surrendered because every person must give an account of himself or herself to the sovereign God at the final judgment.

As Thomas Helwys before him, Leland asserted that religion was fundamentally a matter between God and individuals. Religion did not require a state-supported, established church to survive. On the contrary, "with establishments uninspired fallible men make their own opinions a test of orthodoxy and use their own systems as Procrustes used his iron bedstead to stretch and measure the consciences of all others by." Establishments also favored one particular expression of religion, thus producing "uniformity in religion, which is hypocrisy."

Leland also echoed and thus affirmed the views of Thomas Jefferson (in his 1777 "An Act for Establishing Religious Freedom"):

> Government has no more to do with the religious opinions of men, than it has with the principles of mathematics. Let every man speak freely without fear, maintain the principles that he believes, worship according to his own faith, either one God, three Gods, no God, or twenty Gods. . . .
> It is error, and error alone, that needs human support. . . .

Whereas Isaac Backus was more willing to speak in terms of a "Christian" nation and focused on freedom from government establishment and coercion in religion, Leland was a strict separationist in the mold of Roger Williams. The religious uniformity of the union of church and state, created by Emperor Constantine in the fourth century, had produced persecution and the "shocking monster of [a] Christian nation." Leland declared that a person could be an atheist or a polytheist in America. Special privileges for the religious were anathema and violated the principle of an unfettered conscience.

Leland was no ivory-tower theoretician. He applied his gadfly separationism to specific "church-state" issues. He went much further than most Baptists in questioning the legitimacy of stopping postal mail delivery in deference to a religious day of rest. He opposed religious oaths for office—Backus did not—and questioned the state sponsorship of chaplains. Church and state should be completely separated from the tightening grip of each other's control.

Leland's focus on the individual conscience revealed his rationalism and pietism. While he was clearly a Jeffersonian individualist, he was also, in typical Baptist fashion, a biblicist who sought to model certain New Testament practices that related to the freedom of the individual relationship to God. As Leland understood the Bible, neither Jesus nor the apostles ever gave orders that the civil governments should coerce religious belief. Rather, where complete freedom was the rule, religious revival actually occurred. As voluntary religion reigned supreme in the early nineteenth century, Leland's voice strongly affirmed the role of the common man as opposed to trusting a hierarchical ministry.

Leland's focus on the freedom of the individual conscience not only affected his views of church and state, it affected his ecclesiology. Consequently, he was not interested in reproducing New Testament ecclesiastical polity like most Baptists. Putting his emphasis on individual conversion, church attachment was secondary. He even avoided leading worshippers in the Lord's Supper. The importance of church and communion was left to individual preference.

Leland's trust in the Bible, his distrust of the hierarchical clergy of a state church, his egalitarian faith in the common folk, and his belief in an unfettered conscience before God are summed up in his critical assessment of creeds.

> Confessions of faith often check any further pursuit after truth, confine the mind into a particular way of reasoning, and give rise to frequent separations. To plead for their utility, because they have been common, is as good sense, as to plead for a state establishment of religion, for the same reason; and both are as bad reasoning, as to plead for sin, because it is everywhere. It is sometimes said that hereticks are always averse to confessions of faith. I wish I could say as much of tyrants. But after, all, if a confession of faith, upon the whole, may be advantageous, the greatest care should be taken not to sacralize, or make a petty Bible of it. (Leland, "The Virginia Chronicle," 1790)

Using a typical Protestant aversion to all things Catholic, Leland said that a creed was a "Virgin Mary" between the soul and God. Such props were barriers to direct access of the individual conscience to God.

The General Committee. Throughout the 1770s and 1780s, Virginia Baptists pressured the colonial legislature with petitions in their fight for religious liberty. Regular Baptists submitted petitions in 1770 and 1774 that demanded unrestricted preaching beyond the confines of government approved meetinghouses. On 20 June 1776, Occoquan Baptist Church, led by David Thomas, issued a petition that revealed a shift from seeking toleration to requesting complete religious liberty. The petition was a forerunner of a great influx of petitions that were submitted to the Virginia legislature.

In 1775, Separate Baptists became dominant players in the petition movement to advocate for complete religious liberty. On 12 June 1776, Virginia adopted a state constitution with provisions for full religious liberty and the disestablishment of the Anglican Church. (Section 16 is headed "Free exercise of religion, no establishment of religion.") In the 1780s, a "General Committee," a unified effort of three Separate Baptist associations with cooperation of Regular Baptists, continued the battle for the separation of church and state as new issues arose. John Leland was highly active in the work of the General Committee. The achievement of full religious liberty—a precursor to the blueprint ultimately adopted for the whole nation—was, of course, indebted to the pivotal work of Virginian statesmen, James Madison and Thomas Jefferson. Dissenters, Baptists (and Presbyterians), were some of their strongest supporters.

General Assessment Tax. With the commitment to religious liberty of leaders like John Leland, James Ireland, and other Baptists, it is no surprise to learn of the opposition of Virginia Baptists to a proposal for a general assessment tax that would provide financial support for the Christian faith. With the disestablishment of the Anglican Church, the question arose, What's next? The very popular governor, Patrick Henry, a hero for his "Give me liberty or give me death!" stance during the American Revolution, argued that, because religion was the basis of morality, the new government that was being formed needed a solid moral foundation. Why not, then, have a general tax for religious purposes? Christianity would be established, but the system would be fair because no particular group would be favored over the others. Every citizen would pay a tax to the church of his or her choice. Since religion was good for society, Henry reasoned, the tax should be supported for the well-being of society.

Coming from an eloquent orator like Henry, the plan sounded good. George Washington himself supported the proposed bill. Most Anglicans, recently disestablished, thought it was the best they could hope for in the Revolutionary-era atmosphere.

The primary attack against the proposal came from James Madison, who later became the fourth president of the United States. In his famous "Memorial and Remonstrance against Religious Assessments" (1785), Madison perceived the dangers of any kind of establishment. Who made the government an arbiter of religious truth? Once the government is given the right to establish Christianity to the exclusion of minority faiths, what is to stop the legislators from, in the name of truth, favoring one Christian group over another?

Baptist dissenters understood the heavy hand of tyranny. The Culpeper, Virginia, jail was not a distant memory. They supported Madison and believed government that meddled in spiritual affairs was tyrannical. A compulsory tax implied that religion, if not propped up by the government, would not survive. Madison's warning against tyranny of all types won the day. The general assessment bill was defeated.

In this unwavering defense of religious liberty, some scholars have suggested that Baptists, more than any other Virginia dissenters, effected significant social consequences. By insisting that the property of the formerly established church be sold because it belonged to all Virginians, the gentry class dominated by Anglicans felt the high tide of the egalitarianism of the revolutionary era. In religious language, Baptists wanted religious equality and a freedom of worship unencumbered by state control that characterized the "primitive church" of earliest Christianity.

Not all Baptists in the South were as strong in defense of the separation of church and state as Virginia Baptists. For example, in 1777, South Carolina Baptists resolved that neither the Anglicans nor any Protestant sect be given a favored position by the government. They were willing to call Protestantism the "established faith of South Carolina." Unlike in Virginia, the Anglican Church was allowed to keep its property. In subsequent years, South Carolina Baptists expanded their definition of religious liberty beyond the parameters of Protestantism.

Federal Constitution and the Bill of Rights. Some Baptists, like James Manning of Rhode Island, supported the 1787 ratification of the federal constitution for the new nation. Others, especially in rural areas, were slower to respond favorably to a centralized government authority, given the persecution of dissenters in recent decades. John Leland's fear of centralized hierarchy led him to question the wisdom of constitutional authority, especially when no adequate protection for religious liberty seemed forthcoming from the founding fathers. A legendary Baptist story—in this case still considered historical by scholars—suggests that James Madison met with Leland and agreed to promote a bill of rights that would guarantee full religious freedom for all citizens. Consequently, Leland withdrew his opposition, and decided not to pursue a candidacy opposing Madison for the Virginia delegation to the constitutional convention.

Despite the Bill of Rights in the federal constitution, some states strongly resisted disestablishment. Connecticut maintained its state church until 1818. Massachusetts held to its Puritan past until 1833. In the midst of these ongoing struggles, Thomas Jefferson articulated the view of separation of church and state that became increasingly popular in American society. In a letter to the sympathetic Baptists of Danbury, Connecticut, Jefferson explained his rationale for refusing to observe a government-sponsored national day of prayer. He said that the provisions of the First Amendment built a "wall of separation between Church and State." The Baptist witness for complete religious liberty had never been monolithic, but the views of Roger Williams and John Leland ultimately became identified with American freedom.

Republicanism. Despite their hesitations over ratifying the federal constitution because of religious liberty concerns, Baptists evidently had no problem identifying with the implications of political independence from England. Baptists were quick to support the principles of republican government. They felt that Baptist distinctives were especially compatible with the spirit and direction of the new country. In 1808, William Fristoe wrote a history of the Ketoctin Association of Virginia and added an appendix that gave "reasons why Baptists generally espouse republicanism." With traditional Baptist gusto, he commented that "monarchical government and establishment of religion are twins, wherever the one is, the other appears." The idea of a "national church" contradicted "Christ['s] church in primitive time . . . all that cannot conform to the established system . . . must reconcile themselves to suffering." The freedom and independence found in the Baptist New Testament model of congregational democracy, however, "perfectly corresponds with a government by the people."

In analyzing the growth of evangelical religion in the antebellum South, scholars note the strong connection between popular revivalism and popular support of republicanism. The rapid growth of Baptists, especially among the Separate Baptists, reflected this trend. Some observers view the Separates as a class-based challenge to the authority of the wealthy gentry. Evangelical conversion was made attractive by unequal social conditions. Voluntarism and freedom trumped some of the privileged elements of patriarchal hierarchical society.

Some historians add, however, that Southern evangelicals did not attract a majority of Southerners until the 1830s, and they did so by ultimately appeasing the gentry. Baptists, with their insistence upon modeling early Christianity, their democratic congregationalism, and focus on the individual conscience, however, did not appear to kowtow to the gentry when it came to state-sponsored uniformity and privilege in religion. The Baptist compatibility with America's burgeoning democracy, alongside an evangelism geared toward the laity and the frontier, helped to transform Baptists into the largest denomination in the country at the outset of the nineteenth century.

Free Will and Other Baptists

The eighteenth-century American Baptist story naturally highlights the role of Regular and Separate Baptists because of their numbers and their influential national figures (for example, Isaac Backus, John Leland, Richard Furman, and so forth). Multiple Baptist identities, however, never ceased to populate the Baptist landscape. For example, a German Seventh Day Baptist Church was formed in Germantown, Pennsylvania in 1728. While General Baptists in the South gradually dissolved into Regular Baptist churches, they were the earliest types of Baptists in Maryland, Virginia, and North Carolina. Paul Palmer, Palmer's convert Joseph Parker, and William Sojourner were early leaders. Palmer was especially influential. He started the first General Baptist Church in North Carolina (1727) and in Maryland (1742).

Free Will Baptists. With the eruption of populist religious movements in the years after the American Revolution, Calvinism was modified or attacked with increasing frequency because of its association with the Congregational Standing Order of colonial New England. The growing Methodist movement under Francis Asbury's leadership was an obvious Arminian alternative. One strong reaction to the Regular Baptist tradition in the North was the formation, in 1780, of the Free Will Baptists in New England. Benjamin Randall was the undisputed leader. During the heyday of the First Great Awakening, Randall heard and resisted the message of revivalist George Whitefield. Upon hearing of Whitefield's death in 1770, however, Randall exclaimed, "Whitefield is in heaven and I am on the road to hell." Randall subsequently was converted and became a Congregationalist. In 1775, he became an itinerant Baptist preacher. Like other populist democratic movements of the era, Randall sought to restore the primitive pattern of the New Testament church.

Free Will Baptists recognize June 30, 1780, as the official beginning of their movement. On that day, Randall organized a church of seven members at New Durham, New Hampshire. A new fellowship was needed because Randall had begun to oppose the Calvinistic views of predestination and limited atonement. Rejecting these influential ideas was difficult, Randall said, until God gave him peace in a "cornfield experience" about the truth of the "universal atonement" (all persons could freely accept Christ's offer of salvation) as well as the strength to discard old traditions and return to the Bible. To be a New Testament church, Randall allowed preaching roles for women, practiced foot washing, and had open communion with

Christians of other denominations. Closed communion, from Randall's perspective, was tied to Calvinism's unbiblical idea of limited atonement.

Randall's movement grew throughout New England as he traveled extensively. He often attended more than 300 meetings a year. In 1801, for example, he traveled 2,723 miles and attended 313 meetings. In the process, Randall developed a "connection" of churches that met for fellowship and spiritual guidance. As the spiritual father of the movement, Randall functioned like a Baptist bishop until his death in 1808. He developed monthly, quarterly, and yearly meetings for churches. The first yearly meeting (like a state convention) occurred in 1792. By 1827, all Free Will Baptist churches were sending delegates to a "General Conference." Like other religious bodies in the early nineteenth century, they formed benevolent societies and engaged in social activism. Free Will Baptists were involved, for example, in antislavery activities. They became known as Free Baptists in 1841 when they merged with a small group of "Free Communion Baptists." Although northern Free Will Baptists merged with the Northern Baptist Convention in 1911, a new Free Will denomination, the National Association of Free Will Baptists, emerged in Nashville, Tennessee, in 1935. The group claims the legacy of Benjamin Randall. In imitation of the New Testament church, foot washing is practiced, and continues today.

Relations with Other Christians

Established state churches obviously never wanted to lose their privileged status in the American religious landscape. They did, however, slowly recognize that dissenters were not going away. In some cases, dissenters and the established churches cooperated in surprising fashion. In 1718, when the Harvard-educated Elisha Callender, Jr.—the first native-born American Baptist minister to receive a theological education—was ordained as pastor of First Baptist Church, Boston, leading Congregationalist Cotton Mather preached the ordination sermon and acknowledged that dissenters had been mistreated in years past. After Callender died, Congregationalists commented that he had a "charitable" and "catholic" spirit. Boston Baptists also had Congregationalist ministers for guest preachers during the interim period until a new pastor was selected. Later in the eighteenth century, Isaac Backus suggested that the "ecumenical" ordination service of Callender was a key marker on the Baptist road toward acceptance in American society.

Interdenominational cooperation in the eighteenth century was often the result of the scarcity of ministers in an area. If an itinerant minister came to a region that had no settled minister, believers would allow him to preach. On one of his preaching tours of the South, for example, John Gano preached to a group of Presbyterians. Isolation inevitably led to some cooperation. Urban pastors were also more prone to work with other religious groups on a limited basis. In the South, Oliver Hart once delivered the eulogy at an Anglican funeral and occasionally was the guest preacher at non-Baptist dissenting churches. In 1779, Samuel Stillman, pastor of First Baptist Church, Boston, was the first Baptist ever to deliver the "annual election" sermon for the city of Boston.

Despite instances of respect and the inception of an era of accommodation between Baptists, other dissenters, and religious establishments, strong sectarian tensions still existed throughout the colonial period. During the revivalism of the First Great Awakening, the various religious groups bickered over the acceptability of revival methods and the emotion that accompanied public conversions. In the Middle Colonies, for example, Abel Morgan of the Philadelphia Baptist Association clashed with Samuel Finley of the Presbyterians. In numerous public debates, Finley said that the Baptist insistence on believer's baptism as the only acceptable baptism, as well as the only New Testament method of constituting a church, haughtily de-Christianized all other believers.

In New England, Separate Baptists experienced tensions when they left the Congregationalists over infant baptism. Nevertheless, Isaac Backus wrote about Philemon Robbins, a Separate Congregationalist, who had been harassed by the established church for preaching a revival to Separate Baptists. Dissenters could find a common bond in opposition to the establishment.

The Baptists of colonial Virginia revealed mixed approaches to other Christians. The more persecuted Separate Baptists did not hesitate to call Anglican clergy unspiritual, worldly, and more concerned with their salaries than the gospel. Because Regular Baptists demonstrated a more cooperative attitude toward the government, they were restrained in their criticism. The leading Regular Baptist of Virginia, David Thomas, stood by his Baptist convictions on baptism and church polity, but he asserted that Anglicans possessed many sound articles of the faith. While he defended his right to preach evangelical doctrine to Anglicans, he insisted such preaching should not be done in a presumptuous manner: "If any of our sect have spoken disrespectfully of her as such, I freely allow it was imprudence in them to do so."

The creation of Rhode Island College in 1764 foreshadowed the strong interchurch cooperation present in an academic environment. The school's charter had reserved nineteen of thirty-five trustee spots for Baptists. However, no religious tests were mandated for students or faculty. No avowed atheists or Catholics were allowed admission in the nineteenth century, but by 1770 Jewish students were permitted.

During the eighteenth century, Baptists did not claim that other Christians were not Christian, but the focus on believer's baptism and closed communion remained points of contention. Samuel Jones, in his tract on church discipline for the Philadelphia Baptist Association (1798), urged Baptist churches not to give "letters of dismission" to persons leaving their churches for non-Baptist congregations. A few lines describing a person's character could be issued. These sectarian practices remained throughout the century.

Baptist Women

Before the First Great Awakening, few women had opportunity to speak, much less preach, in American church life. Only the Quakers, who spoke of the inner light in each believer, allowed women to minister. The attitude of Roger Williams typified not only the Baptist response, but the general Christian view, when he said that the preaching of women should be "abhorred."

The focus on individual religious experience in the First Great Awakening temporarily altered the landscape for women in American religion. Dissenting groups on the fringe of Puritan society, such as Separate Congregationalists and Separate Baptists, were more concerned with a divine call than an educated clergy, and they tended to be more tolerant of women who wanted to speak. American society still considered women to be inferior physically and intellectually, but revivalism emphasized the shared experience of conversion. Some historians note that feminine "heart-language" rather than "head-language" characterized emotional conversions. Consequently, women were allowed to publicly tell their conversion stories and some became exhorters ("preaching" from the pew that urged sinners to repent and be converted). Not all Separate Baptists approved, however. Isaac Backus was once interrupted in a service by three female exhorters, but he preferred lay male exhorters.

Regular Baptists of the Philadelphia Baptist Association, who had been less open to the revivalism of the First Great Awakening, addressed the issue of a woman's role in church in 1746 at an associational meeting and

begrudgingly gave women limited avenues to communicate. They acknowledged that the prohibition against women speaking in church was interpreted in an absolute sense by some churches. The association, however,
suggested that women be given at least a "mute voice" and be allowed to
stand or raise their hands to express their opinions on certain matters.
Silence in the church should not exclude a woman from confessing her faith
to demonstrate her conversion, nor should it exclude women from speaking
in disciplinary cases when necessary. If a church objected to hearing a
woman speak, then they should make a brother "a mouth" for her. If women
were allowed to speak, however, they should not "open the floodgate of
speech in an imperious, tumultuous, masterly manner." From their reading
of the New Testament ("Let your women keep silence," 1 Corinthians
14:34) the Regular Baptists concluded that "the silence, with subjection,
enjoined on all women . . . is such a silence as excludes all women
whomsoever from all degrees of teaching, ruling, governing, dictating, and
leading in the church of God."

After a decade of revival fires waned in the North, the fountain of
opportunities for women dried up. The Southern phase of the First Great
Awakening soon brought new avenues. Separate Baptists not only had
women to testify of their conversion experiences, they had women
preachers. In 1770, Margaret Meuse Clay was arrested for unlicensed
preaching in Chesterfield, Virginia, and avoided prison after an anonymous
donor paid her fine. Martha Stearns Marshall was the best-known Separate
Baptist woman. The sister of Separate Baptist patriarch, Shubal Stearns, and
the wife of evangelist, Daniel Marshall, Martha was considered a powerful
preacher who, according to her contemporaries, was "of singular piety and
surprising elocution" and was able to "melt" her audience into tears with her
exhortations. In contrast, Morgan Edwards called her husband, Daniel, "a
weak man, a stammerer, and no scholar."

Martha Stearns Marshall convinced her husband to become a Baptist
and they initially served as missionaries to the Mohawks in New York
before joining her brother, Shubal Stearns, at Sandy Creek, North Carolina
in 1755. Together they preached the Separate Baptist gospel in several
Southern states and in 1771 established Kiokee Baptist Church, the oldest
continuing Baptist church in Georgia.

Martha was not simply an assistant to her husband. After entering the
colony of Georgia, which was still under the rules of an Anglican establishment, Daniel was arrested for preaching without a license. Martha
immediately defended her husband to the constable. Quoting memorized

Bible passages, she again advocated for religious freedom at Daniel's trial. Daniel was convicted, but Martha's witness converted the constable who arrested Daniel and the magistrate who ruled over the case. Martha's career also revealed the challenges of being a woman and an evangelist in the colonial period. She preached, despite the demands of giving birth to ten children. Not suprisingly, one child was named after Martha's aunt, Eunice, who had also been a dissenting female preacher.

Separate Baptists of the South were the most egalitarian of eighteenth-century dissenters regarding women in ministerial roles. One possible reason was that Separate Baptists were popular among lower-class whites in the "backcountry," and revivalism was, in part, a religious alternative as well as a protest against the control of the more patriarchal Anglican establishment. Separate Baptist primitivist biblicism was also a factor. In their zeal to imitate the New Testament church, numerous Separate Baptists churches had women deacons and women elders. The eighteenth-century Baptist chronicler, Morgan Edwards, found forty churches with deaconesses and six churches with elderesses. An elderess had the pastoral function of counseling and ministering to female converts. This openness toward women in ministry was one of the barriers between Separate and Regular Baptists. When they united, a precedent for denominational respectability and centralization had occurred. The Regular Baptist disdain for women in ministry was better suited to acceptance in Southern patriarchal antebellum society. United Baptists moved away from women preaching/exhorting or even voting in church matters.

As other Baptists set out on the road toward respectability at the turn of the nineteenth century, the young Free Will Baptist movement and other new sects in the North (for example, the Christian Connection) affirmed women preachers. Like dissenters during the First Great Awakening, these sects drew many adherents from the lower class and were partially a "Christ-against-culture" response to the rapid social and economic consumerist changes (gradual move to a market economy) of the new century. Historians cite several factors for the eruption of female preaching among these more sectarian groups: the lack of ordained male clergy to meet the needs of churches; the higher percentage of women than men involved in church; and the spontaneity and emotion of the revivals of the Second Great Awakening. Free Will Baptists especially expressed the developing democratization of American religion (explained fully in the next chapter) through egalitarian ministry: all persons could read and interpret the Bible. At the same time, egalitarian ministry was their attempt to duplicate the New Testament church. It was one facet of an intense apocalyptic emphasis—women preachers were one signal of the end-times (Acts 2)—but not a call to equal religious authority via ordination or women's rights in the political sphere.

Historians suggest that Free Will Baptists had more female preachers in the early nineteenth century than any other religious group in America. In the 1790s, Sally Parsons actually traveled with Free Will Baptist founder, Benjamin Randall, and preached and assisted in the creation of churches. (She later married Randall's son.) At an 1803 Quarterly Meeting, three women—Fanney Proctor, Hannah Lock, and Eliza Moore—were listed as "Publick Preachers and Exhorters." At least twenty-seven Free Will women itinerated and preached in the northern states during the first few decades of the nineteenth century.

Just as other Baptist bodies traveled the road to greater centralization and social respectability, Free Will Baptists, with a membership that had grown to 60,000 by mid-century, joined the mainstream with regards to women in ministry. Free Will Baptist leaders yearned for an educated clergy and formed their first Education Society in 1840. Consequently, they became less apocalyptic in their preaching, less open to emotional enthusiasm and forsook their countercultural support of women preachers. Ironically, Hosea Quinby, the son of Dolly Quinby, an early Free Will Baptist preacher, was the first college-educated minister in Free Will Baptist ranks. (In 1853, he became the assistant moderator of the denomination's General Conference.) An 1844 decision of the General Conference made it clear: women should not "bear rule in the church," but should submit to the decisions of the male leadership.

The journey from sect to church for Free Will Baptists meant that leadership was centralized in males—as it was in society and in older, more stable religious groups. By the mid-nineteenth century, rumblings of equal rights for women in America were just beginning with voices like that of "feminist" Elizabeth Cady Stanton, which most denominations considered dangerously radical. Baptists were second to none in declaring the "spiritual gift" of female domesticity: respectable Christian women were expected to develop model Christian homes of virtue but leave roles of authority to men.

Conclusion

During the eighteenth century, the Baptist search for the New Testament church expressed itself in a variety of ways. The Separate Baptist practice of the "nine rites," their use of elderesses and deaconesses, and their fervent evangelism were efforts to restore elements of the earliest Christian churches. While John Leland seemed to care little for church polity and administering the ordinances, he revealed the heart of Baptist worship: preaching a "New Testament sermon." The pivotal role of the association in the Philadelphia tradition found support, Baptists believed, in the practices of cooperating churches in the biblical Book of Acts. Free Will Baptists practiced footwashing and allowed women to preach in order to be faithful to their reading of the New Testament. Attempted faithfulness to New Testament practices continued to dominate Baptist life in the insistence upon believer's baptism by immersion as the foundation of the church.

In the historical setting of the eighteenth century, the struggle to achieve religious liberty in the midst of established state churches was ever present. Isaac Backus and John Leland were influenced by Enlightenment thought. Leland was an unabashed Jeffersonian politician. Still, both leaders were especially shaped by how they read the Bible and by the legacy of their Baptist predecessors. They reflected the tradition of Thomas Helwys, Roger Williams, and John Clarke. Genuine New Testament faith had to be free or it was not genuine. The congregational democracy of Baptist church polity—the church government method that Baptists believed was clearly revealed in the New Testament—was part and parcel with the new nation's democratic ideals.

By the end of the eighteenth century, Baptists had begun the journey toward respectability. There was no turning back, and the tension between imitating biblical faith and yearning for societal acceptance became familiar territory in the widening Baptist landscape.

Antebellum America: Baptist Democratization, Denominational Centralization, and Slavery, or, Baptists and Their Different Bibles

Historians contend that the democratization of American Christianity occurred in the post-Revolutionary era. The environment of disestablishment aided the move away from aristocratic and hierarchical colonial churches to an anticlerical localism. Ordinary believers asserted the right to read the Bible by themselves rather than trust the state-supported clergy. In the era of Jacksonian democracy, Christianity was shaped by the common people, centralized authority met its match in democratic dissent, the individual conscience reigned, and popular sovereignty won the day.

Religious Democracy and Organizational Development

Frontier Revivalism. Baptist growth exploded at the beginning of the nineteenth century. The Baptist stance on religious liberty and a fervent patriotism during the American Revolution began to break down barriers to acceptance in society. The Baptist dual emphases on the independence of the local church and congregational church government went hand in hand with the populist and democratic principles of the Jeffersonian and Jacksonian eras. Baptists and Methodists benefited most from the westward expansion of the nascent country, and each denomination quickly added over 10,000 adherents. From 1800 to 1803 Baptists in Kentucky, for example, increased from 106 churches with 5,119 members to 219 churches with 15,495 members.

This frontier growth can also be seen as an expression of the Second Great Awakening, called by some historians the most influential revival in American history. Camp meetings—the covered wagons camped for days since they could not return home each night—became the place to find God. At the legendary Cane Ridge camp meeting (August 1801, Bourbon County, Kentucky), ministers of several denominations preached to crowds estimated to be 10,000 to 25,000 in number. (Compare this number to nearby Lexington, Kentucky, which had 2,000 residents.) The revival's extreme emotionalism (bodily jerking and "barking" for Jesus) gripped many in the crowds, although some Baptist preachers soon denounced it. Still, frontier revivalism reinforced a Baptist population explosion.

The Baptist emphasis upon a personal experience of conversion matched the individualistic frontier spirit. A revivalistic sermon was essentially a recounting of one's conversion experience peppered by some biblical proof texts. Since education was largely unavailable on the frontier, it was often dismissed as unnecessary for authentic faith. Ironically, the frontier growth of Presbyterians, who helped create the camp meetings, faltered because of educational requirements for ministers. On the other hand, Baptist farmer-preachers and Methodist circuit riders—both of whom preached because they felt a "divine call" from God—adapted to the migratory and decentralized environment of the frontier.

In this age of voluntarism, denominational competition was fierce. Without an established church, a person was free to choose a church without restrictions, and a type of "market Christianity" resulted. Baptist and Methodists preachers would often travel into an area, start a church, and then go to their next "circuit." Before they returned, the rival denomination would sometimes "steal sheep" from the other. Theological battles also raged, mostly over the proper form and importance of baptism. Each group ridiculed the other with sharp attacks and condescending humor. Peter Cartwright, one of the most prominent Methodist itinerants, said that Baptists "make so much ado about baptism by immersion that the uninformed would suppose that heaven was an island, and there was no way to get there but by swimming or diving." Another Methodist itinerant described what he thought was the Baptist obsession with immersion in equally colorful terms: "You Baptists remind me of an ox on a hot day in July. Every time you see a little water you run and jump in it."

Frontier Baptists, of course, were equally colorful in their objection to infant baptism: "You Methodists remind me of a dog with hydrophobia. Every time you see a little water it throws you into a fit." Not to be outdone, a Baptist preacher told a crowd that included some Methodists, "God made the world one-fourth land, and three-fourths water, no doubt having baptism in view when he made it." The ultimate Baptist attack was the appeal to New Testament restorationism, not only in word but in song:

> John was a Baptist preacher,
>   when he baptized the Lamb,

So Jesus was a Baptist,
and thus the Baptists came. (Appalachian folk hymn)

Voluntary Missionary Societies. In addition to revivalism, or partly because of it, the voluntary spirit of the age produced a multitude of religious benevolent societies. Societies focused upon one ministry and drew upon voluntary support from individuals and churches. Many "local" societies were interdenominational in character and included extensive Baptist participation.

Numerous societies developed to advance missionary concerns. The first "local" interdenominational missionary society in America was the New York Missionary Society (1796). Elkanah Holmes, a Baptist minister, worked with Native Americans before Baptists left the Society over its tolerance of infant baptism. On 9 October 1800, Mary Webb led eight Baptist and six Congregationalist women in organizing the Boston Female Society for Missionary Purposes, the first woman's missionary society in the world. Webb, a Baptist, served (from her wheelchair!—she was paralyzed at age five) as secretary-treasurer for fifty years. She was controversial because Baptist men had concerns about her leadership role, but she was inspirational to the Baptist movement as a whole. By 1817 she had corresponded with more than 200 other women's societies around the country.

In the late eighteenth century, some Baptist associations had already practiced "home" missionary outreach. In the early nineteenth century, Baptists, like other Protestants, also formed their own regional/state missionary societies that had a singular ministry focus. National missionary societies soon formed as well. Their development reflected the growth of a national identity in the young country. Some historians suggest that the nationalistic fervor from the War of 1812 helped to propel the missionary advance in denominations. Many societies were again interdenominational in character (for example, the American Bible Society, 1816). The pioneering work of English Baptist William Carey was also a significant impetus to the creation of national missionary societies.

Congregationalists formed the first national missionary society in America in 1810. Baptists followed suit in 1814. The two organizations were linked in unexpected ways. In 1812 a missionary couple, Adoniram Judson, who had helped create the Congregationalist society, and his wife Ann Hasseltine Judson, were traveling to their assignment in India and decided to prepare themselves for meeting the missionary "legend" William Carey by reading scriptural references to baptism. Their study of the New Testament ended with their rejection of infant baptism. Ann later wrote that she did not want to become a Baptist, but the truth of the Bible compelled her and Adoniram to become Baptists. On a different ship, a similar change of theological heart occurred to another Congregationalist missionary, Luther Rice. Uncertainty for the young missionaries loomed when they submitted resignations to their sending agency, but the Judsons went on to Burma and requested support from American Baptists. Boston Baptists, led by Thomas Baldwin, provided some immediate support. Luther Rice returned to the United States and promoted the creation of a national Baptist mission organization.

A National Organization: The Triennial Convention. American Baptists responded with the organization of their first national body, a society to support international missions, the General Missionary Convention of the Baptist Denomination of the United States (usually called the Triennial Convention because it met every three years). Convening at First Baptist Church of Philadelphia, the convention elected Richard Furman of Charleston, South Carolina, as president and Thomas Baldwin of Boston as secretary. William Staughton of Philadelphia, who was known for his strong support of William Carey's endeavors in India, was chosen to be the corresponding secretary. These three men, well educated and cosmopolitan in outlook, epitomized the evolution of Baptists into a respectable national body with a national consciousness. They had "arrived." At the same time, of course, some Baptists cautioned against the increased centralization and steps toward "respectability" in Baptist life. At a church service in Philadelphia the night before the General Missionary Convention was formed, famed religious-liberty advocate John Leland warned against the dangers of aristocratic ministerial control. Just as Israel asked God for a king in the days of Samuel, Leland lamented, people wanted societies with a hierarchy of officers so they could be like their denominational neighbors.

Initially, Baptist enthusiasm for missions was feverish and widespread. Luther Rice, who was appointed to tour America to raise funds, found receptive audiences. The Judsons were appointed to Burma (1814) and published accounts of trials and adventures on the mission field became best sellers in antebellum America. At one point, Adoniram Judson spent nineteen months in jail because of his work. Ann bribed the guards and managed to smuggle food and a Bible to him. Soon afterward, Ann died on the mission field. During his ministry, Adoniram Judson experienced severe eye problems, yet in 1834 he completed a Burmese translation of the Bible. Conversions were slow—the first conversion did not occur until 1819—but determination and sacrifice marked the captivating story of missionaries for supporters back home. Missionaries became Baptist (and Protestant) martyrs. Not unexpectedly, the missionary fervor resulted in almost one hundred missionary appointments in the first twenty years of the existence of the Triennial Convention.

The missionary organization immediately began evolving into an actual convention, that is, it soon supported more than one societal ministry. In 1817, John Mason Peck and James Welch were appointed as "home" missionaries to the Missouri territory. Home mission work included preaching for churches without pastors and ministry to Native Americans. Support from the Triennial Convention was dropped in 1820, but Peck continued his mission work independently. The Triennial Convention dropped its work in home missions in 1826, and a separate society was established in 1832 called the American Baptist Home Missionary Society.

Controversy also occurred after the Triennial Convention decided to take on an educational component, which was the dream of Richard Furman. An institution was needed, Baptist cosmopolitans argued, to train more effective ministers for the inseparable tasks of evangelizing and civilizing the masses. Other denominations had already seen the need for theological training. Consequently, Columbian College (now George Washington University) was chartered on 9 February 1821 with William Staughton as the first president. Yet, education soon became a divisive issue. The school became the obsession of Luther Rice, but he subsequently proved to be a poor administrator of funds. He was accused but exonerated of embezzlement, and in 1826 he lost his official fund-raising position with the convention. Sadly, Rice retired to the South after having lost many of his friends to the controversy. Moreover, many Baptists soon felt the focus on education detracted from missions and the goal of saving the "heathen."

With the withdrawal of support from Columbian College, international missions once again became the sole ministry of the Triennial Convention. Thomas Baldwin and Richard Furman, the two most influential advocates of multiple convention-based ministries, both died in 1825. The return to the societal approach in 1826—called the "Great Reversal"—revealed the ever-present tension in Baptist life regarding the independence of the local church and the pull toward centralization.

Francis Wayland, president of Brown University, epitomized and greatly contributed to the reversal. Elected as the first corresponding secretary of the Massachusetts Baptist Convention (1824) and receptive to convention-style ministries, Wayland soon decided that only societal ministries could protect the local church from a constantly growing giant called connectionalism. Pragmatically, Wayland was intensely committed to foreign missions and the singular focus of the societal method offered a greater chance for missionary success. By 1860, Wayland had moved away from societal methods and said that only ministries controlled by local churches would protect the individual freedom inherent in Baptist life.

Reactions against Denominational Centralization

Campbellism. Conflicts related to the democratization of American religion were readily apparent on the frontier with the "restorationist" movement of Alexander Campbell and its cousin (similar, but separate), the antimissions movement. In 1809, Alexander's father, Thomas Campbell, formed an independent group in Pennsylvania to promote the unity of all believers under the name of "Christian." In 1811 this group constituted itself as the Brush Run Church. In 1812 the Brush Run Church ordained young Alexander, and shortly thereafter Alexander assumed leadership of the "movement."

In the same year, the Brush Run Church affirmed believer's baptism by immersion and in 1815 joined the Redstone Baptist Association. Alexander Campbell began an itinerant ministry throughout the frontier and denounced denominational bickering and divisions. The restrictions imposed by confessions of faith and the doctrinal corruptions that had developed in Christian history needed to be cast aside in favor of a return to the simple faith and practices of the New Testament.

Campbell's message of restoring the Christian church to the New Testament model appealed to many Baptists because of its claim to focus solely on biblical authority rather than inferior tradition and binding creeds. The "reformer's" insistence upon believer's baptism by immersion naturally garnered him a receptive audience. The "no creed but the Bible" motto also supported the democratic antihierarchical populism prevalent on the frontier—each individual was free and able to interpret the Scriptures.

Not all Baptists were drawn to "Campbellism," as opponents called the movement. In 1816, Campbell preached an associational sermon ("Sermon on the Law") that seemed to disavow the authority of the Old Testament. Campbell was also accused of distorting the roles of faith and baptism. He spoke of faith as intellectual assent to the fact that Jesus was the Messiah, but seemed to discount faith as an inner (heart) experience of personal trust. Believer's baptism by immersion was called the final required step of obedience in the salvation process, an idea that caused Baptist critics to label Campbell an advocate of baptismal regeneration, that is, that baptism saves.

In 1823, Campbell began publishing the *Christian Baptist*, in which he not only criticized confessions, but lambasted mission and Bible societies as extrabiblical. Campbell finally left the Redstone Baptist Association in 1825 because of its adherence to the Philadelphia Confession of Faith. Then in 1832, Campbell and his "Disciples" joined with like-minded Barton Stone and his "Christians" to become a new denomination—the "Christian Church (Disciples of Christ)" (often referred to as the "Stone-Campbell Movement"). Hundreds of Baptist churches on the frontier joined the movement, including up to half the Baptist churches in Kentucky. Even the First Baptist churches in some areas left the Baptist fold.

Antimissions Controversy. A full-scale assault, known as the "antimissions movement," was made on centralized missions. One antimissions leader was John Taylor who was converted by Separate Baptists in Virginia and became a prominent itinerant preacher in Kentucky. In 1819, he published his *Thoughts on Missions* which was a severe indictment of Luther Rice and the burgeoning mission movement among American Baptists.

Taylor related that two young Congregationalist missionaries from the east coast visited him and lavished exuberant praise on the missionary movement. However, when they urged him to emphasize mission giving, which would also benefit his own ministerial support, he "smelled a New England Rat." Taylor resented the haughtiness and moralizing of missionaries who felt that if they did not establish churches on the frontier, then the inferior frontier Baptists would surely fail.

Missionaries like Luther Rice and Adoniram Judson, Taylor concluded, were in love with money, power, and prestige. Rice was a "modern Tetzel" (the Dominican preacher of indulgences who was harshly criticized by Martin Luther, thus leading to the Protestant Reformation) and Judson "had the same taste for money that the horse leech has for blood." False teachers in the New Testament always loved money, Taylor noted. Common sense should have suggested that Rice and Judson unite with the English Baptist work of pioneer William Carey when they became Baptists, but their attempt for a separate mission society was, according to Taylor, a way to achieve a grand empire and thus more personal notoriety. Taylor even blistered Rice for obesity and suggested that the "Judas-like money grabber" had never denied himself a healthy meal.

Another influential critic of missions was Daniel Parker, a pastor of several churches in Tennessee near the Kentucky line from 1806 to 1817. At an associational meeting in 1815, the uneducated but commanding preacher harshly attacked mission societies (like the Triennial Convention),

Bible societies, and theological schools as extrabiblical. He later continued his antimission work in Illinois before moving to Texas and establishing the first Baptist church there.

Parker is best known for a unique type of strict Calvinism. His Pilgrim Predestinarian Regular Baptist Church (begun in Crawford County, Illinois, in 1833) was rooted in his understanding of the "serpent's seed." Citing God's message to the serpent in Genesis 3:15 ("I will put enmity between you and the woman, and between your seed and her seed"), Parker declared that after the Fall in the Garden of Eden, the "daughters of Eve" possessed either the "serpent's seed" or the "seed of Christ." Those born with the "serpent's seed" were the nonelect, the Devil's children, and predestined to hell; those born with the good seed were the elect and predestined to heaven. Parker ironically practiced evangelistic preaching; yet, his "serpent's-seed" doctrine aided the antimissions cause. Baptist home missionary Jonathan Mason Peck lamented that Parker was "one of those singular and extraordinary beings whom Divine Providence permits to arise as a scourge to his church."

After initially supporting Luther Rice and a missionary society, frontier Baptists, among others, followed up John Taylor's critique with antimission resolutions. In 1827, the Kehukee Church of Halifax, North Carolina, issued the "Kehukee Declaration" which vowed to discard all missionary societies, Bible societies, and theological seminaries because they were unscriptural. In 1832, the Black Rock Church of Maryland, assisted by antimissions Baptists from neighboring states, issued the more elaborate "Black Rock Declaration." The statement likewise criticized "man-made" organizations that were not instituted by Christ or the apostles in the New Testament and were not the "ancient principles" of Baptists. These extrabiblical false ministries included:

- Tract Societies. Tracts are given more authority than the Bible. Can the publishers be trusted?
- Sunday Schools. Do they preach that education is necessary for salvation?
- Bible Societies. They put power in the hands of a few (the worldly publisher and the educated elitist, a "monstrous combination").
- Missionary Societies. Local democratic churches in the New Testament, not aristocratic societies, are the mission-sending agencies. Missionaries seem to love fame more than souls.
- Theological Schools. They are "a real pest to the church of Christ." They support an aristocracy based on human knowledge.

The antimissions movement was a clear expression of the persistence of biblical primitivism in Baptist life. A literal conformity to the Bible was the cornerstone for rejecting (some would say fearing) new modern institutions like missionary societies. These were viewed as human inventions that attempted to usurp God's New Testament blueprint. When the biblical Jonah preached to the Ninevites, antimissions leaders noted, he had not attended seminary or been sent out by a missionary society. While not all who rejected missions were strict Calvinists who denied any human role in the salvation process, many were, and consequently, they were horrified when they perceived that missionary societies were in reality a manipulative human means of inducing conversions which undercut the role of the Holy Spirit.

The antimissions movement also reflected the era of Jacksonian democracy with its focus on localism and the rights of the common man over against the perceived imperialistic aristocracy of Easterners who advocated a more centralized organization of "hierarchical societies." The conflict revealed strong class and sectional antagonisms on a largely rural, economically insecure frontier. Placing power in the hands of the haughty, educated elite would "sap the foundation of Baptist republican government." Consequently, antimissions advocates abhorred the idea of a paid, professional ministry. They believed that when ministry became a lucrative employment which required theological education for validation, the minister's motivation became suspect, especially for a missionary like Luther Rice who was always, it seemed, asking for funds.

Even the temperance campaigns that Eastern missionaries advocated were repelled. Alcohol—one of the few affordable luxuries for a poor farmer—was not going to be subject to the social control of a wealthier, moralizing, Yankee class. An old frontier story captured the attitude. A traveling preacher was invited to stay at a house on the frontier. When the family was alone, they queried among themselves what kind of preacher the man was. They decided he wasn't a Presbyterian because he was not dressed well enough and he was not a Methodist because "his coat was not cut right." Then one of the daughters looked in his saddlebag for a clue, and, after finding a liquor bottle, confidently asserted, "Ma, he's a Hardshell Baptist!"

By 1844, the antimissions movement claimed more than 1,600 churches with at least 68,000 members. These "hard-shell" or "primitive" Baptists resisted the modernization of the wider Baptist movement for old-fashioned and, in their mind, ancient biblical ways. Baptists in America had experienced their first significant internal conflict. More were to come.

Millenarian Movements. While most of American Christianity had deep roots in England, the revivalistic fervor and voluntaristic spirit among the masses of the new country spawned several new indigenous—native to America—religious movements. Some emphasized perfectionism, attempting to create utopian communities on earth, and some advocated millenarianism, the heralding of the imminent return of Jesus. Several new movements flourished on the frontier in New York state, later called the "burned-over district" (that is, with revivalism). The Shakers, who believed that Christ had returned in the form of a woman—their leader Mother Ann Lee—settled in New York in 1774. The group grew with an influx of Baptist converts. At its pinnacle in the mid-eighteenth century, the movement boasted 6,000 members. Most Baptists strongly opposed the Shakers for their messianic belief in "Mother Ann" and unorthodox practices such as required celibacy and attempts to communicate with the dead.

Baptists also opposed the millenarian movement of the "Church of the Latter Day Saints" (Mormonism) which was led by Joseph Smith. One of the earliest converts and spokespersons for Smith, however, was Sidney Rigdon, who had been a Baptist pastor in Pennsylvania and Ohio for seven years before joining the movement of Alexander Campbell. When Baptists later began mission efforts in the Mormon culture of Utah, they called it "Satan's seat."

The millenarian movement that produced the most widespread publicity about the possibility of Christ's soon return was "Millerism," named for a Baptist "lay preacher" (licensed, but not ordained) from the "burned-over district" of New York. William Miller did a detailed study of biblical prophecy and determined that Christ would return "around 1843." In the mid-1830s, Miller traveled the public lecture circuit and used extensive charts to explain the end of time, a practice still used by prophecy enthusiasts at the turn of the twenty-first century. After a financial panic in 1837, audiences were even more receptive to Miller's message, and in January 1843, he actually specified that Jesus would return between March of 1843 and March of 1844. Miller believed that the Church had fallen away from the apostolic pattern; he viewed himself as a restorer of the genuine New Testament Church.

Many Baptists became avid Millerites. Miller appealed to the individual conscience, the ability of the common folk to read the Bible for themselves, and in good populist fashion, criticized the haughtiness of the learned clergy. Miller's preaching split his Baptist church in Low Hampton, New York, and even attracted the support of Elon Galusha, the twenty-year president of New York Baptists. While he did not acknowledge Miller's specifics about the year 1843, Galusha did preach that believers should "fly to Jesus, swiftly fly, your sins confess," in order to avoid the imminent wrath of God. As a result of his preaching, Galusha was forced to resign his pastorate. Reaction to the Millerite movement contributed to the decline of revivalistic fervor among Baptists in the North.

Miller's following came from across denominational lines, and at its peak it had 50,000 adherents, with as many as a million individuals who were cautiously interested. After the "great disappointment" many lost faith in Miller, but some "adventists" ('advent' referring to the coming of Jesus) said Christ had returned spiritually and looked for new keys to understanding the end of time. Miller's successor was Ellen White, a woman who claimed to have received 2,000 visions from God. White contended that Sabbath worship must be reinstituted before Christ would literally return. Some scholars suggest that White learned about Sabbath worship from tracts and the ministry of the Seventh Day Baptists of New York.

Developing Theological Identity

Theology/Confessions. During the first half of the nineteenth century, the democratization of American Christianity competed with the Calvinism that had dominated the colonial established churches. While Weslyan Methodists led the way with their thoroughly Arminian gospel of free will, the "formal theology" of most Baptists was still Calvinism. The success of revivalism and democratic idealism, which expressed considerable confidence in the abilities of a free common people, softened or 'Arminianized' the practice of Calvinism. In other words, many Baptists still talked like Calvinists but preached like Arminians with a focus on freedom. Baptists focused their preaching on the salvation of the individual and stripped sermons of "arcane doctrine." Some Baptists tied to the lower end of the social scale found no warmth in predestination. In his *Fifty Years among the Baptists* (see also below), Baptist historian David Benedict reported that one Baptist crassly quoted some "doggerel verses," the chorus of which was

> Then fill up the glass,
>   and count him an ass
> Who preaches up predestination.

Benedict, a strong Calvinist himself, criticized the shift in Baptist circles away from what he called the "high authority" of the Philadelphia Confession of 1742. The strong meat of Calvinism was being lost to the "mere water and milk" of Arminianism.

The New Hampshire Confession of 1833 reflected this shift in theological emphases. The strong Calvinism of New Hampshire Baptists was challenged by the influence of Benjamin Randall and the Free Will Baptist movement. Randall also gave significant authority to quarterly meetings which seemed to imply an affinity with centralization. New Hampshire Baptists responded with a confession that emphasized the importance of the local church and omitted any reference to a universal church. The confession still articulated Calvinism, but in much milder terms than previous Baptist confessions. The growing influence of Arminianism in Baptist life was revealed by the declaration that the rejection of salvation was due to a person's "inherent depravity and voluntary rejection of the gospel," and that the perseverance of the saints described only "real believers as endure to the end . . . and . . . are kept by the power of God." In an era when holiness teachers (Methodists and others) were arguing for instantaneous sanctification through the baptism of the Holy Spirit, the New Hampshire Confession maintained that sanctification was a "progressive work" that relied on "appointed means" such as Bible reading, prayer, and self-examination.

Gradually the New Hampshire Confession became the most influential Baptist confession in America. In 1853, J. Newton Brown of the American Baptist Publication Society revised the confession and published it in *The Baptist Church Manual*. J. M. Pendleton, a key leader of Landmarkism, also included it in his 1867 *Church Manual Designed for the Use of Baptist Churches*. Landmark Baptists were especially attracted to the confession's focus on the local church.

Baptist Distinctives. In his book, *Notes on Principles and Practices of Baptist Churches* (1857), Francis Wayland assessed what it meant to be a Baptist. He touted the "exclusive spirituality of the church" (regenerate membership; no infant baptism), the priesthood of believers, and the independence of every local church. Like so many Baptists before him, Wayland linked the importance of the individual conscience to the sole authority of Scripture. "Soul liberty," a term he borrowed from Roger Williams and used to describe the "absolute separation of church and state," was the "peculiar glory" of Baptists. Wayland asserted that Baptist "garments have never been defiled by any violation of the rights of conscience." Soul liberty meant that each believer had the right of private interpretation. The only Baptist creed was the New Testament; besides, denominations that require creeds still had schism. Wayland contended, "The Bible without the hindrance of a creed is allowed to be pure truth." He acknowledged that Baptists had confessions of faith, but "probably not one in ten thousand of our members ever heard of their existence." Baptists were different from other Christians because "we profess to take as our guide, in all matters of religious belief and practice, the New Testament, the whole New Testament, and nothing but the New Testament."

William B. Johnson, the most influential Southern Baptist at mid-nineteenth century, had views similar to Wayland. One year after accepting the presidency of the Southern Baptist Convention (1846), Johnson wrote *The Gospel Developed through the Government and Order of the Churches of Jesus Christ* in which he also affirmed "fundamental principles" found in Baptist life. These "fundamental principles" were God's sovereignty in salvation, "the supreme authority of the Scriptures," the "right of private interpretation" of Scripture, "the independent, democratical, Christocractic form of church government," and a conscious personal conversion experience. Like Wayland, Johnson was anticreedal, but he did support women deacons, a minority position in Baptist life.

Ministry/Respectability. Baptist writers of the early nineteenth century revealed how common-folk Baptists experienced the growing pains of coming of age and the professionalization of their ministry. David Benedict, a pastor at Pawtucket, Rhode Island, for twenty-six years, was one of American Baptists' earliest historians. In 1850, near the end of his career, he published *Fifty Years among the Baptists*, what contemporary readers might call a personal memoir. Reflecting on the status of Baptists, Benedict said that around the year 1800 outsiders considered most Baptists the "dregs of society." These poor Baptists mostly had plain, ugly, log-cabin churches on the outskirts of town almost hoping not to be noticed. Ministers were also common folk who preached extemporaneously, believing that when they opened their mouths, the Holy Spirit filled them with words. Like the Methodists, many Baptist ministers were poorly paid itinerants (the critique being that the established clergy were paid and thus were wolves in sheep's clothing). They were "thirty-day Baptists" serving multiple churches in a month. Congregational life in the early 1800s had an old-fashioned, democratic familiarity with members calling the pastor "elder" and each other "sister," "brother."

Not all Baptists at the beginning of the nineteenth century were poor and uneducated. Philadelphia Baptists were led by William Staughton who read his sermons and utilized the aristocratic practice of renting pews to fund the church's ministries. Brown University educated some Baptist ministers. Benedict's church in Pawtucket, Rhode Island, actually had an organ by 1810. While it was clearly the era of the common man, a few Baptist ministers actually tried to be called bishops.

As the nineteenth century progressed, the rapidly growing, democratized Protestant sects began to yearn for respectability. The creation of the Triennial Convention by urban leaders of cosmopolitan vision (for example, William Staughton and Richard Furman) was a major move in that direction for Baptists. There was a desire to be a national group, do national work, and be like their perceived peers. Baptists also began establishing state conventions; South Carolina was the first (1821). The drive toward respectability sparked the creation of twenty Baptist-affiliated colleges in sixteen states during the antebellum period. By 1850, the professionalization of the ministry was well under way. Benedict said that extemporaneous preaching gave way to written and read sermons. Preachers now used the more fashionable worldly title of "reverend" rather than the biblical "elder." Many ministers were no longer poor and uneducated. Churches who called pastors not only wanted to know if they were "called of God," but if the candidates had attended seminary and had adequate skills in sermon preparation. By 1850, congregations had better facilities. Plain log cabins were replaced by elaborate church buildings, some with stained-glass windows. The informality of lined-out music was trumped by the "scientific performance of worship," of paid singers and organs.

Benedict's description of everyday Baptist life revealed at least some of the tensions between rural localization and cosmopolitan centralization that accompanied the seemingly inevitable journey toward respectability in a free, democratic republic. He was glad that Baptists were no longer the dregs of society, but lamented much of the drift toward respectability. Benedict himself was a man of two worlds. He was nostalgic for many of the old Baptist ways, but he was comfortable in the new, emerging world of modernization. After all, he was from New England, educated at Brown University, an elitist for his day. He knew that respectability was the wave of the future, despite the rumblings of the antimissions movement.

Ecumenism. In an era of intense denominational competition, frontier Baptists did not readily cooperate with other religious groups. During the frontier revivals, differences over baptism were barriers to cooperation. During the antimissions conflict, suspicion of Eastern "aristocratic Baptists" was the norm. Some Eastern Baptists, however, worked with other

Christians in interdenominational missionary efforts. The writings of David Benedict indicate that he and other Baptists had no doubt that their polity and practice of believer's baptism embodied the New Testament church. Benedict was a successionist (believing that Baptists can trace their lineage directly back to the New Testament) who called early Christian fringe groups (for example, the Manichaeans) evangelical Christians. At the same time, he expressed an ecumenical spirit and affirmed that non-Baptists were not all that different from him except for their obvious "error of infant baptism."

Francis Wayland revealed a more typical attitude of caution toward non-Baptists. While he acknowledged his love for Christians in other denominations, these groups had adversely influenced Baptists toward professionalization. They viewed the ministry as a profession rather than a divine calling. Their practice of hereditary membership through infant baptism was the "greatest curse of the Christian church." Despite his position as president of Brown University, Wayland warned that the new equation of ministerial qualifications with education, rather than the "apostolic rule" of divine calling and religious character, was an aristocratic practice that kept the Bible from the laity.

Baptists and the Slavery Crisis

Baptist Slaves. The practice of slavery was introduced in colonial Virginia around 1619 and soon became the accepted way of life in the colonies. With the exception of some Quaker sensitivity, during the seventeenth century colonial America exhibited significant religious apathy toward African slaves. Some colonists evidently doubted that slaves had souls. When conversion was advocated, many whites were skittish about the social implications of "freedom in Christ." In 1667, the courts of colonial Virginia ruled that baptism did not affect a slave's status of bondage.

The treatment of slaves was a concern for some Baptists, but support for slaveholders was the norm. In 1711, the Baptist church of Charleston almost split because of disagreement about a church member's severe treatment of his slave. Some church members sought advice from English Baptists to mediate the situation. The South Moulton church (Devon, England) and the (English) Western Baptist Association supported the rights of the slaveholder. According to the British association, the gelding of a slave was permissible because the Bible affirmed the lawfulness of purchasing slaves. Punishing slaves was necessary to "keep them in order" and to prevent further mischief.

"Uncle Jack, a colored man," evidently was the first recorded African slave to be a member of a Baptist church in America. "Jack" was baptized in 1662 and became a member of the First Baptist Church, Newport, Rhode Island. Existing church records only acknowledge six African slaves as members of Baptist churches before 1750. Significant conversions to Christianity among the slaves began to occur with the flowering of revivalism in the First and Second Great Awakenings. The majority of African-Americans who converted to Christianity became Baptist. By 1790 almost one-third of the Baptists in Virginia were African-American. Historians estimate that slaves totaled twenty to forty percent of Baptist church membership in the antebellum South and comprised the majority of some congregations (for example, First Baptist Church, Petersburg, Virginia).

Long before their interactions with American colonists, however, Africans were strongly religious. The West African culture knew no separation of the sacred and secular. Africans believed that the gods spoke through a frenzied emotional spirit possession; water was a special habitat for the divine. Historians suggest that the pivotal contact point with evangelical (primarily Baptist and Methodist) Christianity was spirited preaching and the emotional conversion experience which gave slaves a sense of dignity and self-worth that helped them cope with their bondage and provided hope for the future. Slaves responded to evangelistic emphases that asserted the equality of all persons in the sight of God and the availability of salvation to all. Baptism perhaps reminded them of African water rituals.

As African-American Christianity grew in the antebellum period, worship found expression in a variety of contexts. Scholars have explored the concept of the "invisible institution," the underground church in which slaves risked severe punishment, "stealing away to Jesus" to worship in secret "hush arbors" away from the surveillance of their white masters. Criticism of the hypocrisy of white Christianity was a dominant theme in recovered slave narratives. They especially condemned whites who prayed with them on Sunday and physically abused them during the week.

More normative worship for slaves was the joint worship service in biracial churches. Segregation was clearly present, of course. African-Americans sat in separated balconies and took communion after the whites (slave or free, in the North and in the South). Slaves and whites heard the same sermon, but the white minister often added a final segment about obedience to masters and the need for docile, submissive behavior by the slaves. Some antebellum Baptist churches did allow testimony from slaves against whites in matters of church discipline.

African-American leadership in antebellum life, while limited, was more possible in the church than in any other social institution or setting. African-American assistants often accompanied white Methodist itinerant preachers. In Baptist life, when a congregation's white minister was unavailable, black preachers sometimes spoke to the biracial audience. African-American preachers were active among Separate Baptists as early as 1766. In 1828, the Alabama Baptist Association purchased the freedom of Caesar Blackwell so that he could preach where he felt called. Baptists, more than other denominations, licensed black preachers up until 1830 when slaveholding states began to restrict preaching by all African-Americans. The rise of African-American preachers has been called the clearest evidence of the democratization of popular American Christianity in the post-revolutionary era.

While some African-American preachers affirmed the "Uncle Tom" message of submissiveness and an escapist theology of deferred freedom in heaven, others developed dual, apocalyptic messages of hope and deliverance. They found hope in the story of the Exodus and were drawn to the picture of Jesus as the Suffering Servant. Black faith sometimes disdained the idea of original sin since some slaves refused to connect their situation with divine predestination. They learned that the God of the Bible was just and thus believed that God would one day reward their suffering with deliverance.

One exceedingly popular African-American Baptist preacher—whites flocked to hear his powerful sermons—was John Jacob Jasper. While he had no formal education, Jasper was able to read the Bible. As a slave preacher, Jasper only preached with permission of his white master. During the antebellum period, he was pastor of a Baptist church in Petersburg, Virginia, and preached twice a week. (The church had 2,000 members after the Civil War.) Funerals, which were marked by a celebratory atmosphere for slaves, were often delayed so that Jasper could be brought to a plantation to conduct the ceremony.

Jasper's most-famous sermon was "De Sun Do Move." Some educated listeners laughed at Jasper's literal rendition of Joshua: "Joshwer . . . tell de sun ter stan' still tel he cud finish his job [of whipping the enemy]. . . . It stopt fur bizniz an' it went on when it got thru." Similar to the double meanings found in "negro spirituals," some historians suggest that slave listeners heard Jasper at a deeper level. God intervened and altered the natural order for Joshua's people to conquer their enemies. Thus, God also would intervene and conquer slavery, which whites said was a part of the natural order.

During the antebellum period whites occasionally allowed slaves to worship separately in their own churches under white supervision. A few independent African-American churches existed under the control of free African-American leaders. First Baptist Church, Williamsburg, Virginia, for example, was begun by whites for blacks in 1776 and an African-American, Gowan Pamphlet, became the pastor five years later. Often the property of African-American churches was held by white trustees and the churches could always be forced to disband.

The first African Baptist church that was led by African-Americans and was completely African-American in membership was most likely the Silver Bluff Baptist Church, Aiken, South Carolina, formed in 1773. The first pastor was "Brother Palmer" (perhaps Wait Palmer of Connecticut who in 1751 had baptized Shubal Stearns). Palmer's successor, David George, merged several church members from Aiken after the disruptions of the American Revolution into the African Baptist Church at Savannah, Georgia. George had been converted by the preaching of George Liele, who helped organize the Savannah church in 1779. Liele, evidently the first officially ordained African-American minister in America, was a former slave who had been freed by his slave master so that he could evangelize slaves at coastal plantations. Family members of the slave master attempted to enslave Liele again when they became heirs of the slave master's property. A British officer stationed in Savannah during the American Revolution thwarted the effort and in 1783, Liele went with the British to Jamaica. He established a Baptist church in Jamaica, and is now acknowledged as the first African-American foreign missionary whose work even predated the first mission work (1792) of the "father" of Baptist missions, William Carey.

The influence of the First Colored (later African) Baptist Church in Savannah continued in the ministry of another of Liele's converts, Andrew Bryan. Under Bryan's leadership, by 1802, the church grew to 850 members and joined with two white churches in the same year to form the Savannah Baptist Association. Still, the church experienced persecution. Bryan, and his brother Sampson, were beaten by local government officials and the church was closed until Jonathan Bryan, Andrew's slave master, intervened with legal assistance. After obtaining his freedom, Andrew

Bryan organized two additional Baptist churches in Savannah and became well known among American and English Baptists.

Before the Civil War, a few African-American Baptist churches also existed in the North. The Joy Street Baptist Church of Philadelphia was organized in 1804. Several members of the First Baptist Church of New York left and formed the Abyssinian Baptist Church when some visiting Ethiopian merchants were told they had to sit in segregated seating. The church's name was taken from the ancient name of Ethiopia, Abyssinia. By the mid-nineteenth century, five African-American associations had been created in the North. By 1822, at least thirty-seven African-American churches existed in antebellum Baptist life.

In addition to the work of George Liele, African-Americans demonstrated an early interest in missions with the creation, in 1815, of the Richmond African Baptist Missionary Society. While the Society was largely sponsored and led by a white Baptist, deacon William Crane, former slaves Collin Teague (or Colin Teage) and Lott Carey were active in mission work. Carey had been befriended by Crane who taught him to read. He had labored in a tobacco warehouse, but had been permitted to collect small leftover bits of tobacco for his own use. Consequently, he raised enough money to purchase freedom for himself and his children.

In 1816 the American Colonization Society was formed to address the "problem" of what to do with freed Africans. Many Americans, including the nation's founding father Thomas Jefferson, felt that repatriating former slaves would free America of the licentiousness of an "inferior" race. Some Christians, including Baptists, realized that the existence of free blacks alongside slaves created tension in the American (especially Southern) way of life. At the same time, some Christians believed that the colonization plan was an unparalleled opportunity for the evangelization of Africa.

In 1821 the African Baptist missionaries Collin Teague and Lott Carey agreed to return and live permanently in Africa and received Baptist support to do so. The inherently prejudiced colonization effort failed, but more than 12,000 African-Americans moved to Africa. Lott Carey earned a reputation as an outstanding missionary and is credited with helping to found the African nation of Liberia in 1822.

Antislavery Efforts. Critics of slavery began to be heard in Christian churches in the years after the American Revolution. These opponents drew upon the biblical theme of Christian equality and the focus on natural rights prevalent in the rising influence of Enlightenment thought. While the South eventually settled into a rock-solid defense of slavery, some antislavery sentiment was expressed in both of the fastest growing revivalist groups in the region, Methodists and Baptists. Methodist leaders Francis Asbury and Thomas Coke were against slavery, and the founding conference of Methodism in America in 1784 promised to excommunicate all Methodists who refused to free their slaves within two years. Resistance was strong and by 1796, Methodist leaders said the subject of slavery was better addressed through moral persuasion than through excommunication.

Baptist voices in the South also denounced slavery. The religious liberty ambassador John Leland of Virginia opposed slavery as a violent deprivation of the rights of nature and decried the harsh treatment of slaves. In 1796, the Ketoctin Association of Virginia declared that slavery was a transgression of divine law and appointed a committee to construct a plan for the general emancipation of slaves. Churches immediately objected and the effort died. In 1802, David Barrow of Kentucky organized "the emancipators." After being expelled from the North District Association of Kentucky Baptists in 1806, Barrow formed the "Baptized Licking-Locust Association, Friends of Humanity" on the basis of an antislavery platform. In the earliest known antislavery tract produced on the Western frontier (*Involuntary, Unmerited, Perpetual, Absolute, Hereditary Slavery Examined on the Principles of Nature, Reason, Justice, Policy, and Scripture*, 1808), Barrow said that the slavery defied the "infallible rule of Scripture." The Bible commanded love, but slavery "works the greatest ill to our neighbor" and contradicted the "golden rule" of Jesus.

Antislavery efforts failed among Baptists (and others) in the South. Attitudes stiffened as cotton became king with the invention of the cotton gin in 1793 and made slavery economically profitable. Historians suggest that antislavery sentiment was further undermined by the psychological reality of racial prejudice and the inability or unwillingness to apply church discipline to slaveholders.

Increased fear of slave revolts also put Southerners on the defensive. In 1822, Denmark Vesey, a free African-American and lay leader in the Methodist Church, planned an insurrection in Charleston, South Carolina. The plan was discovered before it was carried out and white authorities hanged thirty-five slaves. The South Carolina Baptist Convention reacted strongly to the attempted insurrection. Convention president Richard Furman, pastor of the Baptist Church of Charleston, and the most influential Baptist of the South, urged the governor of the state to issue a "Day of Public Humiliation and Thanksgiving" to honor Divine Providence for stopping the insurrection and to warn slaves about the futility of any future rebellions. The bulk of Furman's plea to the governor, however, was an apology "on the lawfulness of holding slaves." Furman's defense became one of the classic expositions of a proslavery argument.

Heightened concern about the emerging abolition movement and the agitations of free blacks also alarmed Southerners. The most radical anti-slavery document was written by David Walker, an African Methodist from Boston who was born a free African-American in North Carolina (some historians speculate he was formerly a Baptist). During 1829–1830, two years before the publication of William Lloyd Garrison's abolitionist magazine, *The Liberator*, Walker published three editions of a vitriolic pamphlet entitled *Walker's Appeal, in Four Articles*. Walker said that the brutal treatment of slaves by the hypocritical "Christian nation" of America was the worst in history; it was worse than the enslavement of the Israelites by the Egyptians before the biblical exodus. Walker encouraged slaves to overthrow their slave masters and follow a "new Hannibal" who would arise to lead an armed insurrection: "'Every dog must have its day,' the American's is coming to an end." According to Walker, God would Christianize the world, but only under black leadership because whites made a mockery of the Bible and apostolic Christianity.

Copies of Walker's pamphlet were circulated in several Southern locales and caused significant shock and fear among slaveholders. Three states—Georgia, Louisiana, and North Carolina—responded to Walker's *Appeal* with laws that forbade teaching any African-American (slave or free) to read or write.

The 1831 slave revolt of "Nat Turner" (the most famous of more than 100 recorded slave revolts) tipped the scales toward a rabid proslavery attitude in the South. Turner was a Baptist lay preacher from Southampton, Virginia. Evidently a mystic given to apocalyptic visions, Turner felt God had called him to deliver slaves from white oppression. He led about sixty slaves to kill fifty-seven whites and remained at large for two months before being captured and then executed. Before his death, Turner allegedly confessed his crime and portrayed himself as an avenging black Messiah demonstrating God's wrath before the imminent "last days." African-Americans later honored Turner as an emancipator, but whites moved toward a hardened proslavery position.

Defense of Slavery. After 1831, closer surveillance of slaves' religious activities became the norm. Most states passed laws prohibiting African-Americans—both free and slave—from preaching. If a black man preached in Alabama, for example, at least five slaveholders had to attend the service.

American colonists (for example, the Puritans) had long cited Scripture to defend slavery. Southern Christians in the nineteenth century developed an elaborate defense using "secular reasoning" and biblical proof texts. Proslavery arguments included at least the following.

- African inferiority was assumed. Africans were considered to be more licentious and intellectually deficient by nature. If set free, they would endanger the stability of society with their idleness and immorality.
- Because of these deficiencies, slaves must be civilized and treated like children. They were children, however, who would never grow up.
- In addition to natural law, slavery was an act of Providence: people were born, predestined into certain ranks. Patriarchy and subordination were the basis of social relations.
- Removing slaves from the hot African climate and a culture of barbarity was an act of Christ-like compassion.
- Being brought to America, even as slaves, provided Africans an opportunity to hear the gospel and receive salvation as opposed to not hearing and going to hell.
- Slavery was sanctioned in the Bible. God would not sanction an immoral act. Numerous biblical passages were cited:
    o   The mark of Cain was the origin of the African race (Gen 4:15).
    o   The curse of Ham (and his descendents through his fourth son, Canaan) subjugated one race to another (Gen 9:25).
    o   The Ten Commandments acknowledged slavery (Exod 20:17).
    o   Levitical laws validated the sale of slaves (Lev 25:44-46).
    o   Abraham and other Old Testament leaders owned slaves.
    o   Jesus healed slaves, but didn't free them.
    o   Jesus' apostles did not criticize slavery.
    o   Paul instructed masters regarding how to treat their slaves and he instructed slaves to be obedient to their masters (Eph 6:5; Col 3:22ff., Philem, 1 Tim 6:1-5).

Proslavery advocates like Richard Furman agreed that some slaves unfortunately had been mistreated. "Husbands and fathers have proved tyrants," Furman explained, but such behavior did not mean that "the husband's right to govern and parental authority" was wicked or unbiblical. To counter such abuses, Furman encouraged fellow Baptists to provide religious instruction—the need for conversion and submissive obedience—to slaves. Throughout the 1830s, Southern denominations practiced this "mission to the slaves" which they believed demonstrated Southern benevolence to grateful slaves. The spiritual welfare of slaves was a part of God's providential design.

In the 1830s and 1840s Northern abolitionists intensified their attack upon the biblical defense of slavery. They asserted that the Bible was against any form of oppression, and accused Southerners of following the letter rather than the spirit of Scripture. Southerners felt such cavalier treatment of the Bible was proof that the Yankees were infidels who denied the authority of the Bible. A defense of slavery was a defense of orthodox Christianity. Southerners accused Northern abolitionists of wrongly mixing politics and religion instead of focusing upon the primary task of the church: evangelism. Slavery had become a "positive good" in the Southern conscience.

Smaller Baptist groups also had an opinion on slavery, especially when it impacted the practice of their faith. For example, in 1855 Seventh Day Baptists of New York issued a resolution to support one of their own, Pardon Davis, who was a prisoner in Louisiana for allegedly helping slaves escape from their owners. They lamented that Davis had to work on the Saturday Sabbath in prison, and then attend Catholic services on Sunday in violation of his conscience.

Formation of the Southern Baptist Convention. As tensions increased over the issue of slavery in American society, Baptists attempted to maintain cooperation in mission endeavors. In 1833, English Baptists, who were important players in the eradication of slavery from the British West Indies, admonished American Baptists to follow suit.

American Baptists, given the diversity of opinion on slavery, attempted to maintain unity in mission work by taking an official stance of neutrality in their societies, the Triennial Convention and the American Baptist Home Mission Society. The issue of slavery was not germane to membership requirements outlined in the societies' constitutions, that is, slavery was not a test of fellowship. Maintaining peace was difficult. Northern Baptist abolitionists formed the "American Baptist Anti-Slavery Convention" in 1840. Elon Galusha, a pastor from New York and current vice-president of the Triennial Convention, was elected president. Northern Baptist abolitionists questioned the proslavery reading of Scripture and asked how Southerners could "claim as property the image of God, bought with the precious blood of Jesus." They declared that Baptist slave owners should confess the "crime" of holding slaves, and leave the South if that is what it took to defeat the practice. Baptists in the South were not pleased that an officer of the "neutral" Triennial Convention was tied to antislavery efforts.

Most Northern Baptists believed the neutrality stance was possible, even preferable, because they favored the gradual emancipation of slavery. Francis Wayland was the chief representative of this approach. He believed that the system of slavery was sinful and should ultimately be abolished, but the call for immediate abolition was unjust. How would the mass of new free African-Americans survive economically? Wayland won Southern friends (Richard Fuller, Basil Manly, Sr.) when he said that the Bible did not command that Christians abolish slavery, nor were slaveholders sinners as long as they treated slaves humanely and helped to prepare them for eventual freedom. Wayland believed that no type of social activism should take priority over the church's missionary endeavors. In an attempt to avoid conflict, Wayland banned the discussion of slavery in his classes at Brown University. Even after the regional split of Baptists, some Southerners attended Brown University because Wayland was president.

In 1841, the Triennial Convention reaffirmed its official neutrality on slavery and said that no new tests "unauthorized by Scripture" should be the basis for cooperation. An olive branch was extended to the South when slavery supporter Richard Fuller of Maryland replaced Elon Galusha as vice-president. In 1844, Southerner William B. Johnson stepped down as president of the Triennial Convention for "health reasons" (to avoid potential conflict with abolitionists?), and a coalition of Northern gradual-ists and Southerners elected Francis Wayland with hopes he could be a mediating influence.

The tension over slavery exploded with fury in 1844. Frustrated and suspicious Southerners wanted an affirmation that slaveholding was no bar to mission service. With some officials of the American Baptist Home Missionary Society involved in abolitionist activities, Georgia Baptists offered the name of a slaveholder, James E. Reeve, for a home mission appointment as a "test case." The mission society simply refused to consider the application because the "test" was an ungenerous maneuver, and more importantly, violated its constitution's stated neutrality. Georgia Baptists openly wondered if a new Southern mission board wouldn't be necessary.

Outraged Baptists from Alabama then demanded an explicit avowal that a slaveholder could be appointed as a foreign missionary. Mission agencies were hiding behind the hypocrisy of neutrality. In resolutions, Alabama Baptists affirmed the perfect social equality of slaveholders and nonslave-holders and the right of individual congregations to judge the morality of their own church members. Alabamians also threatened to escrow mission contributions until a satisfactory answer had been received. The board of managers of the Triennial Convention did not remain silent or neutral. They told Alabama Baptists that threats of monetary blackmail were in vain: a slaveholder would never be appointed. The die was cast.

Baptist leaders in Virginia called for an organizational meeting for a new convention of Baptists. They decried the breach of the constitution of the Triennial Convention as the reason for the schism. They were technically correct. A call for a meeting of concerned Baptists was announced.

The Southern Baptist Convention was created on 10 May 1845. William B. Johnson, the president of the South Carolina Baptist Convention, chaired the committee to form a new constitution and was elected the first president of the new regional body. Convention work would include foreign and home missions. It was declared that the independence of local churches would be fully respected. Kentuckian Isaac McCoy said delegates assembled in Augusta with good feelings; they left with better ones. With hands joined, they sang, "Bless Be the Tie That Binds." What was the tie?

In an explanation detailing the reasons for the Convention's formation, Johnson wrote "An Address to the Public." The schism was not over doctrine because Baptists from the North and South "differed in no article of the faith." No creed was created since Baptists had only one creed, the Bible. According to Johnson, the separation was over missions. The breach of the Triennial Convention's constitution was "FORBIDDING US to speak UNTO THE GENTILES."

Slavery, Johnson explained, was a civil issue: "We find no necessity in relinquishing any of our civil rights." In other words, religious concerns were primarily private, individual issues. According to Southern Baptists, abolitionists wrongly confused politics and religion. Throughout the nineteenth century, Southerners cited missions rather than slavery as the reason for the schism. A few twentieth-century historians, while acknowledging the role of slavery, pointed to tensions between the North and South over the distribution of home missionaries. They also cited a growing ecclesiastical connectionalism in the South (that is, a convention with two mission boards rather than two independent societies).

The issue, however, clearly was the right for slaveholders to do missions. Baptists in the South reflected a growing sectional identity. They were Southerners before they were missionaries. The majority of delegates to the first Convention in Augusta were from Georgia. The fact that they held slaves at a rate six times higher than the average Southerner revealed a definite economic interest in the maintenance of a biblically based slavery. The monetary requirement for representation to the convention, rather than church membership, reflected the affluence of the earliest delegates. The defense of slavery—what has been called the "original sin" of Southern Baptists—necessitated a new religious organization.

Schism over slavery was not unique to Baptists. Both Methodists and Presbyterians split over the issue. The Methodists, whose conflict also involved the question of slaveholding missionaries, split before the Baptists, in 1844. Historians have noted that the creation of separate Southern denominations, while not causing the split of the United States, helped pave the way for it. Baptist leaders (for example, Jesse Mercer of Georgia) recognized that the necessity of religious division was a commentary on the probability of political separation. "Broken churches" were precursors of a "broken nation." If the churches had the courage to separate, the region could also.

Civil War. The Baptist story followed—and helped precipitate—the hardening of sectional lines that resulted in the Civil War. While a few Southern Baptists opposed secession (for example, John Broadus of Virginia), many Southern Baptists strongly advocated succession even before states voted to withdraw from the Union. The creation of the Confederacy was a righteous cause. Alabama Baptist leader, Basil Manly, Sr., gave the invocation at the opening of the Confederacy in 1861. As the war progressed, churches throughout the South had to disband temporarily; twenty-six Baptist churches just in Virginia were destroyed. Tensions with Northern Baptists erupted. Northern Baptist home missionaries received Union permission to assume control of some church buildings in the South, purportedly to save them, but some abuses resulted. At the same time, even Francis Wayland grew frustrated with the hardening attitudes of Southerners. As the southern war effort turned toward defeat, Northerners claimed the victory was vindication from God for America, God's chosen people. Southerners viewed the war as a divine chastisement, but not for slavery. The South was being prepared to be God's unique vessel for virtue, racial purity, and New Testament Christianity.

Conclusion

During the antebellum era of the nineteenth century, Baptists grew rapidly. Already a "democratic" faith of individual conscience and congregational community, Baptists rode the saddle of the democratization of American Christianity. In many ways, American democratization played into Baptist hands and facilitated Baptist growth. Naturally, Baptists were nurtured by the democratization of America. A religion for the common folk had great appeal on the frontier.

At the same time, the growth of the denomination brought increasing centralization. The biblical primitivism of the antimissions movement and the restorationism of Alexander Campbell held sway over many frontier Baptists who did not trust the growing centralization of the more cosmopolitan educated Baptists in the East. The millennial fervor of William Miller also attracted Baptists with its attempt to restore prophecy to the life of the New Testament church.

The growth of organizational centralization was often the result of missionary fervor that spurred the creation of regional and national missionary organizations. The spirit of adventure characterized the world scene, but early missionary Baptists in America like Ann Hasseltine Judson and Adoniram Judson pointed to their Bibles for the command to share the gospel in foreign countries. New Testament Christianity, mission advocates were convinced, said that missions was the duty of the faith.

Slavery revealed the difficulties in the search for a pure biblical faith. Slavery in America cannot be explained without an understanding of the political situation (for example, states rights) and economic factors (for example, cotton was king), but Christians placed the conflict in terms of obedience to the Bible. New Testament Christianity, Southerners declared, was embodied in a literal reading of slavery passages in the Bible which led to one conclusion: slavery was biblical and could be practiced. Northerners, however, looked to the spirit of Scripture and were unwilling to duplicate literally New Testament faith when it was used to oppress people. The North and South essentially had different Bibles and ended up with different pictures of what a New Testament church looked like. The search for New Testament Christianity would become even more complicated with the massive societal changes of the postbellum period.

1850–1950 and Baptists in the North: The Strength of Denominational Efficiency, the Challenges of Rapid Change and Conflict

Historians consider the last decades of the nineteenth century the apex of a Protestant hegemony in America. Protestantism was the "public" religion of the land. After the horrors of the Civil War, Protestant bodies regrouped, multiplied their ministries, and organized themselves into business-like corporations. Centralization and efficiency practically became religious distinctives. At the turn of the twentieth century, a new Protestant publication dubbed itself *The Christian Century*, indicative of the hope and optimism of the future. Northern Baptist life reflected and contributed to this sense of optimism.

At the same time, America's religious map was changing. Immigration changed demographics: more non-Protestants and more non-Christians were becoming American. Industrialization was turning a rural America into a modern urban land. American pluralism was on fast-forward. Scientific inquiry and the use of analytical tools to study the Bible that questioned traditional orthodoxy seemed on an even faster, more threatening track. Permanent divisions within Protestant bodies along liberal and conservative lines resulted. Ideological boundaries began to overwhelm the traditional denominational identities that developed out of the Protestant Reformation. Baptists, like other Christians, responded in diverse ways. Some drank from the modern well, but some resisted the rapid changes in American culture as if they were deadly poison.

Northern Baptist Societies and other Organizations

American Baptist Missionary Union. After the schism with Baptists in the South, Northern Baptists continued to promote missions and ministry through several societies. The "mother" society, the Triennial Convention, immediately changed its name to the American Baptist Missionary Union and continued its aggressive work, especially on the continents of Africa and India, throughout the nineteenth century. Prominent Bostonian A. J.

Gordon served as president of the society for twenty-three years (1871–1894). By 1900, the society had 474 missionaries, and supported about 2,000 churches with about 207,000 members. Reflecting the legacy of Luther Rice, Northern Baptists emphasized educational missions as well as evangelism. (This dual emphasis caused some conflict among supporters.) Forty-four mission schools were established by 1841; the number increased to 1,246 by 1894. In 1910, the society was renamed the American Baptist Foreign Mission Society.

American Baptist Home Mission Society. The American Baptist Home Mission Society (ABHMS) also continued an aggressive ministry in the latter half of the nineteenth century. Henry L. Morehouse was the larger-than-life leader, serving as corresponding secretary twice (1879–1892; 1902–1917) and field secretary (1893–1902). He led the society to expand its work throughout the United States, including Alaska and Puerto Rico. The society reflected Morehouse's ecumenical evangelistic zeal. He commented, "Our chief mission is not to make Baptists, but to do our part as a great denomination in winning the world to Christ." Morehouse hoped that Baptists North and South would reunite, and he never hesitated to send missionaries to the South. By 1869, one-third of the society's missionaries were located in the South and one significant focus of ministry was the education of freed slaves. A Freedmen's Fund was created in 1863, and by 1894, thirty-two schools for African-Americans had been established. While several of the schools had a temporary existence, some endured and prospered.

One such school was Morehouse College, which was established as the Augusta (Georgia) Institute in 1867. The school met initially in the African-American Springfield Baptist Church before moving to Atlanta (1879) where its name was changed to Atlanta Baptist College (1897). In 1913, the school became Morehouse College in honor of Henry Morehouse. Typical of most schools for African-Americans of the late nineteenth century, faculty members were mostly white and this ultimately led to internal conflict. In 1906, missionary appointee of the ABHMS and faculty member John Hope, became the institution's first African-American president. A graduate of Brown University, Hope led the school to increased growth and challenged the "accommodationist" views of prominent African-American and founder of Tuskegee Institute, Booker T. Washington—prevalent at that time—that education for African-Americans should focus on vocational training and agriculture. After providing substantial financial support to help the college survive the depression years, the ABHMS relinquished its control. Morehouse College garnered an international reputation under the presidential leadership (from 1940 to 1967) of the ordained Baptist minister Benjamin E. Mays, who was a graduate of the University of Chicago and the spiritual mentor to the institution's most famous graduate, Martin Luther King, Jr.

Other ministries of the ABHMS included work among Native Americans, immigrants, and various ethnic and language groups. Language departments in several theological seminaries were developed. A German department at the (Baptist) Rochester Theological Seminary was created in 1858, for example, under Karl August Rauschenbusch, the father of the famous social gospel advocate, Walter Rauschenbusch. Work among German Baptists in other areas such as Louisville and St. Louis was also fruitful. By 1882, there were more than 10,000 German Baptists in America. Missionary work among immigrants led to the establishment of the first Polish Baptist Church (1894) and the first Italian Baptist Church (1896) in Buffalo, New York.

The significant influx of immigrants to America with Catholic backgrounds startled Protestants. J. G. Lemen explained, "We must Christianize those masses or they will heathenize our children." Similarly, Samuel Zane Batten, citing with disapproval what he called German Sunday beer gardens, commented, "We must Christianize these foreigners or they will foreignize us." Baptists believed that the Bible mandated the evangelization of these "heathen." In retrospect, efforts to convert immigrants (by both Northern and Southern Baptists) were also a means of "social control" to secure America's traditional Protestant hegemony. This, in part, led to extensive mission efforts in the Western states. By the end of the century, 799 of 1,180 home missionaries were stationed in the West.

The motto of the ABHMS—"North America for Christ"—was challenged by the expanding efforts of the Southern Baptist Home Mission Board in the South and in the "Indian territory." Under the leadership of I. T. Tichenor, Southern Baptists began to assert exclusive allegiance to their mission programs. In one particular case, Tichenor refused to work with veteran missionary J. S. Murrow, who wished to remain dually aligned with both mission groups. Henry Morehouse of the ABHMS objected to these exclusive claims. He felt that Northern Baptists had long ministered in the South and Midwest and should continue to do so. Significant time and financial resources had been invested in areas when Southerners earlier had been unable to organize work.

After a decade of sparring, both Baptist groups met in 1894 at Fortress Monroe, Virginia, and worked out a compromise agreement. Southern Baptists announced that they would cooperate with Northern Baptists in educational efforts for African-Americans. Consequently, Northern Baptists would focus more resources on the Western front. At the same time, Northern Baptists recognized the "handwriting on the wall" and acknowledged the growing territorial identity of Southern Baptists. Morehouse and Tichenor said they were both pleased with the results, but the two giants battled again over the question of territorial boundaries, especially in the "border states," throughout their careers. In 1912, a fragile peace ensued with another "comity" agreement, but by the middle of the twentieth century, both major Baptist bodies asserted national identities without boundaries.

American Baptist Publication Society. The American Baptist Publication Society (ABPS), established in 1824, continued throughout the nineteenth century to serve Baptists North and South. ABPS's most significant leader was Benjamin Griffith, corresponding secretary from 1857 to 1893, who said that the organization was essentially a Sunday school society. Griffith was able to expand ministry efforts with the financial support of his father-in-law, John P. Crozer, a prominent leader in the textile industry (for whom Crozer Seminary was named). The Society employed colporteurs, traveling salespersons of Bibles and other ABPS literature. Between 1824 and 1879, the ABPS produced ninety million pieces (originals and copies) of religious literature.

One creative ministry of the ABPS was the use of chapel train cars to reach the unchurched. The cars functioned as traveling mini-churches and were supplied with a pulpit and enough pews for a small congregation. (Catholic and Episcopal mission societies followed the Baptist lead and had their own chapel railcars.) Prominent industrialists and Baptist laypersons John D. Rockefeller and James B. Colgate provided financial backing for the railroad-chapel ministry and helped secure cooperation with railroads who allowed the cars to be pulled by their trains. The ABHMS also had a chapel-car ministry, which was a sign of its innovative attraction, but according to some observers, was also evidence of the cumbersome nature of duplicated ministry efforts by the two independent societies. Baptist "chapel cars" remained in service for more than fifty years, from 1891 until at least 1946; one car remained on the rails until 1948.

Northern Baptists made other contributions to the publishing ministry. While not an agent of the ABPS, B. F. Jacobs, a local Baptist Sunday school leader in Chicago, helped create the "Uniform Lesson System" in 1872 for use in several denominations. The use of the same Sunday school themes and materials became commonplace among several Protestant groups during the twentieth century.

Women's American Baptist Mission Societies. The first women's-rights convention in America was held at Seneca Falls, New York, in 1848. Its call for equal wages, educational opportunity, and the right to vote was mostly ahead of its time. Throughout the nineteenth century, the norm for Christian women was to embody purity and to teach virtue to their children. Submissiveness and domesticity were the expected characteristics of the biblical woman. Consequently, as America industrialized in the late nineteenth century, women found acceptable ministry opportunities in the venues of missions, temperance, and female education.

American Baptist women became increasingly active in missions with the extensive growth of separate women's societies. By 1900, there were 113 women's societies. While a few women in the antebellum period had been appointed as single foreign missionaries, many Baptists doubted their effectiveness, for they were considered members of the "weaker" sex. In 1861, women from several denominations formed the Woman's Union Missionary Society of America for Heathen Lands in order to support single women missionaries. In 1871, Baptist women in Boston and Chicago (and San Francisco in 1874) formed separate regional mission societies with the goal of appointing women through the American Baptist Missionary Union. These groups eventually merged to form the Woman's American Baptist Foreign Mission Society. Their ministry efforts included ecumenical involvement in orphanages and boarding schools as well as providing nurses and teachers.

In 1877, a Woman's American Baptist Home Mission Society (WABHMS) was organized and promoted the motto, "Christ in every Home." Rumah Avilla Crouse, the society's president for its first thirty years, said that the highest calling of her life was to be a wife and mother. At the same time, she worked to get women more involved in Northern Baptist ministries. Like women in the South, Northern Baptist women were active in the temperance movement against beverage alcohol. Children became "preachers" of the abstinence message with the chorus they were taught:

Pure cold water,
that's the drink for me,
for I'm a young abstainer,
from drinking customs free.

In 1881, the society formed a Baptist Missionary Training School in Chicago, the first one of its kind among Protestants that trained women for missionary service.

The WABHMS was especially active in establishing schools. One mission school is now Spelman College, the oldest and largest historic African-American private undergraduate liberal arts woman's college in America. In 1882, two members of the WABHMS, Sophia B. Packard and Harriet E. Giles, founded the Atlanta Baptist Female Seminary, a school for African-American women, which became Spelman College. Both Packard and Giles served as president. While the earliest students were illiterate, the founders' broad vision was an education of "uplift" focused upon head, heart, and hand (liberal arts and industrial courses). Social injustices such as lynching were not addressed. At the outset, the school was housed in the basement of Friendship Baptist Church of Atlanta, one of the independent African-American churches created soon after the Civil War. The pastor, Frank Quarles, ordained while still a slave by First Baptist Church, Atlanta, had started the church in an old railroad box car. A year after the school's opening, Baptist philanthropist John D. Rockefeller, Jr., gave 250 dollars for the school's operation. The WABHMS also appointed two additional teachers for the mission. In 1884, the school was named Spelman Seminary after Laura Spelman Rockefeller, mother of John Rockefeller, Jr. Northern Baptist home mission leader Henry Morehouse served as the first chair of the school's board of trustees.

Reunification with Southern Baptists. Throughout the postbellum era, Northern Baptists made several suggestions to Southern Baptists about reunification. Numerous factors evidently prohibited any union. Growing differences in theology (Southerners said that Northerners were becoming liberal) and the different approaches to organizational polity (Northern ministries were conducted by independent societies and Southern Baptists were finding their identity in convention polity) were issues. Perhaps more significant was the increasing sectionalism and separate identities due in large part to the "race problem."

Centralization: The Search for Denominational Efficiency

Northern Baptist Convention. Entering the twentieth century, Northern Baptists joined other Protestants who confidently believed it would be the "Christian century." In 1900, a New Jersey pastor, D. D. Munro, proclaimed, "Our denomination is not a puny infant, but a lusty giant. . . . We have numbers; we have wealth; we are an imperial people; we have truth in its blessed integrity." Riding the wave of the quest for denominational efficiency, Northern Baptist societies, long known for highlighting the independence of the local church, made a dramatic methodological shift toward unity and formed the Northern Baptist Convention in 1907. Governor of New York and later chief justice of the U.S. Supreme Court (1930–1934), Charles Evans Hughes, was the first president of the Convention. Societies were still autonomous, but agreed to cooperate in budget planning to avoid duplicating efforts. Associated churches numbered 11,000 with 1,250,000 members. In the Convention's fourth year, Henry Morehouse, who was known as the primary architect of the denomination, told the annual meeting of delegates that the mission of Northern Baptists was to promote the time-honored Baptist principles of the right to private judgment in matters of faith, affirmation of the "authority and sufficiency of the scripture as against imposed creeds," regenerate church membership, democratic church government, a rejection of "sacerdotalism and sacramentalism," and the separation of church and state.

Further consolidation among Northern Baptists occurred in 1911 when Free Will Baptists of the North joined the new convention. New boards were also added the same year: a Board of Education and the Ministers and Missionaries Benefit Board (MMBB). The creation of the MMBB was largely due to the efforts of Henry Morehouse. Seven new seminaries for theological education were opened from 1901 (for example, Central Baptist Theological Seminary) to 1944. In 1912, foreign mission efforts sought efficiency when the decision was made to stop expansion into new areas but strengthen the work in existing mission spots with indigenous leadership. An unabated enthusiasm for the idea of "business Baptists" could be seen in the blunt assessment of pastor Birney Hudson of New Jersey: "There is one word, cold, calculating, deliberate, determined as Omnipotent will. Pile adjectives around it. Make it stand and adorn it. Spiritualize it and make it live. The word is EFFICIENCY." It was a Baptist paradox: modernize, yet remain the New Testament church.

Successful "War drives" during World War I provided an impetus for religious organizations to develop more efficient methods of fund-raising. Northern Baptists optimistically launched a five-year effort, the New World Movement (1919–1924). Using military marketing language, God was called the "general" and each Baptist was a "warrior" on the evangelistic battlefront. The ambitious 100-million-dollar goal fell short; only $45,000,378 was raised in the midst of a difficult economy. The developing fundamentalist crisis among Northern Baptists was also a drain on fund-raising. Fundamentalists were wary of the new convention's shift toward centralization and they were angered by the convention leadership's support of a failed ecumenical effort, the Interchurch World Movement (IWM). Conservative editor Curtis Lee Laws said the IWM "emasculated all Christianity by eliminating all doctrinal emphases . . . because it represented everybody, it was under obligations to offend nobody." Nevertheless, Northern Baptists adopted a unified budget concept in 1924.

Despite efforts toward efficiency and centralization, historians have observed that the Northern Baptist Convention never ceased being a collection of missionary societies. Both the formation of the General Association of Regular Baptist Churches (1933) and the Conservative Baptist Association (1947) resulted from not only theological differences, but frustration with "denominational machinery."

American Baptist Convention. Another denominational reorganization occurred in 1950 when the Northern Baptist Convention changed its name to the American Baptist Convention. Valley Forge, Pennsylvania became the compromise choice for a new convention center. The suggested site— the Interchurch Center in New York which housed the ecumenical National Council of Churches—was rejected. Northern Baptists' recovery of the name "American" was, in part, a reaction to the zealous expansion of Southern Baptists into former Northern strongholds like California. The era of comity agreements was over; the whole nation was now a market for all kinds of Baptist soil.

Theological Movements and Conflicts

Development of Modernism. While there was no established religion in America, a Protestant hegemony of sorts existed in the nineteenth century. A shared pool of Protestant values pervaded much of American life. American religious and cultural interaction, however, began to experience significant changes after the Civil War. Rural areas had a tradition of at least nominal church and family loyalties, but the new burgeoning cities did not have these developed Protestant communities. Immigration challenged the status quo. Whereas Protestantism grew from five to sixteen million between 1860 and 1900, the Catholic Church expanded from three million to twelve million, producing a more pluralistic America.

Secularization occurred despite religious growth. In 1850, most American college presidents were ministers and the schools' primary reason to study nature was to learn about God's creative beauty. In the postbellum period, universities adopted the German scientific model of study, and research was attempted "objectively" based on primary sources and laboratory analysis. Separate professional disciplines developed that were religiously neutral (for example, sociology and psychology), but for some advocates these new social sciences, along with the fledgling study of world religions, raised questions regarding the uniqueness and finality of Christianity. The most significant issue, of course, was the introduction of evolution by Charles Darwin. The question about how to relate science and religion became a battleground.

In response to the advent of "modernity," modernism (liberalism) arose in an attempt to make Christianity intellectually respectable, that is, consistent with the scientific advances of modern culture. The Bible was no longer considered automatically authoritative—no longer accepted as infallible in all areas of knowledge—simply because a religious authority or tradition decreed it to be so. Liberals accepted the new methods of critical biblical study (higher criticism) and tested the Bible's contents for accuracy in light of the best of modern scientific knowledge. For example, belief in traditional doctrines like a literal six-day creation of the world was discarded in light of Darwin's theory of evolution. Belief in literal supernatural miracles was often viewed as a relic of a prescientific age. Liberalism stressed that ethics, not doctrine, was the essence of Christianity. Jesus was the great moral Teacher. Creeds were culturally conditioned dogma of bygone eras. The Bible had to be tested by modern religious experience and/or human reason: these were the ultimate authorities for modern religion.

One Response of the Liberal Tradition: Social Christianity. One area of growing concern to the developing liberal tradition was the rapid urbanization of American society. In the post-Civil War era, rapid and often painful social and economic changes transformed rural, agrarian America into an urban industrialized country. An age of big business, characterized by laissez-faire capitalism, developed. Steel kings, coal barons, and railroad magnates emerged, but profits amassed by the rich did not translate into better wages for laborers. High unemployment, dangerous working conditions, and low wages were only a few of the problems that produced over 14,000 strikes between 1881 and 1894. How should the church respond to urbanization?

Many Christians affirmed the traditional approach that social problems would be solved only after individuals had their hearts right with Jesus. The church should preach individual conversion and focus on personal morality. ("Holiness" could be described by the saying, "I don't smoke, drink, dance, or chew, and I don't go with girls who do.") Many Christians also affirmed the "gospel of wealth" articulated by steel magnate Andrew Carnegie, and largely ignored the direct connection between poverty and current business practices. Be a generous philanthropist if God blesses you with money, Carnegie encouraged, and as for the poor, "help those who help themselves."

The "Institutional Church." Another Christian response to urbanization was a focus on social ministry, that is, the application of the teachings of Jesus to the new social issues of the modern era. One aspect of social ministry popular among Northern Baptists was the "institutional church." Some wealthy, inner-city congregations offered extensive social services (including athletic facilities, hospitals, child care, and even colleges) and were opened day and night during the week. One proponent, New York pastor Edward Judson (son of the influential missionary Adoniram Judson), said that more churches with stellar preachers and state-of-the-art resources needed to minister with "organized kindness" in the most materialistic and densely populated urban areas. By 1900, an unofficial count numbered more than 170 "institutional" congregations.

The best known was Baptist Temple of Philadelphia, led by Russell H. Conwell who was pastor there for forty-three years. In 1891, Conwell's small Grace Baptist Church in north Philadelphia moved downtown. The new structure, patterned architecturally after a Greco-Roman temple, included a 5,000 seat auditorium and a gymnasium. The church established two hospitals and became the largest Protestant church in America.

As other institutional churches developed, they often put "temple" in their names in imitation of Conwell's influence. These "megachurches" at the turn of the century with large auditoriums and office complexes became community centers. However, some Baptists criticized the efforts of the "temple movement." A. C. Dixon represented the conservative reaction when, in his famous *Evangelism Old and New* (1905), he chastised "institutional churches" for de-emphasizing traditional biblical evangelism of the individual for a socialistic message. Dixon bellowed that "swine cannot be made into sheep by change of environment" but by a change of heart through personal conversion.

Conwell's message bore some similarities to Andrew Carnegie's "gospel of wealth." Like Carnegie, Conwell was willing to blame the poor for their plight, and his message of "uplift" contended that people could help themselves. Consequently, Christians should earn wealth to advance the gospel. Conwell delivered his famous lecture, "Acres of Diamonds," more than 6,000 times and earned the reputation as the most prolific orator of his day in America. In his speech, Conwell told a story of a California rancher who sold his home to move to the southern part of the state in the attempt to cash in on the gold rush. After he moved, a little girl found gold while playing in a stream on his former residence. Conwell's message: "Your diamonds are not in far-away mountains or in distant seas; they are in your own back yard if you will but dig for them." This gospel of potential success—available to all—spoke to the yearning for health and prosperity that manifested itself in several religious offerings (for example, divine healing movements, Christian Science) of the day and was a predecessor of the popular "power of positive thinking" preachers of the twentieth century like Norman Vincent Peale.

Conwell's foray into education turned out to be the most famous legacy of the "institutional church" movement. While his church was still named Grace Baptist Church, Conwell became involved in education for workers unable to pay and unable to attend school during the traditional day hours because of job responsibilities. Upon being asked for training by a young man interested in the ministry, Conwell agreed to teach him at night. Word spread and seven young men asked to participate. More students and additional classes soon followed. These classes led to the chartering of Temple University in 1888 and Conwell served as founding president for thirty-eight years. In those earliest students, as Temple University recognizes today, Conwell found his own "acres of diamonds."

The Social Gospel. The "Social Gospel Movement"—known as a subunit in the modernist/liberal tradition—is considered the most radical religious response to economic issues in industrialized America. Carnegie's self-help approach was regarded as inadequate to tackle weaknesses ingrained in the harsh realities of capitalism. The social gospel declared that social structures—not just people—were caught in the web of sin and had to be redeemed. Some of the most influential advocates of the "social gospel" that flowered in the late-nineteenth and early twentieth centuries were Baptists. Walter (originally Walther) Rauschenbusch is acknowledged as the most powerful proponent of social-gospel theology.

Walter Rauschenbusch was raised in the pietistic home of August Rauschenbusch, a leader in the German-American Baptist community. The younger Rauschenbusch followed in his father's footsteps and taught at Colgate-Rochester Theological Seminary, but his theology gradually muted pietistic concerns for the burgeoning liberal tradition in American religion. Prior to his career as a professor of Church History at the seminary (which was almost blocked by trustees' concern about his liberal ideas), Rauschenbusch's stint as pastor of a German-immigrant congregation in the "Hell's Kitchen" area of New York City significantly impacted his understanding of how the gospel must relate to the growing industrialization and urbanization of America. He was stunned by the poverty and unsanitary conditions of tenement housing, and he agonized over the number of funerals that he performed, especially for children ravaged by poverty.

In 1907 Rauschenbusch wrote *Christianity and the Social Crisis*, a widely read book that provided him with public-speaking opportunities to spread his views. Other books followed, including his most famous work, *A Theology of the Social Gospel* (1917). Rauschenbusch was an "evangelical liberal." He did not reject the traditional gospel call for personal conversion, but he added the biblical mandate for social salvation. Social salvation was the regeneration of society; the essence of sin was selfishness and was embodied in the profit motive of capitalism. According to Rauschenbusch, "It is possible to hold the orthodox doctrine of the devil and not recognize him when we meet him in a real estate office or at the stock exchange." The biblical command to love your neighbor was not as simple as it was in the days of an agricultural society where people lived in villages and farms and knew each other. In the dog-eat-dog, competitive nature of capitalism, Rauschenbusch asked,

> Suppose a business man would be glad indeed to pay his young women [workers] the $12 a week which they need for a decent living, but all his competitors are paying from $7 down to $5. Shall he love himself into bankruptcy? . . . If a man owns 100 shares of stock in a great corporation, how can his love influence its wage scale with that puny stick?

Social gospelers like Rauschenbusch feared that rich Christians in bondage to the greed of the profit motive would *pray* for the poor in church on Sunday but then *prey* upon the poor on Monday in their business practices.

The growing tide of premillennialism among evangelicals and Baptists with its indifference toward social reform was distasteful, and according to Rauchensbusch, demonstrated "the despair of monasticism without braving its self-denials." Social gospelers were postmillennialists and believed the virtues of Christianity would gradually make America a more Christianized, democratic society. Typical of "reformers," Rauschenbusch was paternalistic toward the American working class, yet hoped a wellspring of moral indignation on their part would usher in a religious transformation of society. Paradoxically, Rauschenbusch desired the comforts of an upper-middle-class lifestyle and willingly sought the help of Baptist oil tycoon, John D. Rockefeller.

Rauschenbusch's understanding of the Baptist tradition provided support for his belief that a social gospel was the faith of the earliest Christians before the development of a hierarchical organization distorted the biblical message. Writing on "Why I Am a Baptist," he said that "personal experience was the crux" of the Baptist faith. He explained: "Churches based on religious experience, and not intellectual assent to a creed, are genuinely democratic. . . . [In] the insistence on personal experience we are hewing our way back to original Christianity." Because religion required social expression, churches—as independently governed local Baptist churches historically were—should be "Christian democracies that recognize no priestly class or hierarchy of ministry."

Rauschenbusch ultimately viewed himself in typical Baptist fashion as an evangelist. He desired the conversion of America to the social ethics of the Old Testament prophets and Jesus' central teaching about the Kingdom of God. A Christianized America—led by the moral conscience of middle-class America—could model a primitive Christianity that focused on this world rather than a rapture to heaven. Rauschenbusch avoided the excessive optimism of some social gospelers who spoke of ushering in a perfect social order. He recognized that the "Kingdom of God is always but coming." He emphasized a kingdom of evil, although his focus on social demons like alienation and loneliness that resulted from the automated labor of industrial factories, was fiercely criticized by conservatives who disliked his lack of interest in the idea of a personal Satan.

After World War I, the optimistic heyday of social-gospel advocates was chastened. Social Christianity continued to find expression in American religion, however, especially in the work of the ecumenical movement. No group was more involved than Northern Baptists.

Reactions to Modernism: Holiness and Pentecostal Movements.
Evangelical revivalism helped to spawn several reactions to the development of modernism in American religion. Every conservative reaction
warned against the de-emphasis upon personal evangelism and traditional
orthodoxy wherever a social gospel was preached. The focus on personal
faith for some evangelicals found a home in the growth of the Holiness
movement in the late-nineteenth century. The Holiness movement
contrasted modernism's emphasis on the ethical capabilities of people who
were by nature good with a strong focus on the Holy Spirit—the power of
the Spirit to defeat humanity's sinful nature and provide a victorious life of
sanctification. This movement, although heavily dominated by leaders from
the Methodist tradition, attracted an interdenominational audience.

Baptists who spoke of the empowering of the Holy Spirit, especially for
missionary activity, included Adoniram Judson Gordon, pastor of Clarendon Baptist Church of Boston (1869–1895). Gordon was a regular teacher
at the annual summer Bible conferences of another Holiness advocate,
evangelist D. L. Moody. Like most holiness advocates, Gordon defended
women preachers, promoted divine healing and rejected the use of modern
biblical criticism. For seventeen years (1878–1895), he was editor of *The
Watchword*, a journal that promoted New Testament Christianity—"the
primitive faith, the primitive hope, and the primitive charity."

In 1895, C. H. Mason had been a Baptist for two years before he
formed the African-American holiness body, the Church of God in Christ
in Memphis, Tennessee. In 1907, Mason visited the Azusa Street revival in
Los Angeles and returned a Pentecostal believer. The Church of God in
Christ became the largest African-American Pentecostal body in the
country.

Pentecostalism (origins, 1901) can also be seen as a conservative
alternative to modern ways. Like modernism, Pentecostalism made religious
experience central to verifying the Christian faith. Pentecostals, however,
highlighted the personal experience of the Holy Spirit—speaking in tongues
as the sign of Spirit baptism, miracles, healing, and other extraordinary
gifts—in their rejection of the de-emphasis of supernaturalism in modernism. While many early Pentecostals were from the Wesleyan tradition,
several leaders, especially in the young Assemblies of God, came from
Baptist roots. E. N. Bell, the first general chairman of the Assemblies
(1914), had been a pastor of a Southern Baptist church for seventeen years.
J. Roswell Flower, another one of the founders of the Assemblies of God,
acknowledged that Baptist theology was the primary reason for one of his

group's differences with Pentecostals of Wesleyan heritage: the denial of the Wesleyan view of instantaneous, entire sanctification as a "second work" of the Holy Spirit in favor of a doctrine of progressive sanctification (that is, holiness begins at conversion, matures throughout life, and is perfected in heaven). William Branham, one of the giants of the healing revival in the post-World War II era, also came from a rural Baptist background. Ironically, believers who left the Baptist fold for the "full gospel" of Pentecostalism did so in search of fully restoring the New Testament church.

The Fundamentalist/Modernist Conflict. Before 1870, Baptist theologians demonstrated a traditional view of the Bible's sole authority for religious faith. The Bible's factual accuracy was assumed. The blossoming of the modern scientific approach to biblical studies began to influence some Northern Baptist scholars. Eventually Colgate Theological Seminary in New York established itself as a receptive focal point for the "New Theology." William Newton Clarke led the way. He is often considered the first genuine liberal American Baptist theologian and his work, *An Outline of Theology* (1894), is called the first systematic theology from a liberal perspective in America. Characteristically Baptist in his emphasis upon the importance of personal religious experience and personal piety, the evangelical-liberal Clarke described his faith pilgrimage as "Sixty Years with the Bible." In his earlier career, he held to biblical infallibility. By 1880, Clarke had abandoned the traditional method of proving theological points with biblical proof texts and claimed that the Bible reflected different culturally conditioned theological perspectives: "the theology of any age is largely an expression of the Christian experience of that age." Applying the principles of evolutionary theory, Clarke asserted that doctrine evolves and changes in subsequent eras. More conservative Baptists disliked Clarke's theological method and occasionally, but unsuccessfully, tried to oust him from his position at Colgate.

The development of the liberal tradition in Northern Baptist schools moved rapidly forward when the newly established Divinity School of the University of Chicago (1892) affirmed historical-critical methods of biblical study without hesitation, and adapted evolutionary theory to the understanding of religious truth. The school's founding president was William Rainey Harper, an Old Testament scholar who had earned a national reputation while teaching at Yale Divinity School. Harper, the premier Baptist educator of his era, developed the University of Chicago into a major research university. While a devout churchman, Harper did not limit academic freedom with any standard of orthodoxy. The "Chicago School" represented unfettered scholarly discovery, regardless of the outcome for previous definitions of truth.

Strong criticisms of Chicago professors were leveled throughout the "Fundamentalist-Modernist Conflict" of the early twentieth century. Some cite the birth of the Chicago tradition as the earliest tremor of the battle. William Bell Riley, a leading fundamentalist, attended pastors' conferences in Chicago in the early 1890s. In reflections articulated later in his life, Riley remembered that the doctrinal views expressed by President Harper and Professor George Burman Foster were his first exposure to "organized modernism in my denomination."

Several professors of the Chicago School felt the wrath of Northern Baptists who were concerned about modernism. Most offensive to critics was the work of George Burman Foster and Shailer Mathews. Critics railed against Foster's book, *The Finality of the Christian Religion* (1906), in which Foster questioned the reliability of the Bible and adopted a view touted by some scholars that Paul, not Jesus, was the real founder of the Christian religion. His view of Jesus as moral example and "archetype of love for others" sounded at odds with traditional Christology. In reaction to Foster's writings, the Chicago Baptist Minister's Conference expelled him and requested that his church (Hyde Park Baptist Church) follow suit or be excluded from the local association. Foster responded that his critics wanted him "off the earth." Ultimately, more than 225 churches in southern Illinois left Northern Baptist ranks and joined the Southern Baptist Convention.

Shailer Mathews became the most influential representative of the Chicago School. He joined the faculty in 1894 to teach New Testament and eventually became dean of the Divinity School. Mathew's career illustrated the organizational and theological concerns of Northern Baptists in the early twentieth century. He encouraged the formation of the Northern Baptist Convention of which he served as president in 1915. He also symbolized Northern Baptists' ecumenical vision, serving as president of the recently formed interdenominational Federal Council of Churches (1912–1916). Mathews also was a leader in the Social Gospel movement. His *The Social Teachings of Jesus: An Essay in Christian Sociology* was published in 1897.

Mathews helped to define modernism on the American religious scene in two books, *The Gospel of Modern Man* (1910) and *The Faith of Modernism* (1924), the most widely read book in America in the 1920s from the liberal tradition. Mathews described modernism as simply the use of the methods of modern science in order to make traditional, orthodox concepts remain relevant for modern society. He insisted that modernists were evangelical Christians, and he affirmed central, historic tenets such as humanity's need of salvation from sin, Christ as the revelation of God, and the importance of the Bible as the record of God's revelation. Yet, Mathews asserted that such doctrines needed continuous updating in light of the best modern scientific, social-historical analysis available. He contrasted the openness of modernists with dogmatists who used the Bible as a collection of legalistic, infallible declarations. Creeds were "condemnatory" tools of conformity used to "anathematize heretics" and exclude nonconformists from the church. He concluded, "Confessionalism is the evangelicalism of the dogmatic mind. Modernism is the evangelicalism of the scientific mind."

Fundamentalism developed to battle modernism at the doctrinal level. The Bible was the battleground. The dispute is famously known as the Fundamentalist-Modernist Conflict. The fundamentalist response to the challenges of modern culture drew upon several theological and philosophical resources such as revivalism, dispensationalism, and the so-called "Princeton Theology." The urban revivalism of evangelical Protestantism, which flowered in the post-Civil War ministry of evangelist D. L. Moody, continued to focus upon personal conversion and the need to duplicate the practices of the New Testament church, and it upheld the Bible as the unique sacred authority for religious faith. Many evangelicals believed liberalism, with the focus on saving society in its social gospel, was abandoning the Bible's traditional evangelism of saving individuals.

Dispensational premillennialism—as developed and outlined in the late 1800s in England by John Nelson Darby and in the U.S. by C. I. Scofield—caught fire among many evangelicals who discarded the optimistic postmillennialism that had characterized much of American religion (as well as American culture's unique sense of "manifest destiny"). In contrast to liberals, who sought the Kingdom of God via cultural human progress, dispensationalists articulated a pessimistic view of the world. America was still considered "chosen" (as well as Israel), but only Jesus' literal return could usher in any kind of thousand-year era (millennium) of peace and righteousness. A literally interpreted Bible (especially the prophecies and apocalyptic texts) provided dispensationalists their own scientific timetable and hope for the future.

Dispensationalism was popularized at a series of Bible conferences at Niagara, New York (annually from 1876 to 1901), and inspired other Bible conferences nationally which spread the views of premillennialism, biblical inerrancy, and holiness teachings. Among others, two Baptists, A. C. Dixon and A. J. Gordon, were prominent popularizers of the theology. In 1909, dispensationalism gained further support in the commentary notes of the *Scofield Reference Bible*. This new edition of the King James Version of the Bible, edited by C. I. Scofield of what is now Dallas Theological Seminary, quickly became the most widely used Bible among fundamentalists. Increasingly, if fundamentalists ever disagreed on interpreting a Bible passage, they turned to the notes of the Scofield Bible for an authoritative answer.

The "Princeton theology" provided much of the intellectual backbone for fundamentalism. Charles Hodge's infamous remark that "a new idea never originated in this Seminary" revealed the strong Calvinistic tradition of the school and the reliance on confessions/creeds that would later be apparent in twentieth-century fundamentalism. Princeton theologians defended traditional orthodoxy against modern biblical criticism. In 1881, A. A. Hodge and B. B. Warfield articulated a technical view of biblical inerrancy that later dominated fundamentalism (and much of evangelicalism). Inerrancy meant that the Bible was divinely inspired and was without error in its original autographs, and thus was completely trustworthy on any topic that it addressed. Inerrancy attempted to build upon Scottish commonsense philosophy that was still prevalent in American higher education in the 1870s. To correctly interpret the Bible was to read it in its plainest (common) sense. Because the Bible was an inerrant storehouse of factual propositional truths, the orthodox reader was provided a rational, scientific confirmation of his or her faith. The growing liberal tradition felt that the fundamentalist reliance on rational and scientific confirmation of biblical truth was an ironic rejection of the best that modern evolutionary science had to offer.

Other notable events occurred to trumpet the growing concerns about liberalism in American religion. In 1892, Northern Presbyterians passed the "Portland Deliverance" which required ministers to affirm the Princeton theologians' definition of biblical inerrancy. Presbyterian clergy were required to affirm five "essential and necessary" doctrines: inerrancy of the Bible, the Virgin Birth, the substitutionary theory of the atonement, Christ's bodily resurrection, and miracles. The requirements were considered the sine qua non of orthodox faith until Presbyterians chose a more inclusive path in 1925.

Evangelicals defended their faith through Bible conferences, Bible institutes, revival meetings, and mission efforts. The first effort at establishing an organized interdenominational fundamentalist agenda against modernism was the publication, 1910 to 1915, of a twelve-volume series of booklets entitled, *The Fundamentals*. Provided through the financial support of Presbyterian business leaders Lyman Stewart and Milton Stewart, around three million pamphlets were distributed free of charge across America and beyond. Opposition to the liberalism of Baptist George Burman Foster gave impetus to the project. The editor of the first five volumes was a Baptist, A. C. Dixon. In the booklets, the conservative doctrinal tenets that characterized fundamentalism began to take shape. About one-third of the ninety articles affirmed the authority of the Bible and attacked modern biblical criticism. Articles on biblical inspiration touted inerrancy. The "five points" affirmed by Presbyterians in 1910 were defended. The pamphlets, which included nondispensationalist authors, demonstrated a moderated response to liberalism that later gave way to a more strict stance. The "moderate" Southern Baptist, E. Y. Mullins, wrote on the importance of religious experience. In the area of science, naturalistic Darwinianism was rejected, but a limited hearing of theistic evolution received some space.

By 1920, fundamentalism had developed into a well-defined movement. Fundamentalists had a theological litmus test—the five nonnegotiable doctrines. Belief in biblical inerrancy united fundamentalists of different backgrounds (advocates of the Princeton theology were not always dispensationalists) against a common enemy: modernists. These conservatives also had willingly accepted the name of "fundamentalist." Curtis Lee Laws, editor of the independent Baptist newspaper, the *Watchman-Examiner*, apparently coined the term:

> We suggest that those who still cling to the great fundamentals and who mean to do battle royal for the fundamentals be called "Fundamentalists." (*The Watchman Examiner*, 1 July 1920)

Moderation had given way to militant opposition to modernism.

The development of a more stringent fundamentalism had several factors. Some liberals had become more liberal and conservatives were increasingly alarmed. Social and cultural factors were also increasingly evident. An early sense of idealism after World War I was evident in the victory of prohibition, but rapid cultural changes were manifest. Open secularization—public dancing and smoking by both genders, the creation in 1919 of the modern tabloid—accompanied the "roaring twenties." Immigration restrictions increased, and the KKK (an estimated three million supporters by 1923) was revived as cultural fears arose. Among fundamentalists a temperament as well as a set of doctrinal tenets seemed at stake.

Evolution became a symbol of the cultural and theological differences between fundamentalists and modernists. Liberals, especially faculty members of the "Chicago School" like Shailer Mathews, lambasted premillennialists and charged that their pessimistic worldview was theologically incapable of supporting America in World War I. The war, according to liberal postmillennialists, would make the world safe for democracy.

Fundamentalists interpreted the crisis of the war much differently. Affirming that the war was a battle between civilization and German "barbarism," they noted that higher biblical criticism also hailed from German scholarship. German militarism was built on an evolutionary "might is right" philosophy, and theological modernism and its denial of traditional biblical truth was built upon an acceptance of the evolutionary development of religious ideas. Fundamentalists "connected the dots" and said that liberalism's affirmation of the "poison gas" of evolution was a threat to American civilization and to Christianity. To accept evolution was to deny the Bible's accuracy, and to deny the Bible's accuracy was to ultimately end up with another religion besides Christianity. A. C. Dixon said that evolution was a "Trojan horse" full of destruction. Paradoxically, fundamentalists maintained their pessimistic view of human progress, but emphasized a return to the certainty of inerrant biblical truth as the only hope for civilization.

This attempt to connect modernism and evolution was apparent in the work of the independent interdenominational World's Christian Fundamentals Association (WCFA). Organized in 1919 by Minnesota Baptist leader, William Bell Riley, along with Baptists Jasper C. Massee of Boston, and John R. Straton, of New York, the group also encouraged its supporters to establish Bible schools and to purge denominational schools of heretical teachers. Revealing the complexities of determining a short list of required fundamentals, premillennialism was added to the organization's doctrinal litmus test. Battles lines were drawn. Riley boasted that people would look back and call the creation of the WCFA more important than Martin Luther's posting of the "95 Theses" that sparked the Protestant Reformation. Leaders of the movement, especially Riley and Straton (who earned the title, the "Pope of Fundamentalism"), were known by opponents for their censorious spirits. Riley's uncompromising attitude was obvious when he declared that "One who rejects the verbal inspiration of the Bible rejects the Bible itself."

Public confrontations between modernists and fundamentalists exploded in the 1920s and greatly affected Northern Presbyterians and Northern Baptists. The fundamentalist strategy to defeat the encroachments of modernism was twofold: stop the teaching of evolution in public schools and eradicate liberalism from denominations. The methods of purging the denominations had a threefold focus: (re)gain control of theological education, missionary work, and denominational machinery. Doctrinal assent to a creedal litmus test would be enforced to exclude heretics/modernists.

Ironically, the Presbyterian conflict found a Baptist, Harry Emerson Fosdick, at the center of the hornet's nest. Fosdick attended Colgate Theological Seminary where he was influenced by the liberal theology of William Newton Clarke. While pastor of Montclair Baptist Church (New Jersey, 1904–1915), Fosdick was recognized as a talented preacher. (Martin Luther King, Jr. later called Fosdick the greatest pulpiteer of the century.) He also was known as a devotional writer and a professor at Union Theological Seminary. After serving as a chaplain in World War I, Fosdick was invited to be the pulpit minister at First Presbyterian Church, New York City (1918–1925). During this ecumenical experiment, Fosdick became alarmed at the erupting threat of fundamentalism, especially after visiting several Asian mission outposts torn by sectarian theological divisions.

In 1922, Fosdick entered the fray when he preached to his Presbyterian congregation the now (in)famous sermon, "Shall the Fundamentalists Win?" (published and distributed as "The New Knowledge and the Christian Faith"). He warned against the inroads of fundamentalists in Presbyterian and Baptist circles and said that they wanted to exclude liberals from evangelical churches. Attempting to reach out to conservatives, Fosdick declared, "All fundamentalists are conservatives, but all conservatives are not fundamentalists." While conservatives could agree to disagree, he declared that intolerance and the lack of charity were the dominating characteristics of fundamentalism.

Fosdick criticized fundamentalists for creating doctrinal litmus tests. He questioned fundamentalists' insistence upon the historicity of certain miracles (for example, the virgin birth of Jesus), dogmatic beliefs in the literal Second Coming of Jesus, the inerrancy of Scripture, and the substitutionary view of Christ's atonement. Fosdick asserted that science taught that minds were important, but that the narrow-minded attitude of fundamentalists was, "Come, and we will feed you opinions from a spoon.

No thinking is allowed here except such as brings you to certain specified, predetermined conclusions."

Fosdick's sermon was a plea "for an intellectually hospitable, tolerant, liberty-loving church," but it spurred further conflict—as he knew it would. His rejection of traditional Christian beliefs seemed obvious to critics. Because of his suspect view of the virgin birth of Jesus, Fosdick was called a "Unitarian cuckoo" who stigmatized Jesus as a "bastard and His blessed mother a harlot." In the aftermath of the controversial sermon, Fosdick was asked to join the Presbyterian church and have his preaching conform to the 1910 statement of the five necessary points of orthodoxy if he wanted to stay in the New York Presbytery.

Fosdick left First Presbyterian and became the pastor of Park Avenue Baptist Church (1925). Baptist fundamentalist John R. Straton responded to Fosdick with a sermon entitled, "Shall the Fundamentalists or the Funnymonkeyists Win?" Straton considered Fosdick to be a "Baptist bootlegger . . . a Presbyterian outlaw . . . the Jesse James of the theological world." Fosdick retorted that if the orthodoxy embodied and preached by fundamentalists was the standard, then he would "be ashamed to live in this generation and not be a heretic." Fosdick further alienated his Baptist opponents when his church practiced open membership (not requiring immersion). By 1930, with the financial help of Baptist layman and philanthropist, John D. Rockefeller, Jr., the church moved and became Riverside Church. The congregation developed a nonsectarian ministry (ministers did not have to have a certain denominational affiliation) with extensive focus on social ministry, and it was dually aligned with American Baptists and the United Church of Christ.

The Presbyterian conflict had other players involved—J. Gresham Machen, for example, called liberalism a false religion separate from Christianity—but in 1924, partly in reaction to the Fosdick case, Presbyterians rejected the recent requirement of doctrinal conformity to the "Five Points" and said that inerrancy went beyond their Westminster Confession and the Bible's own affirmation about inspiration. They noted that Presbyterians historically had tolerated some diversity in interpreting their confessional statement. Ultimately many Presbyterians, who were doctrinally conservative, refused to side with militant fundamentalist leaders in the battle to take control of the denomination. They opted for a unity based on a zeal for missions, evangelism, and loyalty to the denomination rather than risk a major schism. A similar scenario also played out in the Northern Baptist Convention.

In the 1920s, fundamentalists engaged in a concerted effort to control the Northern Baptist Convention. Leaders had already been speaking at local churches to enlighten the laity against the dangers of liberalism. In 1920, a receptive audience of 150 attended a preconvention rally in Buffalo to launch more visible complaints against liberalism in the denomination. Leaders at the rally asserted that their purpose was to reaffirm the "fundamentals of our New Testament faith." Criticizing Baptist schools and evolution in one swoop, J. C. Massee said, "Our educational cages contain many scholastic monkeys who with their Darwinian complacency confess their parentage." The result of the rally was the creation of the Fundamentalist Fellowship. Influential leaders were again William B. Riley, John Roach Straton, and Massee who were involved in the World's Christian Fundamentals Association. At the meeting of the national convention, fundamentalists successfully pushed Northern Baptists to disavow involvement in the ecumenical Interchurch Movement, and they achieved a victory when the convention authorized a commission to investigate false teaching at all denominational schools. However, fundamentalists, especially Straton, employed harsh rhetoric during the convention and observers said they felt a spirit of intolerance.

School administrators fiercely objected and several refused to participate in an investigation. President William H. P. Faunce of Brown University declined to respond to the convention's questionnaire because the college's charter forbade any type of religious test. He advised other schools to "stand fast in the soul liberty of Roger Williams." When the University of Chicago refused to comply with the questionnaire, fundamentalists accused Dean Shailer Mathews of heresy. The disdain of Baptists who were horrified at the liberal (for some, apostate) direction of the "Chicago School" was readily apparent. Crozer Theological Seminary was also particularly suspect. At the 1921 Northern Baptist Convention meeting, schools generally received a positive report. Fundamentalists were unimpressed and many schools, only nominally associated with the convention, eventually became independent from Northern Baptists.

At the 1922 national convention, the Fundamentalist Fellowship attempted to adopt a creed to safeguard orthodoxy. Leaders promoted biblical inerrancy in their rallies. Militant fundamentalist, William B. Riley, who liked to call liberals "Unitarian Baptists," offered a resolution that the New Hampshire Confession be recommended to churches for their use in order to restore historic Baptist orthodoxy. While most Baptists accepted the conservative theology of fundamentalists, they did not believe intellectual assent and conformity to a creed was necessary or "Baptistic." Cornelius Woelfkin of New York, a former denominational executive, challenged Riley with a substitute motion: "The Northern Baptist Convention affirms that the New Testament is the all-sufficient ground of our faith and practice, and we need no other statement." Fundamentalists lost the vote, 1,264 to 637.

The fundamentalist attack on missionaries also heated up. At the 1922 convention, Frederick L. Anderson, chairman of the board of managers of the American Baptist Foreign Mission Society, defended the orthodoxy of missionaries and denied that attention to doctrinal soundness was inadequate in the appointment process of missionary candidates. Undaunted, fundamentalists produced alleged statements from various missionaries that denied basic doctrines including the virgin birth and the deity of Christ. At the 1924 convention, an official investigative committee was created to examine Northern Baptist foreign missions.

The next year a commission reported that the vast majority of missionaries possessed an "evangelical faith." A few cases of doctrinal problems were identified and a recommendation was made to be more careful in the appointment process. A move to recall identified liberals from the mission field was defeated in favor of allowing leaders of the Foreign Mission Board to handle the matter. The convention chose to follow the "inclusive policy" of appointments advocated by missions leader Frederick L. Anderson. The Foreign Mission Board would "appoint and retain missionaries of varying theological beliefs" who reflected the diverse viewpoints in the churches and who came within the "limits of the gospel." Use of this "inclusive policy" kept the door open for liberal missionaries, according to fundamentalists. Tension even within fundamentalist circles was evident when J. C. Massee, who had participated on the commission and approved its report, resigned the presidency of the Fundamentalist Fellowship, a position he had held for five years.

While the Fundamentalist Fellowship continued to work for change inside the Northern Baptist Convention, a more militant independent, fundamentalist organization to battle modernism was begun outside the convention. The Baptist Bible Union (BBU), formed in 1923, included leaders from across the American continent: T. T. Shields of Canada, William B. Riley from the North, and J. Frank Norris from the South. An impetus to the group's organization was the refusal of Northern Baptists to adopt the New Hampshire Confession. Consequently, the BBU adopted a modified version of the confession as its creedal statement and required a premillennial understanding of Jesus' Second Coming. Advocates highlighted local church autonomy—a reaction against centralization among Northern Baptists who had formed their convention in 1907 and joined the Federal Council of Churches the next year. The BBU, exhibiting the separatist tendencies in fundamentalism, told churches to refrain from giving financial contributions to any mission group or school that failed to affirm the fundamentals of the faith. It also voiced their displeasure with Harry Emerson Fosdick, suggesting that a Fosdick–John D. Rockefeller, Jr. "conspiracy" was afoot to make Baptist schools havens for liberalism. (Throughout the 1920s, Rockefeller contributed gifts that totaled between five and twelve-plus percent per year of the missionary budget of the Northern Baptist Convention.)

As with the Northern Presbyterians, Baptist conservatives who agreed with the militant fundamentalists on most doctrinal issues opted for denominational loyalty and cooperative mission endeavors. Some concessions were made to reach out to these conservatives. In 1925, Eastern Baptist Theological Seminary was established as a conservative seminary (just as Northern Baptist Theological Seminary had been created as an alternative to the University of Chicago in 1913). Faculty and trustees were required to affirm a doctrinal confession. Founders included Curtis Lee Laws who had earlier coined the word "fundamentalist." Ultimately the brand of fundamentalism found in the Baptist Bible Union was regarded as bitterly uncompromising. J. C. Massee, who was called an apostate after his resignation from the Fundamentalist Fellowship and his subsequent willingness to work cooperatively with liberals, summed up the attitude that prevailed among many Northern Baptists toward militant fundamentalists: "I left the fundamentalists to save my own spirit; they became so self-righteous, so critical, so unchristian, so destructive, so incapable of being fair that I had to go elsewhere for spiritual nourishment."

General Association of Regular Baptist Churches. Continued tension among Northern Baptists produced two schisms, two attempts that adherents believed were necessary to restore faithfulness to the New Testament church. In 1933, the Baptist Bible Union disbanded and reorganized as the General Association of Regular Baptist Churches (GARBC). The new name indicated support for "regular" historic Baptist orthodoxy. Headquartered in Schaumburg, Illinois, at the end of the twentieth century, GARBC had more than 1,500 churches. GARBC required that local churches must accept the New Hampshire Confession with an article affirming premillennialism. For these "separatists," dual alignment with other Baptists and cooperation with any group that harbored liberalism was prohibited.

Conservative Baptist Association of America. The Fundamentalist Fellowship remained in the Northern Baptist Convention (NBC) until 1947 when it departed to form the Conservative Baptist Association of America. The "inclusive policy" used by the Foreign Mission Board since 1923 never ceased to irritate fundamentalists. They demanded that belief in the virgin birth be a litmus-test question for missionaries, but the NBC refused to amend its "inclusive" policies to include the specific doctrinal requirement. In 1943, frustrations boiled over when someone they considered liberal, Elmer A. Fridell, was elected foreign secretary of the board. Fundamentalists further complained that in the last two decades, the "inclusive policy" had led to a fifty percent decrease in mission gifts and missionary appointments. Denominational leaders explained several factors for the decline (including the economic depression that paralyzed the country in the 1930s) and defended the "inclusive policy" as the best method to reflect the broad constituency of Northern Baptists. They also cited the convention's 1922 affirmation of the Bible as the convention's faith statement, and rebuffed renewed fundamentalist efforts to require missionaries to sign a specific doctrinal statement. The convention leadership did not trust fundamentalists when they said their confession of faith was not a creed, and fundamentalists did not trust convention leaders when they tried to affirm their orthodoxy.

In December 1943, the Conservative Baptist Foreign Missionary Society was formed. In ensuing years, these conservatives were frustrated that delegates to an annual meeting of the Northern Baptist Convention were not allowed to decide whether to accept the new mission society as a convention agency. Consequently, on 17 May 1947, the Conservative Baptist Association of America was born. Hundreds of churches left the Northern Baptist Convention, formed a "movement" that opposed the centralization of power, and adopted a creedal statement that affirmed the inerrancy of Scripture. At the beginning of the twenty-first century, there was still intentionally no unified budget for cooperating societies, but various mission societies and schools were supported by 1,200-plus churches, most located in the North and West.

Baptist Distinctives. While Northern and Southern Baptists never reunited, both groups laid claim to a similar list of historic Baptist distinctives and asserted that these beliefs faithfully emulated the New Testament. Thomas Armitage, church historian and prominent pastor in the city of New York, and Albert Newman, church historian who taught in Toronto, Canada for twenty years (1881–1901), as well as at posts in the North and South, did not argue for an unbroken line of Baptist churches back to the New Testament. ("Landmarkism" did argue such: see the next chapter.) Both Baptist historians/statesmen, however, contended that Baptist teachings were present from the first century to their day.

Both Armitage and Newman affirmed the typical Baptist emphases of believer's baptism by immersion, local church independence, absolute freedom of conscience, and each individual's right to the private judgment of Scripture, because each person answered directly to God for his or her faith. In his "Baptist Faith and Practice" (1882), Armitage trumpeted Baptist anticreedalism. Why use creeds when the Scriptures were available? While some churches had confessions (articles of faith), they had no authority over individual consciences. Affirming the separation of church and state, Armitage boldly declared that "when a Baptist shall rob one man of soul-liberty, by statue, penalty, and sword, he will cease to be a Baptist for that reason."

Newman made explicit reference to the concept of the New Testament church with his article, "Baptist Churches Apostolical" (1892). "Baptist churches alone of all the churches were Apostolical in spirit and in form," wrote Newman. Baptists were different from the earliest Christians in "minor matters," but not in the essentials. The regenerate church emphasis in Baptist thought was undergirded by the egalitarian affirmation of the priesthood of believers ("every believer is a priest before God . . . the church is a democracy") that was found in the New Testament. However, Newman lamented that Baptists had a standard of orthodoxy, "partly written, partly individual" that

> hamper[ed] the freedom of individual consciences. The amount of bigotry and intolerance to be found in Baptist churches is, when compared with the fundamental principles of Baptists, appalling.

Peace Efforts

*Ana*baptists, not Baptists, are known as pacifists. Peacemaking efforts, however, have been evident in Baptist history. During colonial America, isolated Baptists, including some at the "first" Baptist church in Providence, Rhode Island, called war unchristian. At least a few Separate Baptists, as well as Benjamin Randall and other early Free Will Baptists, decried the bearing of "carnal weapons." In the nineteenth century, prominent Baptists such as Francis Wayland and Adoniram Judson were officers in peace societies. Henry Holcombe, pastor of influential First Baptist Church, Philadelphia, supported the War of 1812 but subsequently denounced war and organized the Philadelphia Peace Society. In a book of sermons entitled *Primitive Theology in a Series of Lectures* (1822), Holcombe argued that "carnal warfare" and the taking of life were not permissible in the primitive New Testament church.

Most Baptists have been quick to support American wars with their patriotism. Support for the Spanish-American War in 1898, for example, reflected the anti-Catholic flavor of Baptist (and Protestant) faith. Prior to World War I, Baptists were outspoken for peace efforts but after Congress declared war against Germany, support was usually immediate. Gordon Conwell of Philadelphia, for example, shifted from preaching peace sermons to assisting the recruitment of personnel for military service. Churches often had special services honoring men on the battlefield and some pastors took leaves of absence to work with the Young Men's Christian Association among the troops.

The work of Baptists in peace groups during wartime was not silent. Baptist pastors, such as Muriel Lester of Britain and Walter Rauschenbusch, assisted in the formation in 1914 of an international Fellowship of Reconciliation, a group that supported conscientious objectors and protested militarism during both World War I and World War II. This ecumenical body spawned several Baptist pacifist groups on both sides of the Atlantic. Influenced by Rauschenbusch, Harry Emerson Fosdick's sermon on the "Unknown Soldier" (1933) demonstrated his turn away from his earlier support of World War I.

At the turn of the twenty-first century the most visible Baptist peace group was "The Baptist Peace Fellowship of North America." Formed in 1984, participants were from various Baptist denominations and included members from Canada, Mexico, Puerto Rico, and the United States. Antecedents were the Baptist Pacifist Fellowship (1939), a group formed by some Northern Baptists but never endorsed by their larger convention, and its successor, The Baptist Peace Fellowship (1960). The name change, which occurred during the "Cold War" fears about an escalating nuclear arms race, allowed persons who were not absolute pacifists to join in peace efforts.

Ecumenism, Religious Liberty, and Women's Leadership

Ecumenism. American Baptists, in proportion to their size, provided more of the national leadership than any other American denomination in the modern ecumenical movement. When the national ecumenical group, the Federal Council of Churches (FCC), was established in 1908, thirty-three Protestant bodies joined. Four were Baptist: Seventh Day Baptists, Free Will Baptists (North), National Baptist Convention (African-American), and the Northern Baptist Convention. Northern Baptist Shailer Mathews was the FCC's first president.

Northern Baptists were also very influential in the ecumenical Home Missions Council (1908), of which Henry Morehouse was one of the founders. Charles Lincoln White, the leader of Northern Baptist home missions after Morehouse, felt that cooperative mission work duplicated the "spirit that prevailed in the earliest Christian centuries." According to some Baptists, the advance in cooperative Christianity would advance the coming Kingdom of God. During World War II, the Home Missions Council, under the leadership of Northern Baptist G. Pitt Beers, cooperated with the FCC and criticized the placement of Japanese-Americans in "internment" camps in the wake of the bombing of Pearl Harbor.

On the international scene, Northern Baptists participated in the early efforts at cooperation (Edinburgh Missionary Conference, 1910; World Conference on Faith and Order, 1911) that eventually led to the creation in 1948 of the World Council of Churches (WCC). American Baptists have been involved extensively in the ministries of the WCC.

Religious Liberty. Northern Baptists spoke clearly about the need for separation of church and state. At the inception of the Northern Baptist Convention, Henry Morehouse said that the convention affirmed this important principle. In 1937, Northern Baptists formed a Public Affairs Committee, and along with Southern Baptists and other smaller Baptist groups, created a religious-liberty agency, the Baptist Joint Committee on Public Affairs (BJCPA).

Despite their ecumenicity, American Baptists remained typically Protestant and hesitant about Catholicism and the continued influx of immigrants into the country during the early decades of the twentieth century. Most American Baptists opposed the 1928 candidacy of Al Smith for president, in large part, because he was Catholic. An exception was the Roger Williams Baptist Association of Rhode Island which declared that political maneuvers to defeat a political candidate because of his religion were inappropriate.

Women's Ecumenical Leadership. Northern Baptist women also participated heavily in ecumenical efforts. None were more influential than Helen Barrett Montgomery. An advocate of women's rights, the licensed minister worked alongside suffrage leader Susan B. Anthony to create the Women's Educational and Industrial Union of Rochester (New York), and she served as its first president. The organization provided assistance to poor women and foreshadowed later public health centers.

Montgomery was extensively involved in Northern Baptist and ecumenical mission efforts. She toured America in 1910, and helped raise one million dollars to assist in the establishment of Christian schools in Asia. She served as president of the American Baptist Woman's Foreign Mission Society for a decade (1914–1924) and traveled overseas with former missionary Lucy Whitehead (McGill) Waterbury Peabody. Their efforts resulted in the publication of mission study guides on various countries, a proposal for a World Day of Prayer, and the creation of the World Wide Guild, which was a support group that encouraged young women to become missionaries. Ironically, the two women later were on different sides of the fundamentalist controversy among Northern Baptists in the 1920s. Peabody served as the first president of the independent, conservative Association of Baptists for World Evangelism.

Montgomery also was a pioneer in other ministries. Elected president of the Northern Baptist Convention in 1921, she was the first woman president of a denomination in America. (A woman has yet to serve as president of either the Southern Baptist Convention or the National Baptist Convention.) Montgomery's *Centenary Translation of the New Testament: The New Testament in Modern English* (1924), intended for the average reader, was the first-ever English translation produced by a woman.

Other Northern Baptist women were leaders in ecumenical efforts. The first president (1908–1916) of the Council of Women for Home Missions was Baptist Alice Blanchard Merriam Coleman. Another Baptist president of this group was Edith Elizabeth Lowry, who served in 1939 as the first woman participant in the National Radio Pulpit. She also served as a home mission coordinator for the National Council of Churches, which American Baptists helped form in 1950 as the successor to the Federal Council of Churches.

While the American Baptist leadership was strongly supportive of ecumenical efforts, not all American Baptists shared the same passion.

When the Federal Council of Churches was formed in 1908, some more conservative Baptists were not interested in cooperating with other denominations that did not consider the New Testament the absolute rule for faith and practice, and who consequently maintained unbiblical elements like infant baptism, grace-giving sacraments, and state churches that denied religious liberty. As ecumenical groups became associated with liberal theology, conservative critics bewailed an "anchorless ecumenism," and they advocated joining the National Association of Evangelicals rather than the National Council of Churches.

Conclusion

In the last half of the nineteenth and first half of the twentieth centuries, American society experienced massive changes. Religion in America followed suit. Baptists were a part of the story. How to modernize, develop centralized efficiency, yet remain true to a biblical faith? Some Northern Baptists—for example, the Chicago School—asserted that biblical faith had to be adapted to the best of modern knowledge to be affirmed. Acceptance of new scientific ideas (evolution; critical methods of biblical study) changed the way the Bible was understood. The search for a literal New Testament church often was considered irrelevant to many modernists, but following the ethical teachings of Jesus was not. For example, advocates of the social gospel like Walter Rauschenbusch became involved in cutting-edge ministries to the urban poor. Rauschenbusch was an evangelical liberal, at heart an evangelist who actually sought to usher in the New Testament church by recovering the social teachings of Scripture. Writers who reflected on Baptist distinctives still talked of the "Baptist Church Apostolical." Baptist distinctives like congregational church government and freedom for the individual conscience were more than relevant in a modern, scientific age.

More conservative Baptist voices found the maintenance of New Testament Christianity in its "primitive form" to be an urgent need in light of the attacks of modernists who they believed had forsaken the Bible. The fundamentalist reaction to modernists was an attempt to defend the "fundamentals" of the New Testament church. Biblical inerrancy was believed to be necessary to holding a pure biblical faith. The growing ecumenism of liberals was considered to be a denial of orthodox essentials. Other reactions to modernism like the Holiness and Pentecostal movements attracted Baptists. A. J. Gordon's acceptance of women preachers and divine healing was rooted in his desire to embody the faith of the New Testament church.

In the century after the Civil War, American religion in the North was increasingly pluralistic and more accommodating of diverse opinions and new religious ideas than the South. Northern Baptists far and wide still spoke of the New Testament as their authority for faith and practice. Beyond that, in the way the faith was practiced, they were often far and wide apart. Some were tolerant of change; some were not; and the two rarely found common ground.

Chapter 6

In Search of a New Testament Church, Southern Style

It is practically impossible to read Southern religion in the decades after the Civil War through any lens but race. Southern religion was, as one historian put it, "baptized in blood." Attitudes toward race impacted relations with the North, mission methodology, and, essentially, all of life. Southern regional identity became identified with religious commitment. To be Baptist was to be Southern.

Like Northern Baptists, but even more so, Southern Baptists developed an increasingly centralized and efficient denomination. While urbanization in the South did not match that in the North, Southerners still were confronted with a changing economic map. Denominational advance was part and parcel with the progress and tensions of the urban-led New South. With the Civil War having contributed to a more politicized ministry, rural and urban Baptists often clashed. Consequently, populist religion found expression in movements that objected to centralization and modernization of culture. More than any other era, rural Southerners focused on Baptists as the *primitive* New Testament church.

Development of a *Southern* Baptist Identity

The Southern Baptist Convention (SBC) was organized on a convention model rather than the society model of the Triennial Convention and other Baptist organizations in the North. As a centralized convention, Southern Baptists desired to support both foreign and home mission boards. For several decades, however, many Southern Baptist churches continued to use some Northern agencies like the American Baptist Publication Society and the nascent Southern mission boards essentially functioned as societies vying and struggling for funds. In the postbellum decades, a general consensus developed that gave structure to the Southern Baptist identity. A sense of Southern Baptist distinctiveness was cultivated and maintained by

- a universal sense of mission rooted in individual religious experience
- a commitment to Southern Culture
- denominational Loyalty

Individual Religious Experience. Southern Baptists found commonality in a universal sense of mission. Baptists were diverse in some theological concerns—some were strict Calvinists; others affirmed a general atonement in their evangelistic practices—and worship styles, but the historic Baptist focus upon individual religious experience was universal among them. Personal conversion was the heart of the gospel. They were mission-minded, evangelistic, and generally focused on personal morality rather than the sins of society. Church discipline was most often enforced against personal "sins" such as drinking, dancing, and card playing. Holiness was usually a function of individual beliefs, not social activism. Southern Baptists became the de facto established church of the South. Not coincidentally, the South was the only region of America where evangelical Christianity became the dominant shape of the faith. In other words, the Southern Baptist focus on revivalistic conversion and acceptance (and promotion) of a segregated "Jim Crow" society helped define Southern evangelicalism.

Southern Identity. From the outset, Southern Baptists found unity in a commitment to a cultural identity. To be Baptist was to be Southern. To be Southern was to defend and contend for a racial orthodoxy of white supremacy that prevailed in the antebellum period and continued in the segregated world of the Jim Crow South. To question this orthodoxy was to commit a heresy greater than any theological speculation.

Segregation replaced slavery as the answer to the "race problem" and was built upon the same biblical rationale. God designed the races to be separate; moreover, African-Americans were considered innately inferior. White ministers were leading defenders of white supremacy. Henry H. Tucker, influential editor of the Georgia Baptist Convention newspaper, *The Christian Index*, expressed the typical sentiment of white Southern Baptists: "We do not believe that all men are created equal as the Declaration of Independence declares them to be; nor that they will ever become equal in this world." Perhaps many Baptists also shared the view of the Baptist layman who wrote in his diary at the end of the Civil War: "It grieves me to think of what the South has suffered and lost, for what? For a lot of worthless niggers, which now are worse than worthless."

These Southern Baptist attitudes were part of the larger Southern response to the Civil War called the "Myth of the Lost Cause." After the War, the "myth"—which was especially promoted by Robert E. Lee's former Confederate chaplain, the Baptist J. William Jones—perpetuated a vision of a united Southern people with a separate cultural identity in place of the failed separate Southern political nation. The American sense of chosenness or "Manifest Destiny" (a concept developed in the 1840s among, especially, Jacksonian Democrats, the term itself was first published in 1845) was "Southernized." Defeat in the Civil War was simply a divine chastening for the South's ultimate purpose. The region was to be a Bible Belt culture that revolved around Anglo-Saxon racial superiority and evangelical Protestantism as cornerstones of society. This collective psyche—called the "Southern way of life"—was the key to withstanding the assault of a Yankee America that was becoming ever more corrupted (secular) and heretical (theologically liberal). Yankee religion and Radical Reconstruction that promoted racial/social equality was especially feared because it would result, according to Jeremiah Bell Jeter, editor of the *Religious Herald* of Virginia, in the "mongrelization of our noble Anglo-Saxon race."

Modern historians have said that these racial attitudes of Southern Baptists (along with other Southerners), were "culturally captive." Or, borrowing a phrase from the prophet Amos, they were "at ease in Zion." Southern Baptists not only defended the status quo of a Jim Crow South, they promoted it. To be Baptist was to be Southern.

Denominational Loyalty. By the end of the nineteenth century, Southern Baptists were developing a strong sense of denominational loyalty around a common programmatic identity/piety (a Foreign Mission Board, a Home Mission Board, a Sunday School Board, and a theological school, the Southern Baptist Theological Seminary). More elaborate programs and agencies were created along the way to provide a "one-stop-shop" for Baptists to live the Christian life. Early work in home missions included the organization of the First Chinese Baptist Church in Sacramento, California. In 1854, J. Lewis Shuck and Henrietta Shuck had returned to the United States from their mission post in China under the auspices of the Triennial Convention and switched allegiance to the SBC. (Henrietta was the first female missionary to China.) The work of the Home Mission Board (HMB) floundered in the aftermath of the Civil War, however, and struggled to survive until a move to Atlanta in 1882 from its original home in Marion, Alabama.

Isaac Taylor Tichenor was the leader of the HMB from 1882 to 1899. He helped not only to save the agency but to define the denominational identity of Southern Baptists. Tichenor, the former president of what is now Auburn University (1872–1882), was a diehard Confederate. Consequently, he was a zealous defender of Southern sectionalism who insisted that Baptists in the South cease their reliance upon Northern Baptist agencies such as the American Baptist Home Mission Society that had served the South for decades. Tichenor used the language of war to make his point: the work of Northern Baptists in the South was an "invasion" and encroached upon Southern autonomy. To cooperate with Northern agencies, then, was tantamount to treason. Tichenor made Baptists proud to be separate, proud to be *Southern* Baptists.

During his tenure, Tichenor greatly expanded the work of the Home Mission Board. He helped to corral Texas Baptists into the SBC as Southerners and pushed the boundaries of Southern Baptist work by challenging (and "defeating") Northern Baptist work in the Midwest. The HMB also developed mission concerns for the education of African-Americans and Appalachian whites under Tichenor. These efforts, in retrospect, often functioned as "social control" to maintain the dominance of Anglo-Saxon superiority in Southern culture. Tichenor has also earned the title of "father of Cuban missions." Historians note that he employed mission methods that reflected the wider Protestant imperialistic exportation of the American culture of the day—true to the antebellum concept of Manifest Destiny. Paternalistically he believed that Cubans, like African-Americans, needed to be "civilized" with Southern Christian values.

Tichenor helped to usher the Southern Baptist Convention into the "New South." Most Southern Baptists were still rural—eighty-five percent of Southern Baptists in the 1920s—passionate localists who looked with disdain at much of the centralizing work of denominational leaders and their increasing focus on agency and program-centered piety. Nevertheless, Tichenor, an urban Baptist—he was a member of Georgia's wealthiest church, Second Baptist Church, Atlanta—helped make Southern Baptists a part of the "New South" movement that pushed the agrarian South to "modernize" by promoting industrialized business. He epitomized the evolving professionalism of Southern Baptist ministry, and he represented the increasing influence of urban professionals in defining what it meant to be Southern Baptist. Tichenor is regarded as the most pivotal figure that stabilized a struggling Southern convention and secured a denominational consciousness that to this day, for many Southern Baptists, has not abated.

James Marion Frost, an ally of Tichenor, also played a key role in the development of loyalty to a Southern Baptist identity. In 1891, Frost garnered support for a Sunday School Board that developed from the work of the HMB. Previous attempts at producing Southern literature were ineffective, but Frost, leader of the Sunday School Board for two decades (1896–1916), succeeded in promoting the use of literature written by

Southern Baptists for Southern Baptists. Once the American Baptist Publication Society broached the idea of black authors for some of its pieces, Frost's goal of a doctrinally correct Southern literature found more ready acceptance. Other Southern Baptists concurred. The Kentucky *Western Recorder* declared in familiar Baptist "apostolic" language:

> Southern Baptists present the world's highest type of Bible Christianity. The responsibility therefore of leading the world is upon us, but if we buy our Sunday-school literature from abroad, we make others, in doing so, our leaders and thus forfeit this high trust.

By 1910, the American Baptist Publication Society had ceased its work in the South.

Denominational identity was seemingly always connected to a passion for foreign missions. The Convention had been formed because Baptist leaders demanded the right of slaveholders to be missionaries. Historians have said that at first the SBC was essentially the work of the Foreign Mission Board. In the early years, mission work was soon initiated in China (1845), Liberia (1846), Nigeria (1850), and Brazil (1859). By 1859, seventeen missionaries had already died. The efforts to establish missions in Liberia and Brazil were not successful. Despite near economic devastation due to the Civil War, mission efforts persevered. By 1900, the FMB employed ninety-four missionaries in six countries. Membership in 113 international churches totaled 6,537 persons.

Mission methodology often revealed the belief in white superiority that was rooted in a Southern identity. On the home front, the promotion of mountain schools was encouraged because the children in the Appalachian region were of pure Anglo stock. On the foreign mission field, African-Americans were initially appointed to work in Africa as assistants to white missionaries. By 1890, the practice had ceased because white missionaries objected to working and socializing with blacks.

Southern Baptists were not the only Protestants to utilize Anglo-Saxon supremacy as a specific mission strategy for world evangelization. The Baptist method was to convert European whites who could then help American whites convert the world. According to James Franklin Love, executive-secretary of the Foreign Mission Board (1915–1928), only whites had the capability of converting all the races. Love said that his assertion was not a show of pride or contempt for "any colored race" but simply a "solemn fact." Ever since the Apostle Paul's call to leave Asia and to preach in Macedonia (Acts 16), Love asserted, "the Anglo-Saxon race has been God's favored people."

Women and Denominational Consciousness. The cultivation of a denominational consciousness was also seen in the missionary work of Southern Baptist women. In the midst of the poverty of the Reconstruction era, Ladies Aid Societies, trailblazers in women's work, raised money to rebuild churches devastated during the Civil War. Since they had little money, their fund-raising efforts included sewing circles, cooking, and selling eggs. With their money, they also supported missions, cared for the poor, and helped to pay ministers whose salaries were often in arrears. Women missionaries, however, were not automatically accepted in Southern Baptist life (or in other denominations). Harriet Baker, who began serving in China in 1850, was the first *single* woman appointed as a foreign missionary. Male missionaries discounted her efforts, and also criticized her for having trouble with the Chinese language. After three years, her supervisor, who was insistent that Baker leave China, finally resorted to persuading a British missionary physician that she had tuberculosis when her symptom was a slight cough. Subsequently, Baker resigned, and doubts about the propriety and physical ability of single women (not under the leadership of a husband) to be missionaries prevailed. Southern Baptists did not appoint another single woman until 1872.

The development of an organized woman's missionary union among Southern Baptists began in earnest in the 1870s. A "Woman's Mission to Woman" movement began in 1868 in Baltimore and was enthusiastically received by Baptist women throughout the South. In 1872, Henry A. Tupper, the new corresponding secretary of the Foreign Mission Board, ushered in a new day when he began the approval of female missionaries, and he strongly encouraged the organization of women's missionary groups in local churches. Two years later, with Tupper's encouragement, "central committees" were created to coordinate mission efforts in states.

The development of women's ministries was not without controversy. In the broader American scene, there was a growing anxiety about a "feminized church." The potential leadership roles for women in missions, fund-raising, and other ministries seemed to contradict the traditional Victorian-era understanding of the New Testament, that the proper sphere for women's moral influence was home and family. As Southern Baptist women began to organize, not unexpectedly some pastors had fears that women's suffrage was on the horizon and invoked the biblical proof text, "Let your women keep silence in the churches" (1 Corinthians 14:34).

Subsequently, in 1885, women messengers from Arkansas were disqualified as messengers to the national convention meeting, and their participation was excluded through a constitutional amendment until 1918. (Until 1901, women had to sit in the visitors' gallery.)

Women continued to organize and a national missions organization, the Woman's Missionary Union (WMU), was officially organized as an auxiliary to the Southern Baptist Convention in 1888. While the women wanted to participate in Baptist missions at the national level, Annie Armstrong, the first corresponding secretary of the infant organization, attempted to calm the waters when she declared that the women did not desire an independent women's organization without ties to Southern Baptists. Neither were they a part of the growing feminist movement that advocated women's suffrage.

As an "auxiliary" group, the WMU immediately became the financial backbone of Southern Baptist mission efforts and became the most effective agent of connecting local Southern Baptists to larger causes. When the Gospel Mission movement—a missions ideology that promoted missions solely by local churches rather than national mission boards—threatened the work of the Foreign Mission Board in the 1890s, Armstrong insisted upon allegiance to the Southern Baptist way of cooperation. "Miss Annie," as Armstrong was known, could be a forceful leader, yet, like many late-nineteenth-century Protestant women, she struggled with the tension between enlarged leadership opportunities and the traditional expectations for women to be submissive and keep out of the spotlight.

If Southern Baptists have saints, Annie Armstrong, and perhaps even more so, "Lottie" (Charlotte) Moon, have been so honored. Moon, an almost legendary iconic figure in Baptist missiology, was a single missionary to China (1873–1912). Her correspondence with local women's groups did much to create a passion for Southern Baptist missions. When invited to preach, Moon answered that "it was not the custom of the ancient church that women preach to men." Moon espoused traditional female roles and evidently broke an engagement with controversial seminary professor, Crawford Toy of Southern Seminary, because of theological concerns. At the same time, Moon was bold and outspoken in her correspondence with administrators of the Foreign Mission Board. She occasionally preached, noted that she was "virtually the pastor" at one of her mission posts, and insisted upon and was given an equal voice in planning the mission work in China. Moon so identified with the Chinese that she ultimately adopted their dress and essentially starved to alleviate the poverty of the girls she taught. Her suggestion to have a special offering for missions was heeded by Annie Armstrong (the Methodists were already doing it, Moon said), and the annual Lottie Moon Christmas offering became (and still is) the most influential financial support for foreign missions in Southern Baptist life. Moon, at her death, was hailed by the *Foreign Mission Journal* as "the best man among our missionaries." Subsequently, a Home Missions Easter offering was named after Annie Armstrong.

When a WMU Training School was created in 1907, Armstrong re-signed as WMU corresponding secretary. She feared that such a school would lead toward advocacy of women preachers. Southern Baptist identity was not yet ready for ministerial equality. Most Baptist men and women concurred with the opinion of Texan B. H. Carroll: "A woman pastor is in flat contradiction of the apostolic teaching . . . [and is a] rebellion against Christ."

Threats to Denominational Loyalty

Landmarkism. The most explicit manifestation of gospel primitivism in Baptist life was the spread of Landmarkism throughout Southern Baptist ranks in the nineteenth century. The intense denominational competition of the frontier provided the context. Alexander Campbell claimed the restoration of the New Testament church; Methodists cited the apostolic poverty (and often celibacy) of their evangelistic itinerant ministers. Baptists did not simply suggest they were restoring the New Testament, but that they *were* the New Testament church. The attractiveness of such a collective identity was readily received by a group often found on the margins of society.

Landmarkism, characteristic of Baptist concerns, began over the his-toric concern regarding the nature of valid baptism. In 1848, James Robin-son Graves, editor of *The Tennessee Baptist*, denounced the views of the more progressive editor of the *Western Baptist Review* (Kentucky), John L. Waller, who accepted the validity of "alien immersion"—immersion administered by non-Baptists. Three years later, Graves led a group "willing to accept and practice the teachings of Christ and his apostles" to issue the "Cotton Grove (Tennessee) Resolutions" that further questioned the biblical authenticity of non-Baptist faith.

Graves's primitivist approach was twofold. First, he asserted that the local Baptist church was the only true New Testament church because only Baptists could trace a direct succession of churches back to Jesus and John the Baptist. Jesus was baptized by immersion in the Jordan River and then established the first church—a local Baptist church—at Jerusalem. Since

Jesus had told the Apostle Peter that the "gates of hell" would never destroy the church (Matthew 16:18), the Baptist church, by prophetic necessity, had always existed. "If Christ has not kept His promise concerning his church to keep it, how can I trust Him concerning my salvation?," queried Graves. Anyone who did not affirm the existence of true (that is, Baptist) churches throughout history, Graves added, really did not believe in the Bible. Second, only the Baptist church duplicated New Testament ordinances and ministry. A genuine local New Testament church practiced believer's baptism by immersion (no infant baptism) and closed communion—the restriction of the Lord's Supper to those baptized Baptist believers. Some Landmark churches even denied communion to Baptists who were not members of their particular local church.

In view of his exclusive focus on the church as a local body of Baptists, Graves argued that only local churches, not mission boards, engaged in missions in the New Testament. Missionaries sent by agencies were removed from the discipline and authority of the local church. Furthermore, because Baptists churches were the only genuine Christian churches, other denominations were considered religious societies—"counterfeit churches"—and their ministers did not have a valid gospel ordination or ministry. Christ had one church, he was "no bigamist," Graves retorted. Consequently, non-Baptists could not baptize (thus no "alien immersion" could be transferred into a Baptist church) and allowing non-Baptists to preach via "pulpit exchange" must not be tolerated. The church of the New Testament never accepted teachers of "recognized heresies." Graves explicitly denied that only Baptists were Christians—he often affirmed "blood (atonement) before water"—but his unchurching of his denominational competitors could easily blur into the de-christianizing of them. According to Graves, the New Testament only spoke of local churches, no universal church.

Landmarkism and its triple emphases of successionism, localism, and exclusivism spread throughout the churches of the Southern Baptist Convention. Graves, a sharp-tongued controversialist armed with a persuasive personality, had earned a hearing on the Baptist frontier because of his staunch defense of Baptist faith against the followers of Alexander Campbell. As a pastor in Nashville in the 1840s, Graves leveled verbal assaults against the popular Methodists and their practice of infant baptism. Subsequently, Graves used the pages of *The Tennessee Baptist*, which was popular throughout the South and Southwest, to disseminate Landmark views as ecclesiological orthodoxy. In 1855, Graves also published an

American edition of *A Concise History of (Foreign) Baptists from the Time of Christ Their Founder to the 18th Century* (original, 1838; Graves added "Foreign" to the original title), by English Baptist George Herbert Orchard, which served as a vehicle to promote the successionist theory that Baptists were *the* New Testament church begun by John the Baptist and Jesus.

Graves coined the term "Landmarkism" when a series of articles that had been written for *The Tennessee Baptist* by one of his colleagues, James Madison Pendleton, was published in pamphlet form with the title, *An Old Landmark Reset: Ought Baptists to Invite Pedobaptists to Preach in Their Pulpits?* (1854). Known as the "theologian" of Landmarkism, Pendleton was pastor of First Baptist Church, Bowling Green, Kentucky, before becoming a professor at Union University in Jackson, Tennessee (1857–1860). While Pendleton's focus in his writings was a rejection of "pulpit exchange," the title, based on Proverbs 22:28—"Remove not the ancient landmark, which thy fathers have set"—became the rallying cry for Graves's followers who felt they were defending the historic Baptist witness to the New Testament definition of the church. Ironically, Pendleton never fully accepted all of the developing tenets of Landmarkism, and in 1860 moved to Ohio because of his antislavery views. Nevertheless, his *Church Manual Designed for the Use of Baptist Churches* (1867) became a standard for local church polity in Baptist circles throughout the twentieth century and is still in print and in use today.

The third well-known proponent of Landmarkism was A. C. Dayton. Dayton was the first Baptist in the South to write a religious novel in order to spread Baptist beliefs. His book, *Theodosia Ernest; or, The Heroine of Faith* (1857), began appearing serially in *The Tennessee Baptist* (1856–1857) before its publication as a two-volume, 945-page apology for Landmarkism, and especially for baptism as immersion. Complete with romance, the young heroine, Theodosia, left the Presbyterian church (Dayton's wife in real life remained Presbyterian) and became a Baptist. Even though "dearer to her than life was Mr. Percy's love; it was her first love; it was her only love," Theodosia chose New Testament baptism over the Presbyterian young man more concerned with his social standing in the community. Her faithfulness to Scripture prevailed—despite the protests of educated non-Baptist ministers—and the happy couple embarked on a ten-day cruise and shared an exposition of the true church with all who would read. Baptists throughout the South made the novel popular reading throughout the nineteenth century, ironically promoting the anti-intellectual legacy of Baptist life.

Landmarkism can be viewed as an expression of the "democratization" of American Christianity that occurred in the aftermath of the disestablishment of religion after the American Revolution. Landmarkers opted for democratic individualism—Graves said that "intense individuality" was "one of the infallible tests of genuine Christianity"—and "localism," the democratic congregationalism of the independent local church. They insisted upon absolute liberty of the individual conscience. Graves identified Baptists with those on the margins of society—poor persecuted commoners. All establishments, especially social castes, which hindered democratic ideals, were criticized. Denominational centralization, in particular, was extrabiblical and invested control in a denominational elite.

In his last book, *Old Landmarkism: What Is It?* (1880), Graves gave full expression to his disdain for denominational centralization. He sounded the warning bell against the dangerous drift of "modern liberalism"—open communion—among Baptists. He lamented that liberal Baptists preferred to associate with non-Baptists rather than Landmarkers. Liberals were also infatuated with the quest for acceptance and popularity that often accompanied denominational centralization. Baptists were in danger of leaving the ancient ways of the primitive church, Graves concluded, because of their "overweening desire to be considered respectable, and to command the admiration of the world. We boast of our numerical strength, our power, and our influence, and the culture of our ministry." Historians have recognized that the rural localism and opposition to centralization and modernization of culture found in Primitive Baptists and Landmark Baptists formed the basis of support for political Populists in the 1890s against the conservative, modernizing urbanites of the New South advance.

Conflict with R. B. C. Howell. Landmarkism's aversion to extrabiblical mission boards was a significant threat to the centralized design for doing missions in the young Southern Baptist Convention. In the 1850s, Graves battled his pastor, Robert Boyte Crawford Howell, at First Baptist Church, Nashville, over Landmark views. Ultimately, First Baptist Church excommunicated Graves for slander and he and his followers established a rival "true" First Baptist Church. At the 1859 meeting of the Southern Baptist Convention, Graves's church was unsuccessful in their effort to be recognized as the genuine First Baptist Church of Nashville (something the church had been able to do in Landmark-dominated association and state meetings in Tennessee). Howell was reelected as president of the SBC and Southern Baptists resisted a Landmark effort to cease doing missions through a centralized Foreign Mission Board. At the same time, Landmark strength was evident when the convention authorized the mission board to transmit funds for local churches who desired to appoint their own missionaries.

Gospel Mission Movement. The strength of the developing loyalty to a programmatic denominational identity in the Southern Baptist Convention was tested by Landmarkism's cousin, the Gospel Mission Movement (GMM). Similar to the failed attempt in 1859 to dismantle the Foreign Mission Board, the GMM emphasized the exclusivity of the local church in mission methods. Local churches alone should select mission fields, send missionaries, and financially support them. Mission boards were contrary to these New Testament principles. The GMM also advocated a total focus upon evangelism, and consequently, frowned upon ancillary mission projects such as schools and hospitals. The driving force behind this Gospel Missionism was T. P. (Tarleton Perry) Crawford, who served along with his wife, Martha Foster Crawford , as Southern Baptist missionaries in China from 1852 to 1893. Crawford attended Union University, a seedbed of Landmarkism, and he was familiar with the activities of J. R. Graves. Crawford also developed some of his ideology independently out of his personal missionary experience and from the missionary views of a Presbyterian minister, John Nevin. Crawford made his first public attack against the Southern Baptist Convention in 1882. In 1892, the Foreign Mission Board severed ties with Crawford after he published the book, *Churches to the Front*, which attacked the board method of mission work. By 1902, the year of Crawford's death, the Gospel Mission Movement had nineteen missionaries in North China. The movement never caught fire, however, and after the death of Martha Crawford in 1909, some of the Gospel Missioners returned to the Foreign Mission Board.

Concern for denominational loyalty was seen in the reaction of Annie Armstrong, corresponding secretary of the Woman's Missionary Union. The controversy that swirled around Gospel Missionism was the only time Armstrong directly intervened in the affairs of a state woman's group and rebuked a mission leader. The object of her consternation was Martha Eleanor Loftin Wilson of Georgia, the most influential leader of mission work in Georgia and the woman who had actually suggested the name for the national Woman's Missionary Union. When Wilson developed sympathy for Gospel Missionism, Armstrong enlisted other national leaders, such as I. T. Tichenor of the Home Mission Board, to undercut Wilson's influence. In 1894, Georgia women temporarily split into two mission organizations when Wilson was told by other state mission leaders that she could not support a group which advocated exclusive local church missions and at the same time work with the centralized efforts of the SBC mission boards. Wilson affirmed her liberty of conscience to support missions through multiple methods, decried the increasing centralization of the denomination, and in classic Baptist individualistic language, defended her leadership of the schism, "I have been led by the Hand that makes no mistakes." Wilson also appealed to her Southern heritage and the icon of states rights to suggest to Armstrong that the national boards should not interfere with the decisions of the state WMUs. Wilson's splinter group did not last; the pull of denominational loyalty prevailed but still did not extinguish Landmark tendencies among Southern Baptists.

The Whitsitt Controversy. The Whitsitt Controversy—eventually involving the resignation in 1898 of William H. Whitsitt as president of Southern Baptist Theological Seminary—also revealed the strength of the Landmark account of history and pointed to the most attractive element of Landmarkism for most Baptists: the claim that Baptists are *the* New Testament Church.

Whitsitt, a church historian, created a firestorm in Southern Baptist life and became the archenemy of Landmark ideology when he contended that Baptists could not trace their origins back to the New Testament, but were birthed in 1641 upon the "recovery" of believers' baptism by immersion in England. Ironically, Whitsitt was raised in a strong Landmark environment. He was a graduate of Union University, and J. R. Graves was a family friend and preached Whitsitt's ordination sermon.

Whitsitt's educational pursuits pushed him beyond the anti-intellectual legacy of Landmarkism. His broadened perspective derived from degrees at the University of Virginia, Southern Baptist Theological Seminary, and study in Germany. Openness to critical study that utilized primary sources led to Whitsitt's reexamination of Baptist origins. He realized that his progressive conclusions would be anathema to the Baptist masses, and thus published his findings anonymously (in an unsigned encyclopedia article) in a non-Baptist publication in 1880. Whitsitt's hesitancy was later expressed in his diary when he said that "to be out of the reach of bigots and fools" he considered having his work published after his death. After years of silence, or at least anonymity, he finally affixed his name to an article on "Baptist History" in *Johnson's Universal Cyclopedia* (1896)—again, a non-Baptist publication—before "going public" in Baptist circles with his book, *A Question in Baptist History: Whether the Anabaptists in England*

Practiced Immersion before the Year 1641? (also 1896). Criticism of Whitsitt's "heresy" and liberalism was immediate.

The Whitsitt conflict revealed a clash of regional subcultures in Southern Baptist life. Baptists on the East Coast, especially Virginians such as William E. Hatcher, were supportive. Theologically trained colleagues at the seminary also defended Whitsitt. The Baptist masses from "western" frontier states such as Kentucky and Tennessee, as well as the Southwest—all hotbeds of Landmarkism—were strongly resistant. Thomas T. Eaton, editor of Kentucky's *Western Recorder* (and a losing candidate to Whitsitt for the presidency of the Louisville seminary in 1895) led the battle against the alleged heresy. Eaton battered Whitsitt in the pages of his denominational paper, which led to the seminary president being censured by several associations. Then in 1897, the Kentucky Baptist state convention passed a resolution requesting Whitsitt's resignation.

Sectional differences were clearly apparent in the opposition of B. H. Carroll, pastor of First Baptist Church of Waco, Texas, and considered by many to be the most influential Baptist west of the Mississippi. The *Religious Herald* of Virginia accused Carroll of exacerbating Landmark tensions in the Southwest. In 1898, Carroll, a trustee at the Louisville seminary, told messengers at the annual meeting of the SBC that he would make a motion at the 1899 convention to dissolve the relationship between the convention and Southern Seminary. With Carroll's involvement, Whitsitt's resignation was a foregone conclusion. In the swirling context of financial blackmail, Whitsitt resigned in order to ensure the survival of Southern Baptists' only seminary.

Subsequent Baptist historians followed Whitsitt by teaching that Baptists had their roots in England, and the successionist claims of Baptist superiority began to weaken. Nevertheless, popular Baptist theology still promoted Baptists as *the* New Testament church. J. M. Carroll—B. H. Carroll's brother—published *The Trail of Blood: Following the Christians Down through the Centuries, or, The History of Baptist Churches from the Time of Christ, Their Founder, to the Present Day*, in 1931. Following Carroll's remarkably extensive "Trail of Blood Chart," groups in the history of Christianity that were persecuted by the Catholic Church were immediate candidates to be proclaimed Baptist churches. (Early Christian schisms like the Montanists and the Novationists, however, bore more similarities to later Pentecostal and Holiness groups, respectively.)

An even more influential Landmarkist work than that of Carroll was Mississippian Joe T. Odle's *Church Members Handbook* (1941), which had sold over two million copies by 1980, and is still in print and a popular "study course" book. Published by Southern Baptists' Broadman Press (now Broadman/Holman), Odle's *Handbook* listed the founders of eleven different denominations but noted that only Baptist churches were instituted by Jesus:

> Those today who claim that they have restored primitive Christianity forget that the church that Jesus built would not have to be restored, for it would not cease to exit. If it did cease to exist for a time, then Christ's promise failed, and we know that is not true.

Landmark Legacies. Some Landmark Baptists ultimately separated from the "evils of conventionism" in order to protect their belief that only a local church could be a New Testament church. The East Texas Baptist Association (later named the Baptist Missionary Association) was the first Landmarkist state organization (1899). About the same time various Landmark groups in Arkansas came together under the leadership of Ben M. Bogard and formed the United States National General Association of Landmark Baptists (1905). These Texas and Arkansas associations—accompanied by some minor splintering—united in 1924 to form the American Baptist Association (ABA). (The "Baptist Missionary Association" name survives as the national Baptist Missionary Association of America and as the state Baptist Missionary Association of Texas.) Currently, the ABA is headquartered in Texarkana, Texas, and in the year 2000 reported 1,760 affiliated churches and a membership of approximately 275,000.

In the latter half of the twentieth century, Landmark ideology was still apparent in Southern Baptist life. The practice of closed communion and the rejection of alien immersion reigned for decades and are still practiced by many Southern Baptists. In 1981, for example, Bell Baptist Association in Kentucky withdrew fellowship from First Baptist Church, Middlesboro, because of the church's acceptance of alien immersion.

The rapid westward expansion of the Southern Baptist Convention after World War II also witnessed strong expressions of Landmark tendencies in regards to ecclesiology and in the distancing of Baptists from non-Baptist religious groups.

Protecting Identity

Church Discipline. A prominent feature of nineteenth-century congregational life was church discipline. Churches were moral courts that enforced codes of conduct and observed church covenants as methods of social control to combat the lawlessness of the frontier society. Discipline was also implemented in an attempt to preserve the purity of the church as the "bride of Christ" and in the process duplicate apostolic Christianity. Discipline was punitive—hypocrites were excluded—but it was also intended to be redemptive—straying saints were restored to the faith. The practice of discipline varied from church to church, but common features—a ritual of church discipline—were often exhibited. At monthly church conferences, which (male) church members were required to attend, charges were heard and the accused were requested to appear for "trial." They could be acquitted, forgiven and restored after a confession, or "excluded." Punishable offenses were diverse, but usually focused on issues of personal morality such as profanity, the use of alcoholic beverages, dancing, card playing, sexual immorality, delinquency at church activities, and doctrinal deviations. For example, in 1879, at First Baptist Church, Gainesville, Florida, church members were excluded for accepting Mormonism (most likely polygamy). The use of alcohol was the most frequent disciplinary offense, but also the one usually forgiven with a plea for restoration. Leniency was usually less forthcoming for sexual sins. While some church members sought restoration, a few simply failed to show up for their trial and others were defiant, guaranteeing their exclusion.

The most frequent reason for disciplinary action was a person's decision to leave the Baptist faith and join another denomination. Since most Baptists believed that they practiced *the* New Testament faith, switching denominations was usually viewed as a serious sin. Letters of dismissal were not granted for persons who left for other denominations; rather, "fellowship was withdrawn" and church members were "excluded as dead" for joining "alien" churches.

The practice of church discipline waned in the decades after the Civil War. Several reasons contributed to the decline. Most revolved around the urbanization of the New South after the Civil War. The focus of urban churches was less on pruning the church membership and more on making churches grow and making church organization more efficient. Larger church facilities were needed; quality musical worship was demanded; higher salaried clergy paralleled less discipline. In general, urban churches were more tolerant than their rural counterparts.

Throughout the heyday of church discipline, the propriety of "popular amusements," especially dancing, was the most "vexed" disciplinary question. Many Baptist leaders, such as Jesse Mercer of Georgia, believed that these activities were the "rock on which discipline floundered." The reaction toward the issue at the influential urban congregation, Second Baptist Church of Atlanta, revealed the changing attitudes toward disciplinary rigor. In 1870, the church unanimously passed a resolution against the "prevalence of worldliness in the form of fashionable amusements, and the extent to which even Christians fall into this snare of Satan." At the next church conference, discussion arose regarding whether the resolution should be published in the city papers as the "standing rule of the church." Almost immediately, a move led by influential former Civil War governor, Joseph E. Brown, to soften the language and limit "worldly amusements" to events "indecent or offensive to good taste" was initiated. One third of the church, it was later admitted, had recently attended a performance of *Hamlet*. In the future, the wealthy church decided that "worldly amusements" could be disciplined on an individual basis, but ultimately each member became free to follow personal conscience on such matters.

Baptist Distinctives. In 1872, in his inaugural address as a professor at Southern Baptist Theological Seminary, William H. Whitsitt reflected upon the contributions of Baptists to American culture. His speech was a good barometer for how Baptists generally understood their core convictions. Whitsitt reminded students of the Baptist commitment to the foundational principle of the sole authority of Scripture for "saving knowledge and faith." He affirmed the "spirituality of the church," that is, the necessity of personal conversion, regenerate church membership, and closed communion. A typical Protestant of his day, Whitsitt harshly criticized the "magical" sacramentalism of Catholicism.

Whitsitt emphasized several familiar Baptist themes: the independence or autonomy of the local church and democratic congregational church government (the best barriers to heresy), the "priesthood of all Christians," religious liberty, and freedom of the individual conscience. He admonished students to continue the Baptist insistence upon the "entire separation of church and state": "the church and its ministers, as such, lose entirely their political position and political power" in favor of spiritual power. Religious liberty, according to Whitsitt, advanced authentic, critically tested faith.

> Everything is open to criticism. No opinions, or creed, or system, is exempt. Theology must enter the lists with other sciences, and bravely defend herself against all comers. There is no longer a covert of defense under the wing of the civil power, whither she may flee in an hour of defeat and distress.

While Whitsitt represented the well-educated progressive Baptist, he warned students not to forget that Baptists were "common people."

> It would be a sad day for Baptists should they ever become the most wealthy and powerful of the religious denominations of America, if they at the same time learned how to push their cause in the halls of legislation, and the drawing-rooms of ministers of state; if they should become the leaders of those circles of society where flippancy is prevalent, and moral and intellectual earnestness are despised. They would forget full soon the simplicity of the gospel and single-eyed devotion to its tenet.

In sum, Whitsitt said, Baptists stood for a "pure Christianity" based on the Bible.

Throughout Baptist history, Baptists have summarized their beliefs in confessions of faith. In the nineteenth century, many local Southern Baptist churches and Baptist associations adopted confessional statements. At the same time, Southern Baptists declared that these confessions were not creeds because the Bible was the sole Baptist creed. Shaler Granby Hillyer, a professor at Mercer University, described the relationship of confessions to the Bible in the life of local churches.

> The Baptists of Georgia, from the very beginning of their development in this State, acknowledged no authority in matters of "faith and of practice," except the Scriptures. It is true, each church had what was called its abstract of principles or its confession of faith. But this abstract, or confession, was adopted by each church, as an independent body, for itself, and it was held to be valid only so far as its subscribers believed it to be in harmony with the Bible. In controversies with their opponents, Baptists never appeal to the confessions found in their church records, but directly and exclusively to the inspired Word. (1902)

John Lansing Burrows of Virginia echoed a similar perspective about Virginia Baptist life. "Personal liberty of interpretation" accompanied any adoption of a confession of faith by an association. And during doctrinal or polity discussions at associational meetings, confessions never were considered authoritative:

> They have always irreverently pushed them aside with the question, What saith the Lord? The uniform reference is to first principles, inspired principles, as furnished by God's Word. They never would attempt to settle differences by quoting human formulations, but at once passed beyond them to find the import of the inspired Word. (1883)

Baptist leaders generally affirmed Calvinism. Professors at Southern Baptist Theological Seminary—Southern Baptists' first seminary, established in 1859—implemented a confessional statement, "the Abstract of Principles" that affirmed the classic Calvinistic emphases on total depravity and election—which is "God's eternal choice of some persons unto everlasting life. At the same time, this confessional standard avoided doctrinal "hot-button" issues such as alien immersion that were divisive in the denomination. Indeed, the focus on rigid Calvinism was modified in local church life by revivalism and concepts like limited atonement never really took hold in popular lay theology. An Arminianized Calvinism meshed more easily with the optimism of the New South advance.

The Search for Denominational Efficiency

Centralization and Expansion. Organizational efficiency was a goal of most denominations in the first half of the twentieth century. Baptists have been dubbed "Business Baptists" for their adoption of the "corporate" model during this era of an increasingly centralized mode of operation. Numerous agencies developed and executive officers were added. The influential Executive Committee (the convention's decision-making center when it was not in annual session) was established in 1917 and a full-time executive secretary-treasurer came ten years later. The Sunday School Board also named its first executive-secretary in 1917. Several new agencies were established that included the Annuity Board (1918), Baptist Brotherhood (1926), Baptist Student Union (1928), and the Education Commission (1928).

Organizational maturation was also seen in the creation of new theological schools. Growth in the Southwest led to the creation of a new seminary in Texas in 1908, Southwestern Baptist Theological Seminary, under the leadership of B. H. Carroll. The seminary eventually became the largest theological school in America. The SBC eventually established six seminaries.

Church growth in America was significant in the latter half of the nineteenth century. In 1850, 15.5 percent of Americans were church members. By 1900, the figure had risen to 35.7 percent of the population. Southerners contributed greatly to the upsurge in church affiliation. Between 1890 and 1906, Southern church membership increased 51 percent, 12 percent greater than the population growth of 39 percent.

Baptists benefited from this focus on organized religion in America. In particular, denominational efficiency and evangelistic fervor contributed to the rapid growth of the Southern Baptist Convention. By the end of the nineteenth century, Southern Baptists surpassed the Methodists and became the largest religious group in the South. Membership in churches grew from one million in the 1870s to two million in 1906 and three million after World War I.

In addition to evangelistic fervor, Southern Baptists (and other groups) benefited from the post-World War II "baby boom" and the postwar religious revival in America. Membership totals climbed to 9,731,591 by 1960. With the breakdown of territorial agreements with Northern Baptists, Southern Baptists were no longer a regional body. New state conventions in Western "pioneer" areas like Arizona (1928), California (1940), Hawaii (1943), and Alaska (1946) revealed that Southern Baptists were South, North, East, and West. Eventually state conventions dotted the North—the historic center of American Baptist life (for example, New York, 1979).

Southern Baptists also developed an efficient fiscal operation to manage its burgeoning corporate structure. Launched a year after Northern Baptist's $100 million New World Campaign, the $75 Million Campaign was a convention-wide fund-raising effort to celebrate the SBC's seventy-fifth anniversary. While convention finances experienced difficulties because of spending based on the $92 million pledged, the $58 million raised was still the largest by far in Southern Baptist history and pointed to the economic potential of the SBC.

The most significant move toward denominational efficiency was the creation of the Cooperative Program (1925), a unified budget administered by the Executive Committee that supported all of the convention's agencies. Previously, the various convention agencies had separate budgets and often competed like societies for funds. With a unified plan, Southern Baptists developed an even stronger loyalty to convention programs since each church—no matter the size—could rightly say it was helping to fund each and every agency. State Baptist conventions adopted the Cooperative Program approach and thus strengthened ties between states and the national body. Most contemporary Southern Baptists do not consider it an exaggeration to call the Cooperative Program the most effective steward-ship method in Christian history and consequently frequently judge loyalty to the convention by the percentage of a church's budget that is allocated to Southern Baptist ministries.

Organizationally efficient and numerically strong, Southern Baptists continued to cultivate a sense of "chosenness" throughout the twentieth century. In the exuberant aftermath of World War I and the nation's belief that it was "called" to spread democracy, Southern Baptists spoke confidently of the unique role of the South and their own missionary mandate. Noted Louisiana Baptist minister M. E. Dodd—known as the "father" of the SBC Cooperative Program—told the 1919 meeting of the SBC that "the Baptist hour of all the centuries has sounded." The following year, influential Kentucky Baptist Victor Masters spared no hyperbole in his assessment: "As goes America, so goes the world. Largely as goes the South, so goes America. And in the South is the Baptist center of gravity of the world."

Theological Movements and Social Concerns

Social Christianity. Southern Baptists normally were not known for the "social gospel" concerns that characterized Baptists in the industrial North during the latter half of the nineteenth and early twentieth centuries. The Southern economy and culture were still largely agrarian. Southerners were wary of the social gospel's connections to liberal theology and were more averse to ecumenical efforts that might compromise their beliefs. Victor Mathews of the Home Mission Board said the social gospel was a "cult of humanitarian service." Baptists who were premillennialists (not a large number in the late nineteenth century) felt that biblical prophecy did not warrant any hope for social progress. In contrast to the postbellum North, the South remained more individualistic in their religious practices, especially in the continued emphasis upon personal salvation in revivalism. Holiness was usually a function of personal morality, not social activism or political activity. Southerners were comfortable with laissez faire economics and individual property rights. Agricultural economic problems were not normally considered complex social/structural issues, as Northern social gospelers preached, but were the result of individual character defects. A focus first on the evangelistic conversion of "lost souls" would result in "better" people who would make a better society. Moral persuasion through preaching, rather than social service, was the key. A "social Christianity" was practiced—for example, mountain schools and orphanages were established—but Southern Baptists were normally "passive reformers" who focused on converting individuals rather than transforming businesses and other social structures.

Orphanages sprang up after the Civil War to care for children orphaned by the war. Gradually several Baptist state conventions supported orphanages. R. C. Buckner of Texas, for example, testified that the Bible's concern for widows and orphans motivated his missionary work on behalf of children. He actually preferred a children's home to adoption because of the family-like structure he envisioned for orphanages.

The creation of mountain schools in the Appalachian region—twenty-six were established in the first decade of the twentieth century—revealed Southern Baptists' desire to educate the poor in order to improve their situations. At the same time, the mission efforts were rooted in racist attitudes of Anglo-Saxon superiority. Corresponding secretary of North Carolina Baptists, John White, told messengers to the 1900 meeting of the Southern Baptist Convention that the mountain folk were "98% Caucasian." Victor Mathews believed that they had the "most pure Anglo-Saxon blood in America." They were converted "children," but untrained. As whites, they deserved help, and under the guidance of Christian education, they would produce greater wealth in their region.

The Social Gospel. A more Northern-styled social gospel concern characterized a small minority of Southern Baptists. From 1880 to 1910, the population of Southern villages and towns had increased by five million people. An urban religious middle class—characterized by newly constructed church facilities and new business opportunities—developed in the New South. While most Southern Baptists remained rural, socially conservative, and repudiated the social gospel as "secular," a progressive minority moved beyond the work in orphanages and mountain schools. They believed that oppression was often created by society's power structures.

One social gospel issue addressed in Southern communities was child labor. In 1902, for example, at least 12,000 children under twelve years of age were being employed in the emerging cotton-mill industry in Southern communities. Editor Frank Barnett of *The Alabama Baptist* made his news journal a major crusader against the exploitation of children. In Birmingham, the one "industrial" center in the South in the early twentieth century, Southside Baptist Church served as an "institutional church"—a practice more common in the North—and opened each weekday and night in order to address social needs in its community.

Progressive activists, in contrast to the traditional localism of rural Baptists, were often urban pastors or seminary professors. Ashby Jones, pastor of First Baptist Church, Augusta, Georgia (1909–1917), promoted the establishment of a settlement home and a hospital in the birthplace of the SBC. Considered doctrinally suspect by some Baptist leaders for his ecumenical perspective (and the most radical Southern Baptist social-gospel minister of his day), Jones said that only a person with a social consciousness could grasp the meaning of Jesus' teachings in the Lord's Prayer when Jesus uttered "thy kingdom come, they will be done on earth." William Poteat of Wake Forest University and faculty members at Southern Baptist Theological Seminary introduced progressive activism in educational curriculums. Biblical scholar A. T. Robertson endorsed the rights of working people and urged the end of child labor. His seminary colleague, Charles Gardner, was open to some socialistic economic theory, encouraged settlement houses for the poor, and advocated interdenominational cooperation to battle social problems. Seminary president E. Y. Mullins had been involved in social ministries during his Baltimore pastorate (1894–1895) and had commented that "greedy, grasping, insolent, and heartless corporations" resulted in the radical actions of striking workers. As Southern Seminary president, Mullins had prominent Northern Baptist proponent of the social gospel, Samuel Batten, speak on campus.

Institutionally, Southern Baptists never progressed far along the social-gospel path. In 1907, the SBC created a Committee on Civic Righteousness (CCR) and a Temperence Committee. In 1913, the Social Service Commission (SSC) was created to take over the work of the CCR, and in 1914, the SSC took over the work of the Temperence Committee. Much of the focus of the SSC, however, was upon traditional matters of *personal* morality, temperance, gambling, and Sabbath keeping. Broader social issues such as peace and labor concerns received only general or vague treatment. Arthur J. Barton, the commission's executive-secretary from its beginnings until his death, adamantly resisted a Northern-styled social gospel. In 1936, an attempt to create a Social Research Bureau failed, revealing Southern Baptists' hesitancy to stray too far from evangelistic emphases. The eruption of World War II, however, awakened social consciences, and social-service work soon flourished among some Southern Baptists.

Temperance Movement. Baptists have not always been shy about social drinking. The earliest Baptists of the seventeenth century drank wine at meals and social events and even in observing the Lord's Supper. Colonial Baptist evangelist and religious-liberty advocate Isaac Backus carried rum in his saddlebag. In 1798, the frontier South Elkhorn church in Kentucky pledged thirty-six gallons of whiskey as part of the salary of their pastor.

In American Christianity, the temperance crusade began in the 1820s with Congregationalist minister Lyman Beecher. Soon temperance societies developed that attacked moderate or social drinking. The movement stalled before the Civil War, but was renewed later when technological advances enabled the production of fermented grape juice. Gradually, Baptists churches developed the position that wine in New Testament communion practices was unfermented, and as they saw the New Testament as the model for practice, they stopped using wine in the Lord's Supper. Social gospelers among Northern Baptists, like Shailer Mathews and the famous pastor Harry Emerson Fosdick, supported temperance for the betterment of society.

Women made indispensable contributions to the success of the temperance movement. The most notable organization was the National Woman's Christian Temperance Movement (WCTU)—the oldest continuing nonsectarian woman's organization in the world—which grew out of the "Woman's Crusade" of the winter of 1873–1874. Annie Turner Wittenmyer was the first president (1874–1879); Frances Elizabeth Caroline Willard—remembered for organizing the WCTU into a potent social force—was the second president (1879–1898). Many Baptist women were originally hesitant about involvement in the WCTU because it advocated women's rights—specifically suffrage—in addition to temperance.

The Woman's Missionary Union was an early advocate of temperance. In 1891, the three-year-old organization adopted a resolution favoring temperance, and in subsequent years advocated total abstinence from alcohol more than any other social issue. Throughout the twentieth century, the WMU worked to keep counties "dry" and to educate youth about the dangers of alcohol. At the state and local church level, many WMU members were also members of the WCTU. Mary Gambrell, for example, helped found the WMU of Mississippi in 1878 and in 1883 helped start a WCTU group in Corinth, Mississippi, where her husband (James Bruton Gambrell) was a pastor. In some churches, WCTU meetings were held in WMU meeting rooms and/or advertised in church bulletins.

The temperance crusade also had a racial aspect. Many Southerners considered African-Americans and Native Americans equally irresponsible with alcohol, and believed that African-Americans were more prone to physically abuse white women while under its influence. In Atlanta, in 1906, alleged reports of attacks by African-American males against whites ignited a racial riot and several African-Americans were killed. Subsequently, the influential pastor of the Atlanta Second Baptist Church, John

E. White, endorsed an editorial in the city's newspaper which argued for the government to strip any saloon of its alcohol license that served African-Americans. Such discriminatory action, White contended, was necessary to protect an inferior race.

Baptists generally supported the passage of the eighteenth constitutional amendment in 1919 and then supported the continuation of Prohibition before it was repealed in 1933. Baptist support of prohibition was an entry into the political realm, but the goal was to reform society by confronting personal sin.

Women, Leadership, and Social Ministry. While Southern Baptist women typically were not involved in the call for political suffrage that led to the nineteenth amendment of the United States Constitution, the Southern Baptist Convention did grant women the right to vote in convention affairs in 1918. Granting women the status of messengers had occurred at the state convention in Texas as early as 1901. Fannie Exile Scudder Heck's 1913 WMU report was the first report received by the SBC in annual session that was written by a woman—but it was read by progressive professor W. O. Carver of Southern Seminary. Finally, in 1929 at the fortieth anniversary of the founding of the WMU, Ethlene Boone Cox, WMU president (1925–1933), became the first woman to speak to the SBC. A resolution was brought, but defeated, that criticized the unbiblical practice of women speaking to men about religion since "Eve tempted Adam" and caused the Fall. Southern Baptists, however, were still not ready to tackle issues of women in ministry. As A. T. Robertson noted, being equal in Christ (Galatians 3:28), had nothing to do with women in positions of ministerial leadership.

Nevertheless, the SBC benefited from the work of the WMU in the financial arena. From 1923 to 1928, the WMU raised forty percent of the convention's contributions to its Cooperative Program. During the Great Depression, the WMU provided seventy percent of the support for home and foreign missions.

As an auxiliary to the SBC, the Woman's Missionary Union was clearly viewed as a submissive ministry, but, ironically, this status gave the organization freedom to determine its own ministry emphases. Consequently, some women—historians disagree as to how much the WMU rank and file were involved—pushed a social application of the gospel. Despite warnings about involvement in "social service," the WMU, led by Fannie Heck of North Carolina, created a Department of Personal Service in 1909, and asserted that social service was its primary mission. The department promoted Sabbath keeping and prohibition, and engaged in projects to combat poverty and child labor. At the local level, associations and WMUs in various congregations supported ministry to orphanages and prisons. In urban areas, they used a survey to map income, employment, and sanitation conditions.

WMU leadership also demonstrated an ecumenical openness in its social service. Fannie Heck, Annie Armstrong, and others participated in charity work with Methodist women and drew resources from Methodist social-work methods. The WMU's *Royal Service* magazine, which was subtly progressive, even quoted from more liberal Northern social-gospel leaders. WMU leaders demonstrated some racial sensitivity. In their publications prior to the Civil Rights Movement, African-American women were called "Mrs.", unlike SBC literature that never referred to African-American men as "Mr." The WMU Training School at Southern Seminary (later named the Carver School of Missions and Social Work for one of its most ardent supporters, seminary professor W. O. Carver) was a pioneer in education when it introduced a social work curriculum into seminary education.

Peace Efforts. Most Baptists supported World War I as a war to spread democracy, but exceptions existed, including, for example, J. Judson Taylor of First Baptist Church, Savannah. In 1917, Taylor was asked to resign his pastorate after advocating pacifism as biblical (ironically, he had written positively about pacifism before the church called him). Taylor later served, however, on the committee that drafted the statement on peace for the the Baptist Faith and Message confession of 1925.

The ebb and flow of attitudes toward war and peace also surrounded World War II. Southern Baptists overwhelmingly supported America's participation on behalf of political democracy and religious freedom. State Baptist papers were harshly critical of conscientious objectors (fifty-two of America's 11,950 objectors were Southern Baptists). After the war, however, strong declarations for peacemaking were issued by the progressive Social Service Commission. In 1951, a commission report questioned the justification of any future war in light of the destructive power of modern warfare. In the midst of the Cold War, the Southern Baptist Convention again took a more traditional "just war" response and attacked the threat of communism.

The Fundamentalist-Modernist Conflict of the 1920s. While the Fundamentalist-Modernist conflict raged in the North, Southern Baptists, who had few theological modernists, experienced a "lighter" version of the controversy. An episode that actually predated the battles among Northern

Presbyterians and Northern Baptists, however, occurred at Southern Baptist Theological Seminary. Crawford Howell Toy, a graduate of the seminary (1860) and later of the University of Berlin (1868), was evidently the first scholar in America to lose his teaching position for supporting modern critical methods of Bible study. Taking his cue from German scholarship, Toy began teaching that readers must separate the kernel of truth from the outer layer of myth. The message of the Bible was divinely inspired even if it was placed in a setting of incorrect science. Backlash against Toy erupted in 1879 when he published explanatory notes on Isaiah 53 in the *Sunday School Times*. His assertion that the "servant of God" did not refer to the sufferings of Jesus Christ, but to the righteous members of Israel, seemed to most Baptists to be an attack on the prophecies of Scripture and gave skeptics ample evidence of the dangers of the newfangled methods of reading the Bible.

Toy's controversial views seemed to seminary administrators to be a "red flag" for fund-raising. James Pettigru Boyce, chairman of the faculty, believed that Baptists would not support an educational institution that tolerated views such as Toy's. The decision to accept Toy's resignation meant that biblical scholarship was expected to reflect the majority views of the Baptist constituency. When Toy subsequently joined the faculty of Harvard University and eventually became a Unitarian, many Baptists were satisfied that the popular teacher had abandoned the Bible.

The Landmark attack against William Whitsitt's debunking of the idea that Baptists could trace their history back to Jesus' baptism by John the Baptist was also, in part, a reaction against the use of modern methods of study—in this case, the use of modern analytical historical tools.

The leading Southern Baptist theologian of the early twentieth century was E. Y. Mullins, president of Southern Baptist Theological Seminary (1899–1928) and president of the Southern Baptist Convention (1921–1924). Clearly neither a liberal nor fundamentalist, Mullins's biographers identify him as the symbol of the "moderate" middle in Baptist life. He was cosmopolitan in outlook, having served as a pastor in Baltimore, Maryland, and Newton Centre, Massachusetts, for fourteen years. Theologically, Mullins's description of the *Axioms of Religion* (1908) provided a list of Baptist distinctives that strongly influenced Baptist identity in the North and South. He highlighted the role of the individual; he gave priority to Christian experience in understanding the Bible which was the final authority for a Christian's faith. He also highlighted freedom: in church-state affairs he called for "a free church in a free state," and in church governance each church must be free (local church autonomy) and each believer must have equal rights (congregationalism). What was most distinctive of Baptist identity, according to Mullins, was "soul competency," that is, the right of each person to go directly to God as the foundational principle of Christian experience. Mullins reiterated and highlighted what earlier Baptists had frequently emphasized: the importance of the individual conscience—the right of private interpretation of Scripture, the need for "soul liberty"—in matters of faith. For Mullins, these "axioms of religion" embodied New Testament Christianity and they—not the faulty history of Landmarkism—were the key to the Baptist claim of being the New Testament church.

Mullins helped guide a moderate path in the Southern Baptist version of the fundamentalist conflict of the 1920s. The Southern conflict bore similarities to the Northern story:

- the dominant issue was evolution;
- teachers at denominational schools were the targets; and
- suspicion toward a centralizing denomination lurked in the background.

Much of the discord came from the antics of the "Texas cyclone," volatile fundamentalist J. Frank Norris, pastor of First Baptist Church, Fort Worth, Texas. Norris has been called a megalomaniac. As a college student at Baylor University he announced that he would one day preach in the greatest pulpit in the world. Ironically, his first church, McKinney Avenue Baptist Church of Dallas, grew from thirteen members to 1,000 in three years. In 1909, he became the pastor of the prestigious First Baptist Church, Fort Worth, and remained there until 1952. Norris's dictatorial style tolerated no dissent, and consequently he dismissed his trustees and deacons in 1911. When 600 members left the church, he called it a needed purification. The next year, he was accused of setting fire to the church facility in order to build a new one. When he was acquitted, he felt practically invincible. Norris took on a second congregation, the Temple Baptist Church, Detroit, for sixteen years (1934–1950), making him the pastor of more than 24,000 members, the largest congregation(s) in the world. His magazine, *The Fundamentalist*, was the most widely circulated religious paper in the South.

Norris's sensationalist methods were reminiscent of the colorful early twentieth-century evangelist, Billy Sunday. He attacked community leaders and his religious opponents. His catchy sermon titles included "Should a

Prominent Fort Worth Banker Buy the High Priced Silk Hose for Another Man's Wife?" and "Shall Uncle Sam Be Made an Ass Again?" (on the eve of World War II). He called Southern Baptist leaders the "Sanhedrin"; Texas Baptist rivals J. M. Dawson of Waco and George W. Truett of Dallas were the "Fosdick of the South" and the "infallible Baptist pope," respectively. A pastor that accepted some of his expelled members was lambasted as a "long, lean, lanky, yellow, egg-sucking dog."

Because of his vitriolic and censorious attitude, the Baptist association in Fort Worth expelled Norris's church in 1922. The Baptist General Convention of Texas followed suit two years later. "Norrisism"—a term coined in the 1920s by L. R. Scarborough, president of Southwestern Seminary and a former member of First Baptist Church, Fort Worth—became synonymous with an intolerant spirit, autocratic leadership, and the refusal to cooperate in Southern Baptist ministries. (Norris quit using Southern Baptist literature and also favored "unbaptistic" practices such as alien immersion and pulpit exchange.)

On the other hand, Norris believed that Southern Baptists were forsaking the New Testament pattern of the autonomy of the local church for the excessive centralization of the "denominational machine." The SBC $75 Million Campaign, chaired by George W. Truett, would, for example, support unscriptural practices not subject to the control of the local congregation. Norris' other complaint was the infiltration of the modernist disease—evolution—into Baptist life, especially at Baylor University. Attacks included verbal assaults and sensationalistic antics. One Sunday Norris brought monkeys to the pulpit to introduce as relatives of whoever accepted evolution. Excessive centralization and modernism were Norris's stated motivations, but surely his battle with Baptist leaders was also a classic struggle for power in denominational affairs.

Ultimately, Norris became the prototypical militant independent fundamentalist in America. In 1926, he harshly criticized the Catholic mayor of Fort Worth. One of the mayor's supporters, D. C. Chipps, came to Norris's church office and confronted him. Norris shot and killed Chipps and the authorities ruled it "self-defense."

The battle over evolution in the Southern Baptist Convention reached a climax in 1925. Convention president, E. Y. Mullins, attempted to mediate the discontent of antievolutionists. He told the 1922 annual meeting of the SBC that denominational schools should teach the historic beliefs of the Christian faith. Evolution should not be taught as fact; at the same time, he argued for "firm faith and free research" in the realm of science. The real issue was the affirmation of supernaturalism in the face of naturalistic claims. In order to maintain unity (and efficiency) in the convention, Mullins and other denominational loyalists led in the adoption of a new confession of faith, the Baptist Faith and Message (1925). The confession, largely written by Mullins, was based on the New Hampshire Confession of Faith. It included a preface that emphasized that confessions were not creeds, but were voluntary formulations of faith. The confession affirmed the sole authority of the Bible for "all religious opinions" but avoided mentioning evolution specifically because the "confession committee," none of whom affirmed evolution, did not believe a theological confession needed a statement on science. The committee did not want to inject the precedent of using science as the arbiter of ultimate truth.

Detractors, especially C. P. Stealey—editor of the (Oklahoma) *Baptist Messenger* who raised the issue of evolution in his paper every week during 1925–1926, and who had been a primary force behind the SBC's adoption of the 1925 confession—continued to press for an *explicit* antievolution statement. In 1926, the SBC adopted the so-called "McDaniel Statement"— from the concluding paragraph of SBC President George White McDaniel's presidential address—as "the sentiment" of the convention. The statement categorically *denied* that humanity, "the special creation of God . . . originated in, or came by way of, a lower animal ancestry." Adoption of the "McDaniel Statement" was followed by the "Tull Resolution" (on motion by Selsus Estol Tull) that urged acceptance of the "McDaniel Statement" by all SBC agencies. Southern Baptists never gave these declarations any creedal weight, however, and the 1925 Baptist Faith and Message had little impact in Southern Baptist life for several decades.

Religious Liberty and Ecumenism

Religious Liberty. Southern Baptist voices for freedom of conscience and religious liberty were not rare in the convention's first one hundred years. They continued to warn against the establishment of religion, a concern articulated by the earliest Baptists of the seventeenth century. One frequent manifestation of the call for religious freedom—and one reason for it—was the persistent Protestant aversion to Roman Catholicism. (From the era of the Protestant Reformation to the mid-twentieth century, Protestants and Catholics regularly called each other 'not Christian.') From the outset, Southern Baptist mission efforts focused on Catholic-dominated countries and in the late nineteenth century even divided mission areas into two sections: "Papal Fields" and "Pagan Fields."

For most Protestants, Catholics, with their divided loyalties to Rome and to America, were incapable of being good Americans. The influx of Catholic immigrants was considered to be a threat to individualism and democracy. For example, in the late 1800s, Seventh Baptist Church of Baltimore considered its ministry especially strategic since the city was the center of American Catholicism and its "gross error." Social gospelers thought the biggest problems of the growing urbanization of America were "rum, Romanism, and rebellion." And these "3 Rs" were interrelated. Would the Pope, the autocrat of autocrats, and in many Baptist minds the Antichrist prophesied in the biblical book of Revelation, try to rule America?

Anti-Catholicism persisted during the first half of the twentieth century. Baptists joined other Protestants in harshly denouncing the candidacy of Al Smith for the presidency of the United States in the election of 1928. Smith was not only Catholic but opposed Prohibition. Baptists warned that the country's moral health was at stake. If Smith prevailed, the decadence of drunkenness that characterized Catholic immigrants would prevail in the country.

Baptist opposition to Catholics persisted through the election of President John F. Kennedy in 1960. With the establishment of better relations between Protestants and Catholics as a result of the changes implemented through the Second Vatican Council (or Vatican II, 1962–1965), some Southern Baptists began interchurch dialogue with Catholics. For example, in 1958, Fred Laughon, pastor of First Baptist Church, Gainesville, Florida, had criticized the Catholic doctrine of purgatory upon the occasion of the death of Pope Pius XII. Laughon had also demonstrated his suspicion of the announced reforms emanating from Vatican II in 1965 when he commented that "unity will not be found by having all Protestants kiss the Pope's ring." By the end of the decade, however, Laughon had begun having the priest from the Catholic Student Center of the nearby University of Florida speak to the church in a spirit of dialogue.

Southern Baptist attitudes toward Catholicism were still mixed at the end of the twentieth century: a revival of the earlier attitude that Catholicism was a "false gospel" occurred among some conservatives, but cooperation especially on conservative "prolife" social issues was increasingly apparent.

For more than a century Americans have wrestled with the issue of religion and the public schools. The disestablishment of the Anglican Church during the Revolutionary War era had prepared the way for nonsectarian public schools. Despite the victory for religious liberty in the infant nation, a Protestant ethos, with Bible reading and devotions, was prevalent in the schools. Around the middle of the nineteenth century, secularization developed rapidly. Horace Mann, "father of public education," allowed for Bible reading (without comment), but favored a focus on teaching general moral principles. A renewed focus on religion in the public schools, however, occurred between World Wars I and II. By 1960, half of the nation's school districts had "religious exercises."

While many Baptists certainly accepted the Protestant ethos found in the public square, voices opposing religious devotions in public schools gave witness to a vibrant affirmation of the principle of the separation of church and state. Virginia Baptists, for example, remained true to their colonial heritage. In 1926, the Virginia Senate considered a bill to require public school teachers to read the Bible in their classrooms. George W. McDaniel, pastor of First Baptist Church, Richmond (and SBC president in 1926—see above), strongly opposed the bill and argued that the United States had made one distinctive contribution to civilization: the separation of church and state. R. H. Pitt, editor of the *Religious Herald*, added that "Virginia Baptists are against any attempt to compel to read the scriptures, to sing hymns, to make prayers, to attend church, or to perform any other act which is religious."

Southern Baptists' call for religious liberty and the separation of church and state found expression especially in the ministry of George W. Truett, pastor for forty-seven years (1897–1944) of First Baptist Church, Dallas. Truett was one of the most legendary Baptist ministers in the convention's history. Like E. Y. Mullins, he served as president of both the SBC and the Baptist World Alliance. One of the legacies of his career was his address, "Baptists and Religious Liberty," given on the steps of the capitol in Washington, D.C., on 16 May 1920, at the seventy-fifth anniversary convention of the SBC. For Truett (and Mullins), Baptists and America were suited for each other: both were democratic and loved freedom. Truett declared that Baptists "have never been a party to oppression of conscience. . . . Christ's religion needs no prop of any kind from any worldly source, and to the degree that it is thus supported is a millstone hanged about its neck."

Support among Southern Baptists for religious liberty resulted in the formation in 1936 of a Committee on Public Relations (actually a renamed "Committee on Chaplains" but with broader responsibilities). In 1937, the Northern Baptist Convention (NBC) followed suit with a public affairs committee of their own. In 1939, the SBC and NBC committees combined forces, and, after being joined by a number of other Baptist groups, became in 1946 (when they opened a full-time office in Washington) the Joint Conference Committee on Public Relations. Finally, the committee became the "Public Affairs Committee" when in 1950 it was renamed the Baptist Joint Committee on Public Affairs (BJCPA). From its inception the BJCPA was funded mostly by Southern Baptists, but was an agency that included at least nine Baptist groups in America. The BJPCA remains a strong voice for the separation of church and state, including, for example, support for the 1963 Supreme Court's decision declaring the unconstitutionality of state-sponsored prayer in public schools.

Ecumenism. As Southern Baptists progressed into the twentieth century, loyalty to a centralized denomination that unified around common programs, especially missions, triumphed in Southern Baptist life. At the same time, Landmark perspectives helped to keep Southern Baptists isolated from the "taint" of ecumenical cooperation with other denominations. Denominational statesman J. B. Gambrell of Texas typified the Southern Baptist attitude: "Southern Baptists do not ride a horse unless they hold the bridle reins." The tendency of Baptists to identify themselves with the New Testament church made ecumenical work difficult.

A few progressive Southern Baptists participated in twentieth-century ecumenical endeavors, especially at the local level. The temperance crusade also crossed denominational boundaries. And Baptists expressed some initial openness to interdenominational cooperation in missions. They attended the London Centenary Missionary Conference (1888) and the World Missionary Conference at Edinburgh (1910). In 1914, the SBC produced its most ecumenical statement, a cautious resolution about cooperation entitled "Pronouncement on Christian Union and Denominational Efficiency."

Still, the Southern Baptist Convention opposed the organized ecumenical movement. All efforts to associate formally with the Federal Council of Churches (1908, which became in 1950 the National Council of Churches) or the World Council of Churches (1948) were rebuffed. In defense of the disassociation, Southern Baptists cited the liberalism of participating denominations and the threat of "doctrineless union" to genuine New Testament Christianity. Regional pride and a feeling of self-sufficiency were also a factor.

Conclusion

The democratization of American religion continued to find expression in Southern Baptist life in the latter half of the nineteenth and the first half of the twentieth centuries. Landmarkism was the clearest expression of the intense localism that dominated Southern religion. It was also the most influential primitivist movement in the history of the SBC. Landmarkism's contention that Baptists not only restored New Testament Christianity but were *the* New Testament church still influences the Baptist psyche with a sense of chosenness and antiecumenical exclusivism.

Beyond the Landmarkers, Southern Baptists strongly articulated a vision of Baptist distinctives that focused upon historic values such as the rights of the individual conscience, the absolute separation of church and state, and an aversion to creedal statements. Baptists believed the New Testament was their sole standard of faith. Southern Baptist women demonstrated that they were biblically minded mission leaders, yet not the feminists that some men feared. Southern Baptists, as did Northern Baptists, gave diverse reactions to the rapid industrial changes enveloping America and to the modern methods of Bible reading. J. Frank Norris helped define fundamentalism. Above all, Southern Baptists developed an intense loyalty to their regional identity as Southerners and as Baptists. Disloyalty was heretical in the land of Jim Crow. Racial prejudice was culturally conditioned "New Testament faith."

Chapter 7

1950 to the Present:
American Baptists Confront the Future

The last half of the twentieth century produced a dizzying array of changes to religion in America. Religious affiliation had meant "Protestant, Catholic, Jew," but now religious pluralism became the norm. The "secular" sixties witnessed the Civil Rights Movement, the feminist movement, the Vietnam War, and a youth "revolution" that featured rock-and-roll music and changing sexual mores. The ice began to thaw in Protestant-Catholic relations with the renewal that accompanied the Catholic decisions at Vatican II. Pentecostalism, a brand-new faith at the dawn of the century, burgeoned. Its theology of the "gifts of the Spirit" entered mainstream denominations in what was called the "charismatic movement." The year 1976 was proclaimed the "year of the evangelical" with the election of "born-again" Baptist Jimmy Carter of Georgia as president of the United States.

In the midst of this whirlwind of social changes, American Baptists confronted the future. They experienced a series of organizational changes; the process of centralization continued. Their ecumenical involvement and their openness to women in leadership put them at the forefront of adapting to the changing modern religious map.

Denominational Centralization

In 1972, the American Baptist Convention underwent a massive reorganization and was renamed the American Baptist Churches in the U.S.A. (ABCUSA). The convention report that suggested the changes (SCODS: Study Commission on Denominational Structure) opted not to use the name preferred by some—American Baptist *Church*—because it seemed to imply "a connectional system, a creed other than the New Testament . . . a possible violation of local autonomy." Organizationally, the denomination had a general secretary and a general board, the major policy-making body. American Baptist churches were divided into thirty-five regions which varied in size from individual urban centers (for example, Chicago, New York, Los Angeles) to the thirteen-state American Baptist Churches of the South (287 churches, 106,407 resident members in 2005). Regions nominated three-fourths of the General Board's representatives. Board members were selected to mirror American Baptist diversity in gender, ethnicity, geography, and age; a balance of ordained and lay leaders was also maintained. Despite the efforts at equal representation, complaints in recent years reflected a sense of dissatisfaction in the lack of local church voice in an increasingly connectional system of governance.

Traditional American Baptist ministries continued in a variety of ways. National Ministries (formerly Home Missions) concentrated on "witness, renewal, and justice." During World War II, American Baptists worked to place about 150 people in noncombatant camps and had 976 chaplains, second only to Methodists. In 1957, Japanese-American Jitsuo Morikawa, director of evangelism of the Home Mission Society, led a shift from personal evangelistic techniques to more of an emphasis on social-action evangelism. American Baptists continued to pioneer in work with immigrants. On the international scene, the focus was upon the training of national workers. The number of missionaries declined from 407 in 1900 to 130 in 2005.

At the turn of the twenty-first century, American Baptists numbered 1.5 million members (the figure for much of the twentieth century). As in other mainline denominations, declines were experienced in Sunday school enrollment, baptisms, and the number of congregations (8,292 in 1928; 5,740 in 2007). Some critics cited the loss of evangelistic emphases in mainline religious bodies, liberal theology, and a doctrinally vapid ecumenism. Some observers noted the declining birth rate among middle-class Americans. Supporters noted that the ABCUSA was ecumenically and socially sensitive—Baptist in honoring freedom, the role of the local church, and the authority of Scripture—and was the most racially inclusive Protestant body in America.

In 1992, a group of conservatives, claiming that American Baptists had succumbed to liberalism and needed renewal, established the "American Baptist Evangelicals." The "hot-button" issue confronting other mainline denominations—homosexuality—revealed strong cleavages in American Baptist life. Different regions took a "welcoming-and-affirming" position, or, in the opposite direction, threatened to leave the ABCUSA unless official statements declaring homosexuality incompatible with the Christian gospel were implemented. In 2005, American Baptists of the West (California) voted to change their name to "Growing Healthy Churches" and explicitly declared that homosexuality was not biblical. Then in May 2006 the board of the American Baptist Churches Pacific Southwest region voted to withdraw from its covenant relationship with ABCUSA over the refusal of ABCUSA to deal with churches having lax policies on homosexualtiy.

Ecumenism

Extensive involvement in the ecumenical activities of the World Council of Churches and the National Council of Churches continued to characterize American Baptists in the latter half of the twentieth century. Critics were never scarce. Like other religious groups, American Baptists were affected by the fears that accompanied the Cold War. A group called the "Circuit Riders Inc." (a group formed in 1928, originally for evangelism) used the method of "guilt by association" when it publicized a list of 660 Baptist clergy who had been affiliated with organizations allegedly soft on Communism. At the 1960 ABC convention, the First Baptist Church of Wichita, Kansas, called the National Council of Churches a Communist organization and asked the convention to repudiate its membership in the liberal, un-American organization. Conspicuously, the NCC's leader at that time was American Baptist Edwin T. Dahlberg. The convention's response was twofold: they declared American Baptists were against Communism and they reaffirmed by a ten-to-one margin their longstanding participation in the ecumenical NCC.

Another decision with ecumenical implications was the convention's shift in 1969 to a more lenient position on "open baptism," long a minority practice among Baptists. The decision whether delegates to the annual national meetings had to be baptized by immersion was shifted to the local church level: the national body would no longer question the baptismal credentials of delegates. Some critics viewed the move as an unbiblical and "unbaptistic" capitulation to ecumenism's lack of doctrinal emphases.

At the same time, American Baptist ecumenical dialogue produced new cooperative alliances. While an effort in 1947 to merge with the Disciples of Christ failed, in 1970 American Baptists and the predominantly African-American Progressive National Baptist Convention formulated an "associated relationship" that focused on cooperative endeavors without organizational merger. In 1973, a similar agreement transpired with the Church of the Brethren.

Women' Leadership

In the latter half of the twentieth century, the issue of women in ministry affected all major Protestant denominations. Following on the heels of increased public roles for women during World War II, and in the footsteps of the Civil Rights Movement, the Women's Liberation Movement pushed for gender equality in all walks of life. In 1963, the World Council of Churches called for an end to gender discrimination in religion, and in the 1970s, all major denominations had national consultations on the role of women in the church. In 1980, the young organization, American Baptist Women in Ministry, held its first national conference.

In American Christianity, Methodists, and then American Baptists, led the way in the ordination of women. In the 1880s, a few Northern Baptist women were ordained. In more recent decades statistics revealed the increasing visibility of women in leadership. A study in 1985 reported that three percent of American Baptist pastors and sixteen percent of the associate and assistant pastors were women. By 2003, the numbers had continued to increase. American Baptists had 1,392 ordained women (twenty-one percent of the total number of ordained ministers) with 1,069 serving in local church ministries. Nine percent of American Baptist pastors (409) and thirty-two percent of the associate pastors were women.

In the latter half of the twentieth century, the most prominent Baptist woman in ecumenical ministries was Joan Brown Campbell. Dually aligned with the ABCUSA and and the Christian Church (Disciples of Christ), she was the first ordained woman to serve as the general secretary of the National Council of Churches (1991–1999), and she was the only woman in the clergy procession of the enthronement of Desmond Tutu as archbishop of South Africa. She also walked with Martin Luther King, Jr. during the Civil Rights Movement, and her congregation in Cleveland was the first in the city to allow King to speak.

Civil Rights Movement

Americans Baptists attempted a progressive response to the Civil Rights Movement. From 1950 to 1966 the convention adopted an annual resolution that attacked segregation and affirmed issues of civil rights: "God is no respecter of persons" (citing Acts 10:34 in 1954). In 1957, churches were challenged to open their membership to African-Americans and in 1962 they were encouraged to celebrate the 100th anniversary of the Emancipation Proclamation.

A "Baptist Action for Racial Brotherhood" was created two years later to provide an organized programmed approach to civil rights. Even the Ministers and Missionaries Benefit Board (MMBB), through the work of J. Martin England, became involved in the civil rights struggle. England set up a regional office in the South. England, a friend and founding resident of Southern radical Clarence Jordan's integrated commune Koinonia Farm, marched with Martin Luther King, Jr. and was the person to whom King gave his "Letter from Birmingham Jail" while in prison. Subsequently, the MMBB was the first organization to publish that now-famous letter.

African-Americans were not always satisfied with the progress of race relations among American Baptists. In 1968, a group of African-American pastors demanded several specific reforms and accused the convention of excluding African-Americans from key leadership positions. The denominational hierarchy made no explicit promises, but the next year Thomas Kilgore, Jr., pastor of Second Baptist Church of Los Angeles, was the first African-American ever elected as president of American Baptists. The massive reorganization of American Baptists (SCODS) also pledged an inclusive approach to future leadership positions.

Charismatic Movement

During the 1960s and 1970s, the Charismatic Movement—the affirmation of Pentecostal teachings on speaking in tongues, baptism of the Holy Spirit, and divine healing—spread through Protestant mainline denominations and Catholicism. Baptist reaction was decidedly mixed.

In 1968, charismatics in American Baptist life organized as the "American Baptist Charismatic Fellowship." Led by Ken Pagard of Pasadena, the group had gatherings and display booths at ABC national conventions. Since 1975, annual summer conferences have been held at the Green Lake national conference center. The most widely known Baptist charismatic academic was Howard Ervin, professor at Oral Roberts University, who wrote several books arguing for the biblical validity of Spirit baptism.

Denominational acceptance of charismatics was not immediate. Many leaders opposed the movement but felt the pluralism of the ABCUSA prohibited official criticism outside the local church. In 1976, however, general secretary Robert C. Campbell expressed tolerance and admonished critics who cited the troubled Corinthian congregation as the only church in the New Testament to practice speaking in tongues: "The church at Corinth had many problems . . . except the chief problem of our churches today: it was never dull." Greater acceptance developed under the leadership of Gary Clark, Pagard's successor, who dropped the divisive word "charismatic" and renamed the movement "Holy Spirit Ministries in American Baptist Churches."

Conclusion

At the turn of the twentieth century, American Baptists could point to their leadership in the areas of civil rights, women's rights, and interfaith dialogue. In some circles "American Baptist" was synonymous with ecumenism. Consequently, not all American Baptists were happy. Growth had stagnated. The future seemed uncertain.

Duplicating the practices of a New Testament church seemed antithetical to the ecumenical emphases of contemporary American Baptists. Nevertheless, they still asserted the Baptist distinctives of the sacredness of the individual conscience, religious liberty, local church autonomy, and the Bible as the authority for religious faith. The more ecumenically minded American Baptists considered their support for women in ministry to be consistent with the liberating spirit of New Testament faith. More doctrinally conservative American Baptists spoke to the need for a literal reading of New Testament faith. Evangelicals who criticized ecumenism as void of orthodox doctrinal concerns said that they were contending for the Bible. The charismatic renewal movement was clearly an attempt to imitate fully the New Testament church.

Looking at American Baptists through the lenses of the search for the New Testament church will continue to be fruitful, and will most likely continue to uncover widely divergent pictures.

Chapter 8

1950 to the Present:
Baptists in the South
Battle for Denominational Identity

In the last decades of the twentieth century, analysts spoke of the "culture wars." Social issues seemed to dominate the national scene. *Roe v. Wade* made abortion a legal option in 1973 and the question of gay rights took center stage. The South became increasingly pluralistic, beginning to catch up with the rest of the country. Economically and politically, "Reaganomics" dominated the 1980s before the presidency of Bill Clinton, a Baptist from Arkansas. In the aftermath of the Civil Rights Movement, the solid-Democratic South turned Republican.

Like the political arena, the American religious map took a rightward turn. The electronic church flourished, with the "PTL Club" of Jim and Tammy Faye Bakker and the like. While Southern Baptists tried to resist Pentecostal influences more than most groups, the spread of charismatic faith continued to make inroads and caused great anxiety for its opponents.

The religious story of the 1980s, however, was the "fundamentalist/moderate conflict" in the Southern Baptist Convention. In some ways, it was a rerun of the theological conflicts that affected Northern Baptists and Northern Presbyterians in the early twentieth century. Doctrinal conformity (or accountability, depending upon one's perspective) became the litmus test for full inclusion in the life of the Convention. Baptists had known conflict before, but never on this scale, and never as much in the public eye. For many observers, the name "Baptist" became synonymous with controversy. At the turn of the twenty-first century, Baptists in the South struggled to put conflict behind them, but their ongoing conflicts were still very visible on the American religious map.

Denominationalism

During the last four decades of the twentieth century, Southern Baptists continued to inculcate a strong commitment to their denomination in the midst of an increasingly pluralistic environment. The 1970s were marked by the height of denominationalism, that is, a commitment to Baptist identity via loyalty to Baptist programs. Baptist young people continued to attend Baptist camps and continued to learn missions in Baptist versions of the Boy Scouts (Royal Ambassadors) and Girl Scouts (Girl's Auxiliary). The year 1976, proclaimed the "year of the evangelical" by secular journalists, witnessed a devout Baptist from Plains, Georgia, Jimmy Carter, elected as president of the nation.

As the challenges of postmodernism and its de-emphasis on traditional denominations surged to the forefront of "doing church" in America, some Baptists responded by moving away from explicit usage of denominational labels. At the end of the twentieth century, Baptist youth often said they were Christian first, evangelical second, and Baptist third. The megachurch/ community church phenomenon, which became persuasive in evangelical America, also impacted Southern Baptist life. The Southern Baptist congregation, Saddleback Church (Lake Forest, California) with Pastor Rick Warren, became one of the largest churches in America.

Throughout the twentieth century, Southern Baptists continued their evangelistic efforts and missionary passion. Support for the Cooperative Program, especially the work of the Home and Foreign Mission Boards, was the pride and joy of most Southern Baptists. "Bold Mission Thrust," an initiative to share the gospel with every person on earth by the year 2000, began in 1977. By 2004, Southern Baptists sponsored more than 5,000 home missionaries and more than 5,000 international missionaries serving in 153 countries.

Southern Baptists entered the twenty-first century with significant organizational restructuring. Baptist Book Stores were renamed LifeWay Christian Stores to appeal to a wider evangelical market. In 1997, the Foreign Mission Board and the Home Mission Board were renamed the International Mission Board and the North American Mission Board, respectively.

Numerical advance continued to characterize Southern Baptists. Membership grew from 13,196,979 in 1980 to 15,044,413 ten years later. The number of Southern Baptist churches increased from 35,404 to 37,974 during the same period. The latest statistics (2005) reported 16,270,315 Southern Baptists in 43,669 local churches. At the dawning of a new century, Southern Baptists claim the title of the largest Protestant body in the United States.

A significant element of the recent growth of Southern Baptists was among ethnic minorities. While almost a completely white denomination in 1970, by 2000 ethnic minorities totaled twenty percent of Southern Baptists. African-American growth was significant. The convention added 1,600

African-American congregations in the 1990s to have more than 2,700 in 2002. In 1995, Southern Baptists offered their first official apology to African-Americans for "historic acts of evil such as slavery." Superseding the observance of Race Relations Sunday, an annual Racial Reconciliation Sunday (1995ff.) dotted the denominational calendar at the beginning of the twenty-first century.

Civil Rights Movement

Throughout the first half of the twentieth century, Southern Baptists, as well as other Christian groups in the South, continued to believe in white superiority, and considered segregation to be the accepted—that is, biblical—way of life. A minority of progressive Southern Baptists, however, pushed for racial equality. Social-gospel proponent Walter Johnson became frustrated with the burgeoning denominational centralization and pushed for civil rights (and peace) outside the traditional institutional framework. He influenced a small "genealogy of dissent" that included Martin England and Clarence Jordan, founders of the interracial commune Koinonia Farm near Americus, Georgia (1942). These social radicals influenced other progressives. Jordan's Cotton Patch Version of the New Testament (1963ff.), folksy paraphrases of New Testament writings in Southern idiom, served to heighten racial awareness. In the parable of the Good Samaritan, for example, the Samaritan turned out to be a Southern African-American.

Progressive thought on civil rights in Southern Baptist agencies had limited success. When the Supreme Court ruled in the groundbreaking 1954 case, *Brown v. Board of Education*, that "separate but equal" facilities were unconstitutional, denominational leaders supported the decision. Still, a denominational call to integrate local churches was not trumpeted until 1968 and it was later than resolutions announced by other denominations. If any group within the local church pioneered better race relations, it was the Woman's Missionary Union. Already in the 1940s some women's groups were doing study courses that discussed racial justice.

During the 1960s, progressive voices within the SBC were found at the Christian Life Commission under the leadership of Foy Valentine. Baptist youth learned about "race relations" in the work of Baptist Student Unions at the college level; at the seminaries, young Southern Baptist ministers were influenced by the progressive, prophetic stands of professors such as Henlee Barnette (Southern Baptist Theological Seminary) and T. B. Maston (Southwestern Baptist Theological Seminary). Southern Seminary made the news in 1961 when Martin Luther King, Jr. preached in chapel and received a standing ovation. Churches across the SBC criticized the visit and threatened to withhold funds. Seminary trustees issued a public statement of regret regarding King's visit. Southern Baptists papers avoided speaking about King until his death; at that point, some editors lamented King's tragic death but others used the occasion to criticize his work.

Southern Baptists were also at the forefront of opposition to the Civil Rights Movement. In the wake of the Rosa Parks-inspired Montgomery bus boycott, a leading local pastor and Alabama state convention president, Henry Lyons, offered a biblical defense of segregation on his weekly radio broadcast. Dallas pastor W. A. Criswell denounced the landmark 1954 Supreme Court decision, which led to an invitation to repeat his criticism before the South Carolina state legislature two years later. He believed that integration was "idiocy and foolishness" and asserted that religious groups should stick with their own kind. At the local church level, the integration of churches was resisted. A few churches slowly integrated; others refused to seat African-Americans and fired pastors who pushed the issue. Desegregation at Southern Baptist colleges and universities occurred begrudgingly but did preserve student eligibility for federal aid. Playing to the anxieties of America's Cold War culture, hard line segregationists asserted that integration was a Communist plot to cripple America. The old religion of the Lost Cause experienced a revival as an Anglo-Saxon, Protestant America was gasping for breath.

In its most extreme form, the desire to maintain Anglo-Saxon superiority was represented in the white supremacist gospel of the Ku Klux Klan. While the KKK found adherents in and out of Southern churches, one of the most infamous leaders was Sam Bowers, a Baptist Sunday school teacher from Laurel, Mississippi, and Imperial Wizard of the White Knights of Mississippi. In 1964, the disappearance of three civil rights workers around the small town of Philadelphia captured the national spotlight and foul play was suspected. The Mississippi Baptist paper, *The Baptist Record*, questioned whether the workers were really missing with the sarcastic headline "Search Begins for Three Million Southern Baptists." (Local church and convention membership totals usually included "inactive" members whose whereabouts were unknown.) The civil rights workers were later found dead, and Bowers served a six-year prison term for masterminding the operation. In 1998, he was convicted of the 1966 murder of another civil rights worker.

"The Controversy"

The central story of Southern Baptists during the last decades of the twentieth century, however, did not focus upon missions, evangelism, or ethnic diversity. Any analysis of ministries during this period is quickly overshadowed by the Fundamentalist-Moderate conflict, or the "Conservative Resurgence," as it was called by the victors. Tremors of this religious earthquake, however, date back to the early 1960s and the "Elliott Controversy." Ralph Elliott, a professor of Old Testament at Midwestern Baptist Theological Seminary, suggested in his book, *The Message of Genesis*, that Genesis 1–11 was "theological history." The importance of the stories—such as Adam and Eve—was their theological message, not whether they were literal history. Published by Broadman Press, the official publication house of the SBC Sunday School Board, the book caused a backlash of protest among some Baptists. Elliott was branded a liberal who did not believe the Bible. Although the Sunday School Board never reissued the book, they initially defended it. They argued that they published a variety of works, which reflected the diversity of theological views held by Southern Baptists. Midwestern Seminary eventually fired Elliott, not over his use of modern historical-critical methods of Bible study, but for insubordination. He refused to revise the book, and he refused to promise that he would not republish with another press.

The convention's response to the Elliott affair was the adoption of the 1963 "Baptist Faith and Message" (BFM) confession of faith. The 1963 BFM was a revision of the 1925 BFM, but the 1963 version retained the 1925 description of the Scriptures as "truth, without any mixture of error," a phrase whose meaning later became a point of contention in convention affairs. As with the 1925 confession, denominational loyalists sought to unify the convention with this voluntary confession. Herschel Hobbs, an influential denominationalist from Oklahoma, emphasized in a preamble the voluntary and noncreedal nature of the confession. Most local churches ignored the confession as they addressed ministry needs in the rapidly changing 1960s.

A second flare-up occurred with the publication of the twelve-volume *Broadman Bible Commentary* at the end of the decade. In 1970, the SBC criticized the 1969 volume on Genesis, primarily because the author, British Baptist G. Henton Davies, said that God's command to Abraham to sacrifice his son, Isaac, could not be taken literally (Genesis 22). Missouri editor Ross Edwards said if the issue was not confronted, the convention owed Ralph Elliott an apology. Charges of liberalism heated up and subsequently the commentary was rewritten by popular Bible teacher, Clyde Francisco, of Southern Seminary.

Theological tension seemed relatively quiet, or at least isolated, until 1979. Actually, a network of persons was developing who believed that seminaries and other denominational agencies needed to be purged of liberalism. The most visible group was the Baptist Faith and Message Fellowship, organized in Atlanta in 1973, which featured Charles Stanley of First Baptist Church, Atlanta. Russell Dilday, a pastor in Atlanta at the time, felt the winds of creedal conformity blowing. In a 1975 sermon he preached that Baptists were a noncreedal people whose commitment to the priesthood of believers meant that no Baptist should demand that other Baptists conform to his interpretations for them to work together. Nevertheless, the following year Dilday, like most Southern Baptists, suppressed the doubts caused by local fundamentalist stirrings and expended his energies on adopting Southern Baptists' "Bold Mission Thrust," the ambitious plan to take the gospel to the entire world by the year 2000.

With the election in 1979 of Adrian Rogers, pastor of Bellevue Baptist Church, Memphis, as convention president, the transformation of the Southern Baptist Convention began in earnest. A political strategy to elect a series of convention presidents who affirmed biblical inerrancy—called the sine qua non of orthodox evangelical theology—was devised by architects Paige Patterson of the Criswell Biblical Institute and Houston layman Judge Paul Pressler. According to the plan, the convention presidents used their appointive powers to select committees that remade trustee boards of SBC institutions into bastions of conservative inerrantist theology. While many of the presidential elections at annual SBC gatherings were contested and close, the Patterson-Pressler plan was remarkably successful. The 1985 convention drew 45,000 messengers, the largest meeting in the history of the convention. It was also the most controversial, with Charles Stanley's parliamentary methods constantly challenged as manipulative by critics.

By 1990, the "conservative resurgence" of the Southern Baptist Convention was a fait accompli. Leaders proclaimed that a "new reformation" had occurred; they announced that liberalism had been soundly defeated and historic, orthodox, conservative, Baptist theology had been restored. Agencies and seminaries had been purified. (W. A. Criswell, revered pastor of First Baptist Church, Dallas, and conservative icon, speaking at the 1988 SBC Pastor's Conference in the heat of the battle between SBC moderates and conservatives, said that moderates are the same as liberals, that "A skunk by any other name still stinks!")

"Conservative versus liberal" was not how many Baptists assessed the controversy. Conservatives were really fundamentalists and liberals were really moderates. Since both groups were Bible-believing Baptists, moderates declared the insistence upon the theory of biblical inerrancy was unnecessary, confusing, and a red herring. While some theological diversity was readily apparent in the SBC—such had always been the case in Baptist life—moderates viewed the controversy as primarily a political power struggle between "freedom and control." They warned that a "galloping creedalism" was usurping biblical authority and trampling historic Baptist biblical distinctives including "soul competency," the priesthood of believers, the separation of church and state, and the freedom of conscience.

A "lightening rod" between the warring groups was the Baptist Joint Committee on Public Affairs (BJCPA)—a religious-liberty agency that represented practically every major Baptist body in America—and its colorful executive-director, James Dunn. According to his opponents, Dunn's cardinal sin was his harsh denunciation of President Reagan's 1982 proposal for a school prayer amendment. Most leaders of the "conservative resurgence" rejected the strict separation of church and state that was extolled by the BJCPA in favor of an accommodationist approach that believed government could (and should) facilitate the free exercise of religion without breaching the establishment clause of the First Amend-ment. Consequently, conservatives opposed the 1963 ruling of the Supreme Court that banned state-sponsored school prayer and strongly supported President Reagan.

Dunn retorted that state-sponsored voluntary prayer was an oxymoron. He denounced President Reagan for playing "petty politics with prayer" and for being "deliberatively dishonest" by siding with reactionaries who suggested that God had been kicked out of the public schools and the decline of American society was the result. In his typical picturesque fashion, Dunn declared, "It is as if the Divine could be dumped into a wheelbarrow and carted out. The charge that everything went wrong because they threw prayer out of schools is patent poppycock." Dunn concluded, "The God whom I worship and serve has a perfect attendance record, never absent or even tardy," and added that prayers would be voiced to God as long as schools had tests.

Throughout the 1980s, Dunn and leaders of the "resurgence" sparred. Dunn warned that fundamentalist leaders with their advocacy for school prayer, tuition tax credits, and school vouchers were practicing a civil religion (mixing of traditional religion with national life until the two became indistinguishable) and aping the political agenda of the "Religious Right." He called Southern Baptists back to the tradition of Roger Williams and John Leland and their heritage of complete religious liberty. Dunn's opponents, however, considered his views too liberal, too secular, and out of step with Southern Baptists. After several attempts in the 1980s, in 1991, the SBC withdrew its support from the Baptist Joint Committee.

When by 1990 the "fundamentalist takeover" was assured, many moderates felt disenfranchised and decried the loss of a great denomination. They lamented that their plea for genuine cooperation and "unity amidst diversity" in order to carry out the convention's raison d'etre—missions—had been scuttled in favor of doctrinal conformity, pastoral authoritarianism, the subordination of women, and the political agenda of the Religious Right. With conservatives in control of all denominational agencies and employing only like-minded supporters, moderates were resigned to defeat and disillusioned about the future.

Local churches took a variety of approaches to "The Controversy." Some took a fast track to a moderate or fundamentalist stance; others tried to ignore the battle and simply remained Southern Baptist. Some churches, despite problems with political maneuverings by the denomination's conservative leadership, believed an almost total focus on mission support would prevail over any political/theological infighting. They believed that Baptists—because of their love for cooperative missions—would never let the pendulum swing too far in one direction. Ultimately, for these Baptists, decades of deeply rooted commitment to the Southern Baptist Way (especially to the Lottie Moon Christmas Offering for Foreign Missions) and undying loyalty to a Baptist programmatic identity prevailed. This sense of loyalty was clearly expressed in the attitude of James Griffith, a Georgia Baptist leader, when he said he would not reduce his support of missionaries and risk hurting their work. In 1987, despite a conservative victory on the horizon, Griffith declared: "I don't let nobody blow smoke on my blue skies."

By 1990, "The Controversy" was over at the national level, but skirmishes continued during the next decade at the state and local levels. A few dissenting churches (or individuals from SBC churches) formed the Cooperative Baptist Fellowship (CBF), which eventually distanced itself completely from the SBC. These churches, having felt stampeded by a fundamentalist victory, believed that to say the denominational skies were blue was to never look up. The CBF achieved steady but slow growth by the turn of the century. In addition to emphasizing Baptist distinctives, such as separation of church and state and the priesthood of believers, the CBF fashioned itself as a "fellowship" that honored local church autonomy. The CBF partnered with ministries, but did not govern them with trustees. In contrast to the SBC's views on the "rule of the pastor" and the prohibition of women in pastoral roles, the CBF articulated an egalitarian "servant leadership" view of ministry of both women and men. Some critics noted, however, that CBF churches were rarely as open to women pastors as the CBF leaders were.

The crowning achievement of the "conservative resurgence" in the SBC came with the adoption of a revision of the 1963 confession, the "2000 Baptist Faith and Message." New items included a statement that excluded women from the pastorate, a statement on the submission of the wife to the husband in family life, and the importance of doctrinal accountability. Ironically, the statement on the Bible did not use the word "inerrancy," though inerrancy was assumed without question. Denominational employees and seminary faculty were required to subscribe to the confession. Moderate critics said the fundamentalist adoption of a creed was complete.

"The Controversy" produced some additional consequences. Some independent fundamentalist Baptists joined forces with Southern Baptists after the defeat of the moderate group; the most notable addition being the nationally known televangelist, Jerry Falwell. Citing theological liberalism as the primary reason, Southern Baptists distanced themselves from mainline Protestant churches and other Baptists by withdrawing from the Baptist World Alliance in 2004. At the same time, Southern Baptists cooperated more extensively with other conservative evangelical groups in missions and in the public arena (for example, prolife concerns and Republican politics). At the turn of the twenty-first century, a resurgence of Calvinism was occurring among Southern Baptist conservatives, especially among young people. Noticeable Calvinists included seminary presidents Al Mohler of Southern Baptist Theological Seminary and Danny Akin of Southeastern Baptist Theological Seminary.

Women's Leadership

Ministerial leadership positions were more restrictive in Southern Baptist life than in American Baptist churches. A few women served on church staffs in the early 1900s and increasingly so by the 1940s, but they were "directors" rather than "ministers" of education/children/music. From 1927 to 1958 only five women served on the SBC's executive committee. In 1963, Marie Mathis was the first second vice-president of the national convention. In 1964, Addie Davis was the first woman ordained by a Southern Baptist church (Watts Street Baptist Church, Durham, North Carolina), but she had to relocate to Vermont to pastor a Baptist congregation. In recent decades, women served on various denominational committees (up to twenty percent in some agencies), and individual churches ordained around 1,900 women. The Southern Baptist Convention, however, declared that the Bible prohibited women pastors and, consequently, the convention took official steps to deny leadership roles to ordained women in denominational positions. At the turn of the century, most Baptist women in the South who sought ordination did so from churches affiliated with the Cooperative Baptist Fellowship.

Charismatic Movement

A small group of Southern Baptist pastors were involved in the charismatic movement (including John Osteen in Houston) that flourished in the latter half of the twentieth century. Southern Baptists leaders, however, responded with increasing hostility. W. A. Criswell, of First Baptist Church, Dallas, called speaking in tongues "gibberish" and "near heresy." Commenting on the idea that women were associated with speaking in tongues at the Corinthian church in the New Testament, Criswell said the charismatic movement was a "woman movement. You stop the women from speaking in tongues and the practice will absolutely disappear from the earth."

Several churches that affirmed charismatics were excluded by associations in 1975, but only Texas passed a resolution warning of "potential dangers." In subsequent decades, the SBC continually tightened its stance. In 1987, the Home Mission Board moved to restrict its missionaries from speaking in tongues. In 2005, the International Mission Board decided to disqualify any new missionary candidate who practiced a "private prayer language." In 2006, tension erupted with Dwight McKissic, African-American founder of the 3,000 member Cornerstone Baptist Church of Arlington, Texas, and trustee at Southwestern Baptist Theological Seminary, preached a chapel sermon at the seminary. In his address, McKissic criticized the SBC's new policy and announced that he practiced a private prayer language. Despite his trustee status, the seminary initially refused to make the sermon available to internet listeners even though other chapel sermons were available. The school's board of trustees then passed a resolution forbidding employment to anyone who affirmed or practiced speaking in tongues.

Some other Southern Baptists also continued to identify themselves as "Spirit-filled." In 1989, Ron Phillips, a leader of the "conservative resurgence" in Tennessee in the 1980s, said that he had a "Spirit-filled" experience. Subsequently, his church, Central Baptist Church of Hixson (Chattanooga), became "Abba's House." In 2006, the congregation numbered around 3,000. Phillips sponsored annual "Fresh Oil" and "New Wine" conferences and reported that more than 600 Baptist churches participated. While still Southern Baptist, Phillips felt increasingly excluded by the new restrictive convention policies toward speaking in tongues.

Pentecostal influences were evident in other Baptist venues. The Pentecostal Free Will Baptist Church, incorporated in 1959, in North Carolina, still existed as a small restorationist Baptist group. Independent charismatic television personalities James Robison and Pat Robertson (who ran for the presidency of the United States), were formerly Southern Baptist ministers. The most profound, yet possibly under-recognized Pentecostal influence in Baptist life, was "praise and worship," "contemporary Christian music" that was popular with Baptist youth, and utilized in "contemporary" worship.

Baptist Distinctives

Southern Baptists do not claim a separate list of Baptist distinctives. They affirm the "classic" list of defining traits that includes believer's baptism by immersion, personal religious experience, salvation through Christ alone, missions and evangelism, priesthood of believers, religious liberty, congregational church government, the importance/autonomy of the local church, confessionalism, the sole authority of the Bible for faith and practice, and the Lordship of Jesus Christ. What was distinctive was the way some of the distinctives functioned as Southern Baptists entered the twenty-first century.

- "Priesthood of believers" still meant that all Christians had direct access to God, but its corollary, "soul competency," (*the* distinctive for E. Y. Mullins) was criticized for allowing private interpretation of the Bible, a gateway to heresy. The priesthood of the laity was also paired with and subordinated to the authority of the pastor—the "ruler" of the local congregation.
- Biblical authority meant an affirmation of biblical inerrancy; the Bible was "without error" in all areas of reality (for example,

including historical and scientific detail); consequently, inerrancy necessitated the exclusion of women from the pastorate (and often from the deaconate).

- Confessions had more creedal force, especially in the employment of denominational employees.
- Religious liberty no longer translated into a strict separation of church and state. Support for the placing of religious symbols such as the Ten Commandments on public property was commonplace.
- Cooperation in missions and evangelism was to be with other conservative evangelical or "doctrinally orthodox" Christians.
- Local churches were autonomous, but associations and state and national conventions demanded doctrinal accountability for participation.

As they had throughout their history, Southern Baptists were known for their passion and commitment to missions and evangelism. They sought to be biblical in faith and practice, and desired to embody the New Testament Church. The essential defining characteristic of twenty-first-century Southern Baptists is a doctrinal consensus of conservative, evangelical, inerrantist theology. Unified in doctrinal orthodoxy, Southern Baptists are committed to evangelizing the world for Jesus Christ. The sense of chosenness, a trait found throughout their history, still inspires the Southern Baptist vision. In hyperbolic terms, conservative giant Adrian Rogers expressed this optimism regarding the significant role of Southern Baptists in God's future providence:

This is going to sound like megalomania, but I believe that the hope of the world lies in the West. I believe that the hope of the West lies in America. I believe that the hope of America is in Judeo-Christian ethics. I believe that the backbone of that Judeo-Christian ethic is evangelical Christianity. I believe that the bellwether of evangelical Christianity is the Southern Baptist Convention. So I believe, in a sense, that as the Southern Baptist Convention goes, so goes the world.

Independent Baptists (Southern Baptist Cousins)

After the "Fundamentalist-Modernist Conflict" of the 1920s and 1930s, some ideological descendents of the earlier fundamentalists helped develop a "neoevangelical" movement. These conservatives included Baptist leaders such as Edward J. Carnell and Carl F. H. Henry at the new interdenominational school, Fuller Theological Seminary, Pasedena, California (founded in 1947), and editors like Harold Lindsell at the evangelical magazine, *Christianity Today*. Evangelist Billy Graham, fundamentalist in theology, epitomized the new conservative that willingly cooperated with other Christians in evangelistic work.

Other descendents of the earlier fundamentalist battles were "Independent Baptists" who continued to preach a militant separation from liberalism. Prominent leaders included Bob Jones, Sr., Bob Jones, Jr., and John R. Rice. When Billy Graham accepted cooperation with mainline Protestants for a New York crusade in 1957, he was condemned as a compromising traitor. At issue was the degree of separation required of an orthodox believer. Rice did not cooperate with anyone who cooperated with liberals. Jones Sr. refused to cooperate not only with liberals, but also with conservatives (for example, Southern Baptists) who worked with liberals.

Independent, separatist, fundamentalist Baptists were the most-radical expression of mistrust of denominational centralization. Local churches were completely autonomous and were not officially a member of any larger connectionalism (though they might join together for "fellowship"). Denominationalism was considered contrary to the faith of the New Testament church. Independent Baptist rhetoric reacted strongly to any perceived compromise of the faith. In his book entitled *Bobbed Hair, Bossy Wives, and Women Preachers: Significant Questions for Honest Christian Women Settled by the Word of God* (1941), for example, John R. Rice declared, "I have no doubt that millions will go to hell because of the unscriptural practice of women preachers."

Independent Baptists, with their insistence on doctrinal conformity to the Bible's unchanging commands, believed that the Civil Rights Movement was an attack on America's Christian civilization. Martin Luther King, Jr. couldn't be trusted because his theological liberalism was evidence of apostasy. Intermarriage was unbiblical, damaged the purity of the superior white race, and created social chaos. Bob Jones University, the most visible independent Baptist school, was segregated from 1927 to 1971 until it succumbed to the threat of government sanctions. The school admitted married African-Americans only if they were married to other African-Americans while single students had to agree to date within their race. John R. Rice, founding editor of the popular *The Sword of the Lord* magazine, contended that African-Americans were mostly to blame for their poverty. Claiming not to be prejudiced, Rice admitted that heaven would be integrated since blacks would not be morally deficient there as they were on earth. The responsibility of the church was to evangelize lost sinners for heaven; it was not to engage in communist-inspired plots to undermine a democratic civilization patterned on the Bible's teaching about racial separation.

The most visible Independent Baptist individual in the last decades of the twentieth century was Jerry Falwell, founding pastor of Thomas Road Baptist Church and founder of Liberty University, Lynchburg, Virginia. Falwell was a graduate of Bible Baptist College in Springfield, Missouri, a school associated with the independent Baptist Bible Fellowship (1950) that was formed by dissidents who had split from the country's most famous fundamentalist in the early twentieth century, J. Frank Norris. Falwell was originally a segregationist and a typical dispensationalist who avoided involvement in social issues. However, his cofounding of the "religious-political right" organization, the Moral Majority (1979), whose membership initially included a majority of independent Baptists, was the signal event in the greater involvement of religious conservatives in American politics. In 2005, some independent Baptists, along with some individual Southern Baptists, formed the International Baptist Network. Utilizing a revision of the New Hampshire Confession of Faith that they called the "Georgia Baptist Confession," the group, some of whom called themselves "the face of twenty-first-century Baptists," was potentially viewed as an alternative to the Baptist World Alliance.

Conclusion

In the latter half of the twentieth century, Baptists in the South exhibited diverse ways of being Baptist, a diversity consistent with the whole tenor of Baptist history. Pentecostal Free Will Baptists and Independent Baptists both were extremely literal in their search for New Testament Christianity. The charismatic tensions among some Southern Baptists revealed the strength of Pentecostal restorationism in the wider American religious culture. Regardless of the decade, Southern religion was impacted by its racial legacy.

The "Controversy" that engulfed the Southern Baptist Convention revealed the conservative direction, not only of Southern religion, but of Southern culture in general at the end of the twentieth century. Moderate to liberal voices existed, but in minority patterns. At the turn of the twenty-first century, some analysts said that Southern Baptists were fragmented and damaged, with hope for a genuine Baptist identity to be found in a renewed focus upon ministry at the local church level and in ecumenical association and participation. Others noted that Southern Baptists were still the largest

Protestant body in America and more prepared to lead an evangelical renewal movement than ever before.

At the outset of the twenty-first century, the theological buzzword in American religion was "postmodernism," a concept that maintains that the modern reliance upon reason and absolute truth was passé. Some "postmoderns" claimed that truth was relative to each individual's situation, and personal choice (a type of religious consumerism) was emphasized. For an increasing number of Christians, traditional denominational affiliations mattered little. Finding God "in community" became commonplace.

Postmodernism's willingness to diminish traditional denominational loyalties in favor of adapting contemporary cultural forms produced a variety of Southern Baptist reactions. In 2006, Emir Caner, a professor at Southwestern Baptist Theological Seminary, articulated the position of the Southern Baptist leadership by insisting upon one hundred percent fidelity to the SBC's "2000 Baptist Faith and Message" doctrinal statement. Criticizing postmodern churches that attempted to use culture to reach the American masses, Caner retorted, "It is not our call to be a twenty-first-century church." Instead, he insisted, "It is our call to be a first-century church in a twenty-first-century world." Given the historic Baptist tendency to interpret theological issues through the lenses of the New Testament church, Caner's response was typical.

Chapter 9

African-American Baptists: From the Slave Cabin to a National Podium

In the postbellum period, African-Americans separated from white churches in droves and formed their own congregations. Some white Baptists initially wanted African-Americans to continue to worship under white supervision. African-Americans desired equality and whites were unwilling to give it. Consequently, independent local African-American churches were birthed all across the North and South.

The church was the central institution of the African-American community. It was not only the religious center, but the social and educational center as well. Naturally, preachers, who had played such an important role in the organized social life of slaves, became Republican political leaders during the Reconstruction period when African-Americans (temporarily) had civil rights. When "Jim Crow laws" prevailed (1876–1965), the church continued as the primary agent of socialization in the African-American community. Ministers maintained the most prestige in the black community and were accorded significant power.

From Slave Cabin to the Pulpit

While the strongly emotional preaching of African-American pulpiteers like John Jacob Jasper continued to flourish after the Civil War, black preaching was not monolithic. A calmer style and more educated approach was apparent, for example, in the ministry of Peter Randolph, a slave who became a free man in 1847. Randolph reminded whites that if whites were not all alike, then neither were African-Americans. He pastored Baptist churches in his native Virginia as well as Boston after the Civil War. He actually was accused of having an "aristocratic church." He allowed women to vote, had mixed seating (males and females), and frowned upon excessive emotionalism in worship. He made friends with influential white pastors, such as Jeremiah Jeter of Richmond and A. J. Gordon of Boston.

In his autobiography, *From Slave Cabin to the Pulpit* (1893), Randolph validated and reminded people of the African-American struggle. Given that Americans in the Jim Crow era were likely to forget (or continue to distort) the harsh realities of slavery, Randolph wrote to set the record straight. He remembered the savage beatings of slavery in chilling fashion and poignantly told of families being separated by the slave trade. He blamed the North and well as the South for the terrible plight of slaves. Why did the North give the South control over the black population? After the War, African-Americans were greatly disappointed to find that "instead of forty acres and a mule, they had to return to their former masters barefooted" and beg for work. Even after the slavery era, Lynchings and burning at the stake were still prevalent crimes against African-Americans.

Despite the horrors of slavery, Randolph expressed confidence in his race. The use of emotion in worship was simply part of the "progress of humanity"; African-Americans were deeply religious people. As African-Americans were given educational opportunities, they would continue to make progress. Randolph implored his readers to follow the Golden Rule: Do unto others as you would have others do to you. "On this rests the joy or sorrow of America."

National Baptist Conventions

African-Americans not only established churches, they organized regional missionary societies, state conventions, and national conventions. "National Baptist Convention" is the main title of several African-American Christian denominations, including the National Baptist Convention, U.S.A., Inc.; the National Baptist Convention of America, Inc.; the Progressive National Baptist Convention; and the National Missionary Baptist Convention of America.

In August 1866 the Consolidated American Baptist Missionary Convention was organized, but it disbanded in 1877. In 1880, in Montgomery, Alabama, the Baptist Foreign Mission Convention (BFMC) was created. (In in some sources the "Baptist" part of the name changes positions: Foreign Mission Baptist Convention.)

William W. Colley was instrumental in the development of the BFMC and its emphasis on missions to Africa. Colley, the only African-American Baptist to work for both a white and an African-American mission society, was initially a missionary for the Southern Baptist Convention. Appointed in 1875, he served with W. J. David, a white missionary from Mississippi. While a few white missionaries worked willingly with African-Americans, David was typical of those that did not. He treated Colley as subordinate and inferior, despite the fact that they worked in West Africa. In 1879, Colley returned to America and declared that African-American Baptists needed a separate mission society that would not be subject to white discrimination. Colley's efforts helped encourage the creation of the BFMC in November 1880.

In 1883, Colley was among the first missionaries appointed by the BFMC. He returned to West Africa where the difficulties of missionary life were rampant. Adjusting to the African climate was a challenge, regardless of a person's background. Of the first dozen missionaries appointed by the BFMC, eleven either died or became ill and had to return to America.

African-American Baptists of course had a special interest in missions to Africa. They viewed it as a biblical duty—fulfilling the New Testament "Great Commission" to share the gospel to the world—and also as a racial responsibility because they were "sons of Africa." Salvation for Africans meant spiritual and material uplift (racial progress). African-American missionaries never condoned American slavery, but they came to believe that it was a part of a divine plan for them to acquire Christianity and Western civilization so they would become God's special messengers to save Africa. Recalling Psalm 68:31 (KJV)—"Princes shall come out of Egypt; Ethiopia shall soon stretch out her hands unto God."—African-American Baptists were convinced that God had a special destiny for Africans.

As black disenfranchisement and the intensity of white superiority increased in the American South, African-American Baptists formed a separate national organization. The BFMC, which was really a regional body, along with two other conventions (one focused on education—the Baptist National Educational Convention, 1893—and one on home missions—American National Baptist Convention, 1886) consolidated their efforts and in 1895 formed the "National Baptist Convention of the United States of America" (NBCUSA). The organizational meeting of this National Baptist Convention was at Friendship Baptist Church, Atlanta. E. C. Morris of Helena, Arkansas was the founding president of the convention, and served as president for the rest of his life (twenty-seven years).

The trigger event for the formation of the National Baptist Convention was the decision of the American Baptist Publication Society (ABPS, white Northern Baptists) to restrict black authors from writing for white audiences because of complaints from their Southern Baptist readers. Consequently, when NBCUSA saw that cooperation with white Baptists was contingent upon the subordination of African-Americans, in 1896 they formed the National Baptist Publishing Board (NBPB). Ultimately, the efforts of Northern Baptists to establish educational institutions for African-Americans in the South had not resulted in a permanent working relationship. The paternalistic attitudes of white Baptists, both in the North and South, were unacceptable to African-Americans.

Some historians consider the creation of the NBCUSA to be part of an emerging black nationalism in America that focused on self-determination. The energy of the convention's early years, however, was marred by schism. In 1897, several pastors, especially from Virginia and North Carolina, separated and formed the Lott Carey Baptist Foreign Mission Convention (LCBFMC). They feared a diminished focus on foreign missions in the new NBCUSA and they questioned the need to completely separate from white Baptists. Many of the pastors were agents for the American Baptist Home Mission Society and had been educated by schools it supported.

North Carolinian Calvin S. Brown was the first president of the LCBFMC. Brown strongly believed in cooperation with white Baptists who had provided much humanitarian and educational work for African-Americans after the Civil War. Initially Brown believed that the "common people" needed white assistance. He noted that whites were strong and educated and rich, whereas blacks were weak and ignorant and poor. Brown, in a vein similar to Booker T. Washington's accommodationist approach to cooperation with whites, did not want to emphasize any connection between white racism and the preaching of the gospel. Consequently, leaders of the National Baptist Convention felt that the LCBFMC was willing to perpetuate racial subordination in order to receive financial support from white Baptists. The National Baptist Convention connected the gospel and racial progress.

Eventually LCBFMC modified its stance on the cooperation/independence issue. As Jim Crow laws were enforced, cooperation with whites, North or South, was increasingly difficult. At the turn of the twenty-first century, the LCBFMC was still at work seeking "to be a premier mission agency of the African Diaspora." Many of its churches are still dually aligned with American Baptists.

A second schism in the NBCUSA occurred in 1915 over ownership and control—especially regarding the distribution of funds—of the National Baptist Publishing Board (NBPB). Under the leadership of Richard Henry Boyd, the NBPB had earned more than two million dollars during its first decade. (In addition to Baptist literature, the NBPB marketed the first African-American *dolls* in America.) Boyd clashed with convention leaders, however, over the distribution of funds to other denominational agencies. In order to state its legal claim to the publishing house, the convention incorporated as the "National Baptist Convention, *U.S.A., Inc.*" (NBCUSA).

Boyd and his supporters said the NBPB was independent of the National Baptist Convention and responded by forming a new denomination, the "National Baptist Convention *of America*" (NBCA; in older sources, often referred to as the NBC "unincorporated"; it eventually did incorporate in March 1987).

The NBCA experienced schism during its incorporation process: again, control of the publishing company was an issue. In 1988, the National Missionary Baptist Convention of America (NMBCA) was formed in Dallas, Texas. This convention, however, does not see itself as a new body. The NMBCA reports that it was founded in 1880 (origins of the Baptist Foreign Mission Convention) and "restored" in 1988. The R. H. Boyd Publishing Corporation, which refers to itself as "a global name in publishing for over 100 years," works with the new convention and sponsors an annual summer "National Baptist Congress" that focuses on Sunday School and other educational work. At the end of the twentieth century, the NBCA reported 3.5 million members and the NMBCA reported three million members.

Throughout the twentieth century, the National Baptist Convention (incorporated) was the most influential African-American Baptist national body. Leaders continued to be highly respected and were granted intense loyalty by many adherents. J. H. Jackson served longer than any president (1953–1982). Controversial national headlines accompanied the five-year presidential tenure of Henry Lyons (1994–1999) when he was forced to resign and was convicted in federal court for the misuse of funds. In 2005, the NBCUSA was headquartered in a new "Baptist World Center" in Nashville, Tennessee, and reported 7.5 million members. National Baptists had sixty-two state conventions and 341 district associations. (The NBCUSA is routinely cited as the oldest continuous African-American Baptist convention in America—although of course the NBCA and the NMBCA could and do make the same claim, since they also can point to direct kinship with the original 1895 NBCUSA organization, and even back to the 1880 BFMC.)

Theological and Baptist Distinctives/New Testament Church. African-American Baptists were generally no different in their doctrinal emphases than their white counterparts. They valued the Calvinistic bent of orthodoxy (all have sinned and cannot save themselves) found in late nineteenth century Southern evangelicalism. At the same time, African-American ministers preached "racial uplift" and the brotherhood of man. Unlike some whites (especially in the North) who adopted a "scientific racism"—blacks and white did not derive from a common species—African-American ministers asserted that all races were of "one blood."

African-American Baptists have emphasized the gospel of *freedom* and *social justice* throughout their history. For example, E. C. Morris, the influential founding president of the National Baptist Convention, called Jesus Christ the "great liberator" who created a "common brotherhood" that crossed racial lines wherever the gospel was believed. Christ, he said in a 1900 sermon, provided soul freedom *and* physical freedom.

In the 1920s, Adam Clayton Powell, Sr. embodied the call for social justice. Powell was a pioneer in having a soup kitchen for the poor after his Abyssinian Baptist Church moved into Harlem, New York. His son, Adam Jr., expanded the congregation's social ministry to include employment placement as well as providing help to African-American workers who participated in labor strikes. Revealing the ties between religion and politics in the African-American tradition, Adam Jr. was elected to the New York city council and in 1944 was elected as New York's first African-American member of Congress.

The "Baptist identity"—a roll call of Baptist distinctives—was usually less apparent in African-American life than in white Baptist writings. In the early years of organizational Baptist life, however, Baptist statesmen emphasized that white and African-American Baptists had the same essential biblical beliefs. They also identified with the restoration of the New Testament church.

In two early annual convention sermons (1898 and 1900), E. C. Morris emphasized to his African-American colleagues that they, as Baptists, could trace their existence directly back to Jesus and John the Baptist, the great Baptist preacher. Was Jesus a Baptist, Morris asked? Of course, since a Baptist was identified by believer's baptism by immersion. Morris also called for other Baptist emphases: congregational church government and the "absolute separation of church and state."

With this preaching about Baptist distinctives and New Testament primitivism, Morris apparently sought to bring a sense of dignity, pride, and heritage to his African-American audiences. Consequently, Morris asserted that all Christians needed to be brought under the biblical church polity of Baptists. In 1898, he was one of the first Baptists, white or black, to call for a unity of all Baptist groups that eventually resulted in the formation of the Baptist World Alliance (BWA, 1905). Throughout the twentieth century, African-American Baptist preachers continued to focus on apostolic doctrine as the foundation of their beliefs. In the arena of religious liberty, civil rights concerns were supported by calls for the free exercise of religion and freedom of the conscience. On the other hand, at the start of the twenty-first century, some African-American Baptists, like some conservative white Baptists, were less concerned with the establishment issues in church-state separation. They were willing to support accommodationist positions that affirmed the use of school vouchers and government-funded "faith-based initiatives."

Progressive National Baptist Convention

Because of the influence of the NBCUSA in the African-American community, the president of the NBCUSA functioned as the unofficial spokesperson for "Black America." He had the prized platform on issues in African-American social and political life. Consequently, strong authoritarian leaders characterized the history of the NBCUSA presidential office. The question of "term limits" to avoid an excessive concentration of power inevitably became an issue.

J. H. Jackson was elected president of the NBCUSA in 1953 and pledged to implement term limits on the presidency. In 1956, however, he did not fulfill the pledge and consolidated his power base. Not surprisingly, in 1958, Jackson's church, Olivet Baptist Church, Chicago, voted him life tenure as pastor.

An anti-Jackson group developed in the NBCUSA that pushed for term limits, but who were also opposed to his conservatism on civil rights methodology. At the 1956 convention a symposium was held on the subject and several spoke against gradualism (work for change within the legal system), the position favored by Jackson and the NAACP. After the symposium, Martin Luther King, Jr. addressed the convention and delivered "Paul's Letter to American Christians" which was wildly received by the audience. King reiterated his now-famous call for nonviolent protest and the willingness to go to jail to achieve integration. He lamented:

> When you stand at 11:00 on Sunday morning to sing "All Hail the Power of Jesus Name" . . . you stand in the most segregated hour of Christian America. They tell me that there is more integration in the entertaining world and other secular agencies than there is in the Christian church.

Jackson loyalists and detractors clashed at the 1960 convention. King supported the presidential candidacy of Gardner C. Taylor, pastor of the 11,000-member Concord Avenue Baptist Church, Brooklyn. Taylor was elected, but Jackson declared the election invalid and it was sent to federal court. The clash became tragic the next year when a shoving match on the platform resulted in the fall and death of pastor A. G. Wright from a fractured skull. Jackson won the election in court, and retorted that Wright's death was the result of King's support of Taylor.

In the aftermath of the violent convention, L. Venchael Booth pushed for a new convention, and in November 1961 the organizational meeting of the Progressive National Baptist Convention (PNBC) met at Booth's church, Zion Baptist Church, Cincinnati. Thirty-three delegates from fourteen states registered at the organization meeting. While King and Taylor originally were not in favor of a split, they soon became leaders. King preached annually at convention meetings of the PNBC until his death in 1968. Historians affirm that the PNBC "movement was undergirded by Dr. Martin Luther King, Jr.'s struggle for freedom for African-Americans," and that the "PNBC provided a denomination home for Dr. Martin Luther King, Jr. and many of the Baptist leaders of the Civil Rights Movement," all of whom "became important forces in the life and work" of the PNBC.

Gardner C. Taylor ultimately was acknowledged as one of (or the most) influential African-American preachers in America during the latter half of the twentieth century. He served as pastor of Concord Baptist Church in Brooklyn from 1948 to 1990, building the membership from 5,000 to 14,000. During Taylor's tenure, the church was involved in social ministry. A grade school, a home for senior citizens, and the Christ Fund—a million-dollar endowment designed to invest in Brooklyn—were established.

When the PNBC was created, its platform included a progressive civil rights agenda, a commitment to PNBC presidential term limits, and the creation of the office of general secretary. The PNBC was more socially progressive than the NBCUSA, and joined the World Council of Churches, but, at the turn of the twenty-first century, women had yet to be involved in leadership positions. The PNBC maintains close cooperative ties with the American Baptist Churches in the U.S.A. (ABCUSA), a cooperation highlighted by the election in 1969 of Thomas Kilgore as the first African-American president of the ABCUSA. Later, Kilgore was president of the PNBC (1976–1978), and to date is the only person to be president of both the predominantly white ABCUSA and the predominantly black PNBC. Headquartered in Washington, D.C., in 2005 the PNBC reported 2,000 churches and 2.5 million members.

Civil Rights Movement

Martin Luther King, Jr. is known as a cultural hero for his contributions to the Civil Rights Movement in American history. For his leading role, Americans honor King with a national holiday. While King was a national figure, he affirmed that he was at heart a Baptist preacher. The son of a Baptist pastor, King himself was a pastor throughout his public career, first at Dexter Avenue Baptist Church in Montgomery and then with his father at Ebenezer Baptist Church, Atlanta.

For Martin Luther King, Jr. and others the Civil Rights Movement was a spiritual movement of liberation. With African-American churches serving as the base for the movement, the discipline of prayer was central to confronting the demon of racism. Local communities held prayer vigils for racial justice and prayer meetings often preceded marches for freedom.

The protesters in the 1954 Montgomery bus boycott, which King led after Rosa Parks's refusal to give up her bus seat to a white man, were galvanized by the message of the radical love of Jesus as found in the Sermon on the Mount. Members of King's Dexter Avenue Baptist Church (and others) were assured that their dissent for freedom was a demonstration of New Testament faith. As the bus boycott unfolded, the inspiration of Mahatma Gandhi's views on nonviolence also became influential. King later commented, "Christ furnished the spirit and motivation, while Gandhi furnished the method" of nonviolent love. King further admonished civil rights supporters to hate segregation, but not the segregator, for he too was created by God. In his influential "Letter from Birmingham Jail," King wrote that civil disobedience was rooted in the moral law of God. Moral laws were to be followed; laws such as segregation that degrade sacred personhood were not.

For King, the Civil Rights Movement was the embodiment of the social gospel (which he learned through the writings of Baptist Walter Rauschenbusch and ethicist Reinhold Niebuhr). King believed the Civil Rights Movement was a preview of the "beloved community," an integrated society of brotherhood. In the famous 1963 speech in Washington, "I Have a Dream," King captured his desire for a completely integrated society in which everyone was considered equal in the eyes of God and everyone had equal opportunity: "I have a dream that one day on the red hills of Georgia, sons of former slaves and sons of former slaveowners will be able to sit down together at the table of brotherhood."

Besides King, other (though not all) African-American leaders—such as Ralph Abernathy, Jesse Jackson, and John Lewis—involved in the Civil Rights Movement were Baptists. The Southern Christian Leadership Conference (SCLC), which began in 1957, initially had mostly African-American Baptist leaders. While not all Civil Rights workers were religious, the movement in the key city of Birmingham was overwhelmingly Baptist. When the city outlawed the NAACP in 1956, Fred Shuttlesworth responded by forming the Alabama Christian Movement for Human Rights (ACMHR). Ninety-eight percent of the group were church members and eighty-seven percent of those were Baptists (sixty-two percent were women but they usually observed traditional gender roles and raised money through bake sales).

Shuttlesworth, pastor of Bethel Baptist Church, was Birmingham's unquestioned civil rights leader. After the victory of the bus boycott in Montgomery, he announced that the ACHMR would challenge segregation laws in Birmingham. Shuttlesworth's house was bombed, but he survived and his working-class coworkers considered him divinely selected to lead the battle against segregationists. Liberation and equality, he contended, were rooted in a literal reading of a divinely inspired Bible. Birmingham was a modern Babylon which oppressed the poor; white moderates with empty talk about their support of civil rights were "New Testament Pharisees." Shuttlesworth preached in the style of a blistering confrontational biblical prophet. While middle-class African-Americans thought he possessed a "holy arrogance" and questioned his confrontational style, historians consider Shuttlesworth an unsung hero. His invitation to King to come to Birmingham and help fight for integration was a turning point in the Civil Rights Movement.

Women's Leadership

As did white women, African-American women formed local and state women's societies in the 1880s. They also realized that education was a key to "uplift" and responded favorably to educational initiatives offered by Northern Baptists (for example, Atlanta Baptist Female Seminary, now Spelman College). When the new National Baptist Convention was organized, little opportunity for female participation was offered. As a result, a Woman's Convention (WC) was created in 1900 as an auxiliary to the NBCUSA. The "righteous discontent" of the women opposed the inequality they received in the church.

The Woman's Convention provided a place for women to have a public forum about issues of racial and gender discrimination. The women also organized settlement houses, job training centers, and child care facilities, and some supported the suffrage movement. Women had supportive and adversarial relationships with male leaders. Evangelist Virginia Broughton, for example, traveled throughout the South forming women's Bible study groups called "Bible Bands." Her husband demanded to know when she would stop her missionary trips and she retorted, "I belong to God first, and you next, so you two must settle it."

The one woman most responsible for changing the status of women in African-American Baptist life was Nannie Helen Burroughs. She was the founding corresponding secretary and later long-term president (1948–1964) of the Woman's Convention. At the initial meeting of the convention she challenged the status quo with her speech, "How the Sisters are Hindered from Helping." In 1901 the NBCUSA suggested that the women's group become one of its boards. Sarah Willie Layten, the first president of the Woman's Convention, favored the idea, but Burroughs disapproved because it meant that they would come under the control of the men who had previously not been receptive to their participation. The Woman's Convention sided with Burroughs and by 1907 had 1.5 million members.

Before her career in religious work, Burroughs was educated in Washington, D.C., but subsequently was rebuffed at her attempt to teach in the city because she was African-American. In 1909, the Woman's Convention helped Burroughs establish the National Training School for Women and Girls in Washington. As the school's president, Burroughs pushed classical and industrial education (self-sufficient wage earners and "expert homemakers"). Students had daily Bible study and a required course in black history. The curriculum addressed the "three B's: the Bible, the bath, the broom; clean life, clean body, clean house." In this combination of progressive ideas and traditional gender values, Burroughs had adapted the self-help agenda of Booker T. Washington.

Tension with male leaders surfaced occasionally concerning oversight of the training school. In the 1930s, NBCUSA leadership attempted to acquire the school's deed but Burroughs refused and was labeled a "noncooperative officer." In 1964 the school was renamed the Nannie Helen Burroughs School and, in 2006, continued as a private elementary school under the sponsorship of the Progressive National Baptist Convention.

Burroughs also was a pioneer in the work of the NAACP. She was never timid. Regarding Americans who refused to stand up for equality, justice, and human rights, she believed they were "small Hitlers."

Peace Efforts

African-American Baptists were involved in Christian peace efforts. Howard Thurman, an African-American Baptist leader in the peace group, Fellowship of Reconciliation, wrote *Jesus and the Disinherited* (1949). He had influence upon Martin Luther King, Jr., the most visible Baptist pacifist in the latter half of the twentieth century. King preached that the Vietnam War violated Jesus' command to love the enemy and the oppressed of the world. In contrast, the American government's military buildup had plundered the war on poverty. With blunt rhetoric, King concluded, "If America's soul becomes totally poisoned, part of the autopsy must read Vietnam." In subsequent decades, translations of King's sermons circulated in East Germany before the fall of the Berlin Wall (1989).

Charismatic Movement

Pentecostal theology and "megachurches" were increasingly evident in African-American Baptist life at the beginning of the twenty-first century. This was apparent in the ministry of the "multidenominational" Full Gospel Baptist Church Fellowship. Before hurricane Katrina (2005), Greater St. Stephen Baptist Church of New Orleans reported a membership of 18,000. In 1994, the church's pastor, Paul S. Morton, led in the founding of the Full Gospel Baptist Church Fellowship. Its first conference at the Louisiana Superdome in 1994 reportedly attracted 25,000 participants. According to Morton, God instructed him in 1992 to "change a generation" and "bridge the gap" between Baptist and Pentecostal faiths. The Fellowship affirmed charismatic gifts—baptism of the Holy Spirit as a second work of grace and speaking in tongues—and acknowledged the Baptist distinctive of the autonomy of local churches. At the same time, the movement found supporters across the globe. The Fellowship was constructed upon an episcopal hierarchy with Morton the "International Presiding Bishop" and a "Tiers of Leadership" that included a bishop's council, a college of bishops, general, state and district overseers, and in the local church, senior pastors, ministers, elders, and deacons.

One of the "founding bishops" of the Full Gospel Fellowship was Bishop Eddie Long, pastor of the Greater New Life Baptist Church of Atlanta. Long led the church from a membership of 300 in 1987 when he became pastor to more than 25,000 in 2006. In 2001, the church dedicated the New Birth Cathedral, a fifty-million-dollar complex that seated 10,000 for worship. Long developed an international television ministry and acquired the reputation of a "gospel of prosperity" preacher (that is, God wants believers to be rich).

Traditional African-American Baptist denominations noted some membership losses to the "full gospel" megachurches. They objected to their charismatic theology and opposed their strong episcopal structure as threats to Baptist polity. Morton responded to critics with the theme of the Full Gospel Baptist Church Fellowship: "[We are] the movement that gives Baptists the right to choose." In 2006, William Shaw, president of the NBCUSA, criticized the consumer-focused prosperity gospel as "a capitalistic devotion to personal privilege."

Conclusion

African-American Baptist Christianity began in slave cabins and secret worship services amidst the oppression of whites who proclaimed faith in Jesus. Black preachers, from the days of slavery to the turn of the twenty-first century, held places of honor and prestige in the African-American community. They were religious/social/political spokespersons. An influential politician, for example, was often introduced with his ecclesiastical title, the "Reverend" Jesse Jackson.

The search for the New Testament church among African-American Baptists emphasized the same Baptist distinctives as whites. African-Americans who adopted believer's baptism by immersion also wanted to model a biblical faith. As the leadership of E. C. Morris revealed, however, identification with the New Testament church brought a sense of dignity and identity usually not given to them by fellow white Christians.

For a people historically oppressed in *the* land of freedom, the search for genuine religious faith had to battle the racial demons of Jim Crow laws and discrimination. African-American Christians asserted that the American dream of freedom was not incompatible with New Testament faith. While not all civil-rights leaders rooted their work in religious values, Martin Luther King, Jr. and Fred Shuttesworth, among others, preached that civil rights and human dignity were rooted in the equality found in the teachings of Christ. Decades earlier, staring oppression in the eyes, Peter Randolph opined that Jesus' "golden rule" was the cornerstone for any genuine progress in America. African-American Baptist life, naturally then, talked less about being *the* New Testament church, and more about how biblical faith involved the political and social struggle for freedom. Anything less was "pharisaical."

Chapter 10

Baptists: An International Movement

Introduction

Baptists are a worldwide movement. Baptists began in England, expanded into America, and later into Europe. Eventually missions extended the Baptist witness to every continent on the globe. Diversity in Baptist life is ever present on the international scene; at the same time, most Baptists have united for fellowship in a Baptist World Alliance. International Baptists have generally had smaller organizations than Baptists in America, yet many of them have survived even in the midst of persecution from established state churches.

Baptists in England

After their formative years in the seventeenth century, English Baptists entered into a period of stagnation despite the passage of the English "Act of Toleration" in 1689. (The full title is instructive: "An Act for Exempting Their Majestyes Protestant Subjects Dissenting from the Church of England from the Penalties of Certaine Lawes.") Religious indifference that accompanied the "age of reason" was one factor for the decline. Historians have suggested that the General Baptists were hindered by a backward-looking sectarianism that argued over the legitimacy of hymn singing and excommunicated church members if they married persons who were not General Baptist.

Eighteenth Century. The drift toward Unitarianism affected several religious groups in England and was the primary reason for decline among the General Baptists. Reflecting the shift away from belief in the supernatural during the "age of reason," Matthew Caffyn, a General Baptist messenger, spread an Arian view of Christ, that is, that Jesus was not fully divine. In 1686, the national General Assembly attempted to avoid a schism and urged unity around the six principles of Hebrews 6:1-2. However, this approach sidestepped the issue of the divinity of Christ. Churches in the Midlands withdrew from the General Assembly because of the toleration of heresy. Further attempts at reconciliation failed; the willingness to maintain fellowship with persons who advocated unitarian ideas resulted in decline among the General Baptists in the eighteenth century. The number of churches decreased from 146 in 1715 to sixty-five in 1750.

The Particular Baptists also struggled with stagnation in the eighteenth century. While they were more numerous than the General Baptists, the decline was significant: 220 Particular Baptist churches existed in 1715 but only 146 by 1750. Whereas General Baptists were prone to excessive centralization, Particular Baptists were extremely reluctant to organize nationally. They did not hold a national assembly from 1689 to 1812. Hymn singing caused some consternation among Particular Baptists, but the real reason for decline was the growth of a strict Calvinism, which had little if any focus on evangelism.

John Skepp and John Brine were early advocates of strict Calvinism but John Gill was its most prominent spokesperson. Gill was the pastor of the Horsleydown church in Southwark, London for more than fifty years. His writings totaled more than 10,000 pages, and he was the first Baptist to write a verse-by-verse commentary on the entire Bible. Gill's most influential work was *The Body of Divinity* (1769). To counter the rationalism of the "age of reason," Gill spoke of a "heart," experiential religion, "a fire that burns in love of Christ." The church should focus on worship of God. At the same time, Gill's preaching style was scholarly and void of emotion.

Gill and other strict Calvinists affirmed the limited atonement—Christ died only for the elect—and affirmed that the elect had been chosen before the fall of Adam and Eve without any regard for human merit ("Supralapsarianism"). Gill affirmed a double predestination: some were elected to salvation and some were elected to damnation. Consequently, to invite sinners to accept salvation or to preach repentance and forgiveness to unconverted sinners implied the heretical Arminian idea that Christ died for all persons. Gill thus focused his preaching on exposition of doctrine for the elect.

Gill's writings were often the only theology that some Baptist ministers read. He was influential in England and America. An abridged edition of his multivolume work, *The Body of Divinity*, was edited and promoted by William Staughton, the prominent colonial pastor of Philadelphia (*Gill's Complete Body of Practical and Doctrinal Divinity*, 1810). Gill had strong opponents, however. His contemporary, Robert Hall, said that Gill's writings were so dense that they read like a "continent of mud." Josephy Ivimey, an English Baptist historian, asserted that Gill needed to learn what Peter and Paul really said about Christ. At the same time, some modern historians question whether Gill was totally against "sharing the gospel" as the phrase "hyper-Calvinism" suggests.

During the latter half of the eighteenth century renewal occurred among both General and Particular Baptists. The evangelical revival of Methodist founder, John Wesley, had caught fire in England in the 1730s. Baptists did not participate directly given Wesley's Arminian theology and acceptance of infant baptism. Converts of the Wesleyan revival, however, influenced the Baptist movement.

Dan Taylor led the most significant renewal movement among General Baptists. A convert at the age of nineteen (1757), he concluded that infant baptism was not biblical. Taylor and his independent Methodist followers requested baptism from some neighboring Particular Baptists, but were rebuffed because of their Arminian theology. Taylor's group found a General Baptist church to baptize them; consequently, they became a General Baptist congregation and joined the Lincolnshire Baptist Association. Confronted by what he felt was a heretical view of the divinity of Christ, Taylor recruited other like-minded Baptists and in 1770 formed the "New Connection of General Baptists." Taylor's goal was to restore New Testament Christianity: "to revive experimental religion or primitive Christianity in faith and practice."

Churches in the New Connection insisted upon believer's baptism by immersion for membership (many General Baptists were practicing open membership) and ministers initially were required to sign a confession and to affirm a personal conversion experience. Congregations—including women!—sang hymns and appealed to the working classes. Churches were established in the towns most affected by the developing "industrial revolution." Taylor led the annual meeting of the New Connection for forty-five of forty-six years. He even attended the older General Assembly of the General Baptists, but withdrew in 1803 after it accepted a professing Unitarian. The older General Baptists ultimately became Unitarian.

Particular Baptists moved beyond the strict Calvinism of John Gill in the latter half of the eighteenth century. In 1781, Robert Hall, Sr. published *Help to Zion's Travellers*—an expanded version of a sermon he preached at the annual meeting of the Northampton Baptist Association two years earlier—which encouraged "experimental" religion for all hearers. English historian Joseph Ivimey called the sermon the dawning of a new era in the history of English Baptists. The most influential critic of strict Calvinism was Andrew Fuller, pastor at Kettering (1782–1815). Fuller's 1785 book, *The Gospel Worthy of All Acceptation*, developed an "evangelical Calvinism" that eventually provided the theological foundation for the Baptist missions movement. Fuller opined that if strict Calvinism continued to reign, the Baptist movement would become "a perfect dunghill in society."

"Fullerism," as Fuller's theology came to be called, said that "faith in Christ is the duty of all who hear." Fuller was still a Calvinist; he believed in a limited atonement and that God chose the elect regardless of human merit. However, it was the biblical duty of believers to share the gospel with unbelievers. Only God knew the elect, and ministers must preach as if all had the possibility of accepting Christ. Preaching that invited listeners to repent was God's method of saving the elect. Unlike Gill, Fuller believed that the primary function of the church was evangelism. While doctrine was not unimportant, an exclusive focus on it unfortunately had made the *definition* of faith the essence of faith.

Like the American revivalist Jonathan Edwards, whose writings influenced Fuller and others in the Northampton Association to distance themselves from strict Calvinism, Fuller spoke of the moral capacity to respond to the gospel. When critics charged that evangelical Calvinists were Arminian, Fuller strongly denied it. However, his preaching moved in that direction. While some Baptists continued to read John Gill, "evangelical Calvinism" won the day. Fuller's writings were also influential with American Baptists and they helped usher in the mission movement of William Carey.

Nineteenth Century. The nineteenth century has been called the "Great Century" in missions. In addition to the atmosphere of the evangelical awakening, travel and communication were easier than ever. It was a period of colonial expansion: a *pax brittanica* with the strength of the British Empire. Denominational and interdenominational missionary societies became plentiful.

While Moravians and the African-American Baptist George Liele engaged in foreign missions before William Carey, the English Baptist, Carey, is known as the "father" of modern missions. Carey was influenced by the emergence of "evangelical" Calvinism among some Particular Baptists and became convinced that the New Testament required Christians to practice the "Great Commission" (to take the gospel to the uttermost parts of the world, Matthew 28:18-20). Carey also was influenced by the adventurous culture of his day. He read and reread about the South Sea adventures of the famous Captain Cook and placed a map of the world on the wall of his home.

Carey called himself a plodder; indeed, the beginning of his ministerial career was inauspicious. After being baptized, he began to preach occasionally. He was encouraged by a seasoned minister to be ordained, but after preaching a "trial" sermon, the church declined to ordain him. Eventually Carey became pastor at Moulton while he continued as a village shoemaker.

In 1787, Carey asked the Northampton Association to discuss foreign missions, but he was rebuked by the respected senior minister, John Ryland, Sr. who said, "Sit down, young man. You are an enthusiast! When God pleases to convert the heathen, He will do it without consulting you or me." Then in 1792, Carey published his plea for international missions, *An Enquiry into the Obligations of Christians to Use Means for the Conversion of the Heathen*. He noted that seventy percent of the known world population was non-Christian. If baptism concerned Baptists, Carey implored, world missions should likewise. Why else baptize?

At a meeting of the Northampton Association in 1792, Carey preached his famous missionary sermon, "Expect Great Things from God; Attempt Great Things for God" (Isaiah 54:2). When no specific action appeared imminent, Carey tugged at the coat of Andrew Fuller, the presiding officer, and begged, "Oh, sir, is nothing to be done? Is nothing again to be done?" Consequently, Fuller, who was known to support the need for missions, and other evangelical Calvinists formed the Baptist Missionary Society (BMS). Fuller was elected secretary of the BMS and became its primary fund-raiser. The offering taken at this first meeting was spontaneous and placed in Fuller's snuff box, which ironically was adorned with a picture of St. Paul's conversion experience.

In 1793, William Carey and John Thomas were appointed as missionaries to India. The great things that were expected did not come quickly. It took seven years before two Indians were converted to Christianity. Poverty, illness, and potential death hounded missionaries. The culture of martyrdom that surrounded pioneering missionaries was embodied in the story of Carey's wife, Dorothy.

Dorothy Carey initially refused to go to India. Her family had been tied for five generations to their small village life and she was expecting a fourth child. When William's trip was delayed, she consented to go to keep her family intact. Her sister agreed to make the trip as well. In India, Dorothy never adjusted. Her sister married and moved away. Peter, a five-year-old son, died of dysentery. With William absent for long periods because of missionary trips, Dorothy battled depression and ultimately went insane. She lived her last thirteen years (d. 1807) in a small padded room, sometimes interrupting the night silence of the missionary compound which the Careys called home with moaning and shrieking. William often translated Scriptures by candlelight outside of her room.

As the "father" of modern missions, Carey's contributions were immense. In 1800, Carey and two other missionaries began the Serampore Mission. During his forty-one-year missionary career, Carey's methods included a focus on learning the native culture, establishing native churches and training an indigenous ministry. Carey emphasized putting the Bible in the vernacular: he translated the Bible into six languages and portions of it into twenty-nine others. He helped to found Serampore College, the first Christian college in Asia. He also called for an ecumenical approach, challenging world missionaries to unite for annual conferences. Carey also took interest in transforming Indian culture. He worked, for example, to eradicate the practices of infant sacrificing and widow burning.

Carey's work clearly influenced others to be involved in missions. In 1795, the interdenominational London Missionary Society—which sent the first Protestant missionary to China—was formed. The British Baptist Missionary Society became a significant contributor to global mission efforts. Carey's work also influenced American Baptist leaders who in 1814 formed the Triennial Convention in support of international missions.

Significant events in English Baptist life in the nineteenth century included a move toward denominational centralization similar to the American story. Particular Baptists began discussing organization in 1812, and in 1832 the national organization became complete and took the name "Baptist Union." In 1891, several Particular Baptist and New Connection General Baptist associations joined to form the present "Baptist Union of Great Britain (and Ireland)." Open and closed communion were acceptable; Calvinistic emphases had been modified.

Despite the centralization of Baptist life, some Baptists, including a smaller group of Calvinistic Strict and Particular Baptists, remained separate. These Calvinists, who today are sometimes called (Sovereign) Grace Baptists, clearly preferred John Gill to Andrew Fuller. Some were evangelistic but others refused to offer invitations of salvation to sinners. Gospel primitivism was apparent in the practice of closed/strict communion and the refusal to call ministers "reverend." Some denied that Baptists were Protestants, that is, Baptist teachings were traceable back to the New Testament church, long predating the so-called Protestant Reformation.

The most-famous English Baptist preacher of the late-nineteenth century was Charles Haddon Spurgeon. Converted as a teenager in a

Methodist meeting, Spurgeon soon became a Baptist after he affirmed believer's baptism as scriptural baptism. In 1853, the "boy preacher" was called to pastor the historic church at Southwark, London, which had earlier been home to John Gill. When Spurgeon assumed the pastorate, the congregation had eighty people in a 1,200-seat auditorium. Practically an "overnight hit," Spurgeon's church overflowed and he soon commanded crowds of 10,000 in London. In 1861, the 5,500-seat Metropolitan Tabernacle—later named the Spurgeon Tabernacle—was built.

Spurgeon was a prolific writer—more than 200 books—and was known for his philanthropy. He helped the poor with housing needs and founded two orphanages. He was best known as an evangelist, however, who believed that saved individuals rather than social activism was the key to helping society. Around 3,800 of his sermons, which used simple language for the common people and down-to-earth illustrations, were published and read widely even in America. He was a Calvinist, but his evangelism functioned otherwise: "I fear that I am not a very good Calvinist because I pray that the Lord will save all of the elect and then elect some more."

Spurgeon was not always popular, however. In 1864, he angered Anglicans when he said that "baptismal regeneration" had led millions to hell. On one occasion, the Anglican William Wilberforce retorted that he did not envy the humor or success of Spurgeon with the comment, "Thou shalt not covet thy neighbor's ass."

Similar to the story of the fundamentalists and modernists in America, Baptists in late-nineteenth-century England were involved in a conflict over new currents in theological study. Spurgeon was at the heart of the conflict, which was dubbed the "Downgrade Controversy." In the spring of 1887, two unsigned articles (attributed primarily to Robert Shindler, Spurgeon's close associate and biographer, with input from Spurgeon) appeared in Spurgeon's journal, *The Sword and the Trowel*, and contended that the "downgrade" of religion in eighteenth century England was the result of a neglect of Calvinism. The articles implied the same would happen in their day: "Earnest attention is requested for this paper. . . . We are going downhill [*downgrade*] at breakneck speed. . . . [Denominations often] got on the downgrade [when they abandoned Calvinism]."

In August 1887, Spurgeon added his lament. He wrote that theological error and worldliness of the clergy among Congregationalists and Baptists were crushing the faith. While he affirmed biblical inerrancy, Spurgeon focused his subsequent attacks upon the lack of sound doctrine. He asserted that the Baptist Union included pastors who denied the divinity of Christ, the inspiration of Scripture, and other heresies with their modern biblical-critical methods. According to Spurgeon, "A new religion has been initiated, which is no more Christianity than chalk is cheese." Spurgeon wanted the denomination to adopt a conservative confession—its only doctrinal test was believer's baptism by immersion. To Spurgeon's dismay, the leadership of the Baptist Union reacted negatively to his criticisms. They demanded that Spurgeon name the names of the alleged heretics, but he refused.

John Clifford, the leader of the Baptist Union, represented an alternative vision to Spurgeon. Clifford emphasized social reform and ecumenical cooperation. He affirmed open membership as a key to fellowship of the universal church. He advocated biblical authority as opposed to biblical inerrancy. He placed more trust in religious experience than assent to written statements. Consequently, Clifford was against creeds and rebuffed Spurgeon's efforts to require doctrinal conformity. Efforts at reconciliation failed and Spurgeon left the Baptist Union in October 1887. Very few churches left the union to follow Spurgeon and he remained bitter until his death. Depending on the source, the Spurgeon legacy was evangelism, coercive conformity, or both.

A third prominent English Baptist at the end of the century reflected the influence of evangelical renewal movements outside the Baptist family. F. B. Meyer, a pastor in London, was internationally known for his ministry in the "holiness movement." He was influenced by and worked with Dwight L. Moody, the famous American evangelist, in England and America. As an adherent of "Keswick holiness" (named for the annual "Keswick Convention" where it was first developed about 1875), Meyer preached that believers could experience an "enduement" of the power of the Holy Spirit for Christian living. In Baptist life, Meyer helped initiate a "prayer union" of Baptist ministers and participated in the Baptist Forward Movement which performed social ministry to the poor, and helped create the office of deaconesses which assisted women in need. Scholars suggest that after Anglicans, Baptists were the most receptive to Keswick teachings.

Throughout his ministry, Meyer affirmed Baptist distinctives. When the Downgrade Controversy raged, he opposed Spurgeon's call for a creed since the New Testament advocated unity through holy Christian living rather than forced doctrinal statements. He helped to mediate the conflict. As his ministry extended in the twentieth century, Meyer's leadership roles were found more in nondenominational venues. In that regard, he foreshadowed the de-emphasis upon denominational identity that has become a part of the contemporary Baptist story.

In the eighteenth and nineteenth centuries, English Baptist women ministered more through the written word rather than through positions of church leadership. Some women shared the gospel by penning deathbed testimonies. At the same time, these testimonies often pictured the ideal woman as the virtuous homemaker. As the Sunday school developed in the late-nineteenth century, women found a place to teach and embody spiritual concerns.

Writers of spirituality have renewed interest in Anne Dutton. A writer of hymns and doctrinal tracts (for example, *A Discourse upon Walking with God*, 1735), Dutton also carried on extensive correspondence with the evangelical leaders of her day like George Whitefield (whom she supported) and John Wesley (she disliked his Arminianism). Some analysts of the past called Dutton a religious fanatic; some now see her more as an "ordinary mystic" who acted as a spiritual director through her writings. Reminiscent of medieval mystics, Dutton spoke of experiencing union with God. As a "Baptist mystic," the Holy Spirit led her to commune with Christ the "beloved," the Christian's "spouse," through Scripture.

As in America, English Baptist women supported mission endeavors. The Baptist Missionary Society, however, would only ordain men and would not commission single women for service. In 1867, a significant work developed in India, later called The Baptist Zenana Mission (1897). Women were appointed as missionaries to work with women in zenanas— the high-caste Hindu dwellings that did not allow the company of men outside the family. In these missions, women worked as doctors and teachers and biblical translators. When the mission merged with the Baptist Missionary Society in 1914, some of the autonomy that women experienced was lost as male leadership took over.

Twentieth Century. In the early twentieth century, English Baptists, like their American counterparts, focused on being an "efficient" church in terms of organizational business methods. Still, like other religious groups in Britain, Baptists became smaller in size. In 1921, the Baptist Union had 3,068 churches with a total membership of 442,000. In 1981, the figures had dropped to 2,058 churches and 170,000 church members. By 2006, The Baptist Union of Great Britain reported 2,150 churches and 150,000 members. Some analysts blamed the lack of doctrinal focus for the Baptist decline. Others noted that Baptists emphasized open membership and were leaders in the ecumenical movement. Others cited the increased secularization of Great Britain.

English Baptists of the twentieth century reflected the increasing diversity of Baptist identities. Many, especially denominational leaders, were involved extensively in ecumenical endeavors. They were key players in the founding of the Baptist World Alliance (1905) and the European Baptist Federation (1948). In 1919, John Howard Shakespeare helped form the Federal Council of Evangelical Free Churches. Shakespeare also worked to have dissenting churches reunite with the Church of England; however, most Baptists maintained a commitment to local church independence and refused to accept the idea of episcopal leadership. Many other English Baptists, including Ernest Payne, the general secretary of the Baptist Union from 1951 to 1967, were strongly ecumenical. Payne served as a leader in the World Council of Churches.

Support for women in ministry developed extensively during the twentieth century. In 1894, a Mrs. Stockford was the first woman delegate to the Baptist Union. In 1890, the Deaconess Order was created, which focused on social ministry; by 1919 the Baptist Union approved the order. By World War II, women were serving churches in pastoral ministries. In 1979, the office of deaconess was dissolved so that the women then serving could be ordained. Finally, in 1998, Patricia Took of London was named the first woman superintendent in the history of the Baptist Union.

In the 1950s, a renewed interest in Reformed theology developed in England. In this environment, Reformed Baptist churches arose which were more evangelistic and more willing to practice open communion than their doctrinal cousins, the Strict and Particular Baptists. Reformed Baptists also used elders whereas Strict Baptists preferred congregational polity. While both groups believed that their church order followed the divine pattern of the New Testament church, the two Calvinistic groups never united.

Fundamentalism never raged in English Baptist life as it did in America. Still, some Baptists declared their allegiance to fundamentalism. One fundamentalist home was the historic church of Charles Spurgeon, the Metropolitan Tabernacle. The current (2008) Tabernacle pastor, Peter Masters, for example, is an independent Reformed Baptist. After Masters became the church's leader in 1970, the congregation withdrew from the Baptist Union. In 1975, Masters created the London Reformed Baptist Seminary. In 1995, Masters published a thirty-page essay in *The Sword and the Trowel* entitled "Are We Fundamentalists?" The answer was Yes. According to Masters, the essentials of fundamentalism included *exclusiv-*

ism (Jesus is the only way to salvation); *biblicism* (belief in biblical inerrancy); *creationism* (acceptance of a literal six-day creation); *believism* (only use New Testament methods of proclamation); *evangelism*; and *separatism* (separation from the world and from false doctrine). So-called "Evangelicals," according to Masters, do not hold to this "authentic biblical Christianity."

English Baptists were influenced by the Pentecostal/charismatic movements that impacted the broader evangelical world. Many English Baptists opposed Pentecostalism, but some fertile ground was cultivated. In 1915, for example, Donald Gee, later a prominent international spokesperson for Pentecostalism, was first exposed to Pentecostal beliefs at Duckett Road Baptist Church of London. When the church's pastor, Albert Saxby, was encouraged to limit Pentecostal expressions of worship, he resigned and Gee, one of the church's musicians, also left and joined a Pentecostal church.

The charismatic movement of the 1960s and 1970s also impacted some English Baptists. While some charismatic believers remained in churches affiliated with the Baptist Union, others became independent. In the 1970s, a "house church" movement called "Restorationism" attracted some English Baptists. Adherents affirmed the imminent Second Coming of Christ and submitted to the spiritual direction of "shepherds." Critics cautioned that the movement was dictatorial. At the turn of the twenty-first century, the interdenominational Spring Harvest Movement helped popularize contemporary Christian music in Baptist and other churches. The movement, which began in 1979, drew more than 50,000 to an annual Easter conference, the largest Christian conference in Europe.

In the midst of an increasing pluralism at the turn of the twenty-first century, English Baptists exhibited diverse theological perspectives. Some maintained a symbolic view of the Lord's Supper, but increased attention to a more sacramental view was evident. For example, Baptist theologian H. Wheeler Robinson argued for a relationship between baptism and the reception of the Holy Spirit. Open-membership policies—not requiring believer's baptism—increased. Reminiscent of early Puritan Separatists, English Baptist theologians concentrated on the meaning of the church as a covenant community. Some analysts described English Baptists as either "sacramental" or "evangelical," but at least a few people could be described as both.

At the end of the twentieth century, The Baptist Union of Great Britain had no formal confession or creed. Baptist distinctives, including the authority of the Bible, priesthood of all believers, religious freedom, believer's baptism by immersion, believer's church, and evangelism were affirmed. Each church "has liberty, under the guidance of the Holy Spirit, to interpret and administer His laws." With the increasing secularization and pluralism of England, accompanied by the declining influence of the Church of England, seventeenth-century-type-dissenter calls for religious freedom diminished in frequency.

Conclusion. For many English Baptists at the turn of the twenty-first century, with the focus on ecumenism, the search for New Testament Christianity appeared diminished or even absent. Still, ecumenical faith was an attempt to reconnect with a common faith of the universal church. Emphasis on the biblical language of "covenant" was rising. As in America, restorationist Pentecostal streams at last were making some significant impact in Baptist waters. Charismatic Baptists were a part of the restoration of New Testament spirituality. Smaller groups like the Strict and Particular Baptists remained faithful to their primitivist reading of the New Testament.

The Baptist Movement in Europe

During the seventeenth and eighteenth centuries, the Baptist movement was Anglo-centric and concentrated in Britain and its colonies. International expansion began with the modern mission movement of Englishman William Carey. While Baptists first appeared in France in the 1820s, the European Baptist movement grew out of Germany in the 1830s. English Baptists developed in the context of English Puritan-Separatism; the context for European Baptists was German Pietism—an eighteenth-century evangelical movement that focused on personal heartfelt religion, small groups, and devotional Bible reading. Due to persecution during the Reformation era, many Anabaptists had settled in Europe, and consequently European Baptists have felt a close identification with Anabaptists. Mennonites were more prone to join Baptist churches in Europe, and Mennonite "converts" were especially numerous in the early Russian Baptist movement. Nevertheless, historians do not find a direct historical link between European Baptists and Anabaptists. Government authorities throughout the nineteenth century, however, equated Baptists with the much-maligned Anabaptists. The relentless intense persecution that accompanied dissenter religion, especially in Eastern European nations with totalitarian governments, sometimes brought dissenters together across denominational lines. Governments as well often lumped dissenters together for purposes of controlling religion.

The story of European Baptist life revolves around the ministry of Johann Gerhard Oncken. Known as the "father of German and Continental Baptists" Oncken is considered the fountainhead of all Baptist activity in Germany, Sweden, Denmark, Austria, Hungary, and Romania, and his influence played a significant role in countries such as Russia, Switzerland, and Yugoslavia. Even South African Baptists felt his shadow.

Johann Gerhard Oncken. German native Johann Gerhard Oncken was baptized into the state-supported Lutheran Church. However, he grew up in a British environment which prepared him for his pioneering work in missions. After working nine years with a Scottish merchant, Oncken claimed a conversion experience in an evangelical "independent" church in London. He served as a missionary with the British Continental Society and as an agent for the Edinburgh Bible Society. He became intensely devoted to the task of distributing religious tracts. At the age of twenty-three (1823), Oncken settled in Hamburg, Germany, continued his evangelistic-tract ministry, and aligned with the English Reformed Church. He also began drawing crowds to his preaching at "house church" meetings which were in turn shut down by the government.

Oncken's turn to Baptist life came in stages. He first expressed doubts about infant baptism in 1826 and turned down support to undertake theological studies to become a Lutheran minister. Much like other missionaries before him (Luther Rice, Adoniram Judson), when Oncken rejected the validity of infant baptism, he claimed that his decision was based on his reading of the New Testament. He contacted the Scottish evangelist, Robert Haldane, and asked him to administer believer's baptism. However, Haldane suggested that Oncken, in the manner of Baptist pioneer John Smyth, baptize himself. Oncken believed Haldane's advice was unbiblical and rejected it. He decided to wait for a "Philip" (Acts 8:38) to provide him with scriptural baptism.

American Baptists helped to solve Oncken's crisis of religious identity. Oncken shared his story with a sea captain who reported it to the American Baptist Missionary Society of Boston. On a study trip to Germany in 1833, Barnas Sears, a Baptist pastor in Hartford, Connecticut, met with Oncken. With Oncken about to travel to Poland, no decision about baptism was made. The following year, on 22 April 1834, Oncken and six others—his wife included—were baptized by Sears secretly at night in the Elbe River in order to avoid local authorities. The next day the first German Baptist Church was founded with Oncken as its pastor. Believer's baptism was needed, they believed, to organize a church on the "primitive model" of the

New Testament. They also adopted articles of faith and a covenant. Despite his extensive missionary travels, Oncken remained pastor in Hamburg for most of his career.

Oncken's missionary philosophy was summed up in his motto: *Jeder Baptist ein Missionar* ("Every Baptist a missionary"). A church that rallied around this commitment, instead of leaving ministry to ministers and deacons, was "almost infallible." A united congregation was a genuine model of the New Testament church. J. R. Graves, father of Landmarkism, believed that Oncken's commitment to the Baptist church as the New Testament church was so great that he called the German leader a "Landmarker."

A Triumvirate of Early Leaders. From 1834 to 1884 Oncken was an appointed missionary of Northern (American) Baptists. He spoke English very well and this allowed him to develop contacts in America and Britain. His extensive missionary travels spanned Europe and beyond (for example, Russia). He preached, helped organize churches, emphasized personal evangelism and continued his distribution of religious tracts. He often took tracts and Bibles to ships so that the Christian message might spread. The expansion of German Baptist work was also due to the work of two of Oncken's colleagues, Julius Johannes Wilhelm Köbner and Gottfried Wilhelm Lehmann. The trio was referred to as the *Kleeblatt* ("clover leaf").

Julius Köbner, the son of a Jewish rabbi, became a Christian before meeting Oncken. After hearing Oncken preach, however, Köbner experienced a more profound sense of salvation. Oncken baptized him in 1836. On a mission visit to Copenhagen, Oncken and Köbner baptized eleven converts, and in 1839 this group formed a Baptist church, the first in Denmark or in any part of Scandinavia, where much later Köbner served as pastor (1865–1879). Köbner compiled the first hymnbook for Danish Baptists, including many hymn lyrics he had written himself.

Before Oncken's adoption of Baptist beliefs, Gottfried Lehmann was also involved in a religious tract ministry. The friendship they had, however, became estranged by Oncken's defection to the Baptists. After studying the New Testament on the issue of baptism, Lehmann invited Oncken to Berlin with the intention of defending infant baptism. Lehmann was overwhelmed by Oncken's rhetorical skill and lucid explication of believer's baptism. On 13 May 1837, Lehmann, his wife, and four others were baptized. On the next day the first Baptist church in Berlin was founded with Lehmann as its pastor.

Germany. From the outset, Oncken and his church at Hamburg were victims of persecution. False rumors about secretive nighttime baptisms prompted Oncken to baptize during daylight hours. Increased scrutiny and harassment resulted. On various occasions, state-supported clergy successfully had Baptist meetings stopped. In a now legendary confrontation, the police chief from Hamburg bellowed, "Oncken, as long as I can lift my little finger I will put you down from preaching this Gospel." Oncken replied, "Mr. Burgomaster, as long as I can see God's mighty hand above your little finger, I will preach this Gospel."

In an 1840 conflict, Oncken and two colleagues were arrested. He was in prison for a month and his property was seized and auctioned by the state to pay for the court proceedings. Some Baptist meetings were subject to mob violence and even forced christenings where Baptist children were given infant baptisms against their parents' wishes. Persecution against the Baptists began to wane after they earned trust for their charitable work in the aftermath of the "Great Fire of Hamburg" in 1842 that displaced thousands of residents. Despite almost two decades of persecution, by 1848 German Baptists had increased to twenty-six churches with about 1,500 members. The "Revolution of 1848" finally brought religious toleration to German Baptists and other dissenting Christian bodies outside the state Lutheran church.

Like English and American Baptists, German Baptists organized beyond the local church for cooperative work. In 1849, fifty-six representatives convened the first European Baptist confederation called the "Union of the Associated Churches of Baptized Christians in Germany and Denmark." The Union was modeled after the American Triennial Convention and met every three years. A confession of faith, originally written by Oncken and Köbner in 1837, was adopted. The confession revealed dependence upon the English Second London Confession (it is still followed). In this earliest declaration, a moderate Calvinism and closed communion were advocated. The church was called to be the New Testament church (to imitate the apostolic model) and religious liberty was affirmed in the demand that a believer's conscience was subject only to Christ.

Having experienced persecution, early German Baptists were staunch advocates of religious liberty. In 1848, shortly after publication of Marx and Engels's *Manifesto of the Communist Party*, Julius Köbner wrote his *Manifest des freien Urchristenthums an das deutsche Volk* (*Manifesto of Free Primitive Christianity of the German People*), a strong declaration for full religious freedom. He detailed past abuses of "persecuting and inquisitory" state churches and told of the mistreatment of dissenters who had converted to "real Christianity" (this language reflected the German pietism of Johann Arndt). Köbner cited Roger Williams and declared—most likely drawing on the most radical words in *The Mistery of Iniquity* by the early English Baptist Thomas Helwys—that religious freedom must be for every person, "whether they be Christians, Jews, Mohammedans, or whatever." Calling himself "the apostolically minded Christian," Köbner proof-texted the New Testament (for example, "My Kingdom is not of this world," John 18:36) to argue for the separation of church and state.

In the 1850s, changing tides in the German government brought more persecution to the Baptists. Some German Baptists immigrated to the United States. Religious toleration finally prevailed, however, and German Baptists continued to grow. By Oncken's death in 1884, Germany had 150 Baptist churches with more than 31,000 members. The Hamburg Baptist Seminary, which Oncken permanently opened in 1880, became the training ground for the spread of the Baptist witness and his influence throughout Europe.

In the twentieth century, German Baptist history is often told through the lenses of international conflict. Many observers felt that German Baptists were "used" by Nazi propaganda when the Baptist World Alliance was held in Berlin in 1934. As World War II wreaked havoc on Germany, German Baptists, as did all Germans, felt the devastation. In the postwar era of Communism, Baptists were necessarily split into East German and West German Baptists. German Baptists reunited, however, when the reunification of East and West Germany was achieved in the 1990s.

Throughout the twentieth century, German Baptists developed cooperative relationships with other smaller groups. In 1942, they joined (under government pressure) with the Plymouth Brethren and Pentecostals in the Union of Evangelical Free Church Congregations. While the Pentecostals (and some Plymouth Brethren) later left the union, Pentecostal practices also influenced some German Baptists in the twentieth century. After World War II and the greater frequency of ecumenical activity, German Baptists shifted from closed to open communion. In 1992, German Baptists decided that each congregation should decide whether they affirmed women in the pastorate. At the turn of the twenty-first century, German Baptists totaled about 115,000 and participated in the Baptist World Alliance.

Sweden. Baptist growth in Sweden was closely connected to the evangelistic efforts of Johann Oncken and German Baptists. In 1845, Gustavus Wilhelm Schroeder, a mariner who had adopted the Baptist faith in America two years earlier, went to Sweden and met another mariner/missionary, Frederick Olaus Nilsson. Schroeder challenged Nilsson about the New Testament's view of baptism; consequently, Nilsson sought an answer, went to Hamburg, and in 1847 was baptized by Johann Oncken. Upon his return to Sweden, Nilsson organized the first Baptist church of Sweden (1848) at Frillesas near Gothenburg. He declared that a New Testament church had been born since "Baptist principles are the only Apostolic, the only true ones." Subsequently, Nilsson was banished by government authorities and became a pastor in Copenhagen for two years (1851–1853). After a seven-year ministry in America, Nilsson was able to return to Sweden.

During Nilsson's absence, Andreas Wiberg emerged as another Swedish Baptist leader. He began a journey toward a Baptist identity after meeting Oncken and Julius Köbner. A pamphlet that Köbner gave Wiberg was evidently influential in his decision to become a Baptist. After affirming that believer's baptism was mandated by the New Testament, Wiberg visited the exiled Nilsson in Copenhagen and was baptized. After a three-year ministry in America, Wiberg returned to become pastor of the Baptist church in Stockholm. He became the most influential leader of Swedish Baptists—he published the first defense of believer's baptism in Swedish—and helped form the General Conference of Baptists (1857). His writings also resulted in the adoption of a Baptist identity by some Finns. Subsequently, Wiberg led Swedish Baptists to work closely with American (Northern) Baptists.

Similar to the story of other European Baptists, Swedish Baptists often suffered religious persecution from the state-supported Lutheran church and pleaded for religious liberty. Religious freedom for dissenters, despite earlier laws granting toleration, finally became a reality by the middle of the twentieth century.

The Swedish Baptist story illustrated the occasional challenge that Pentecostal beliefs posed to Baptists abroad. Lewi Pethrus, the leading international Pentecostal from Sweden, was baptized into a Baptist church at the age of fifteen. He later served as an evangelist and as pastor of the Baptist church in Lidkoping (1906–1911) and at the Filadelfia Church of Stockholm (1911–1913). When Pentecostalism burst onto the global scene in the first decade of the new century, Pethrus and his Stockholm church joined the movement. In 1913, Swedish Baptists expelled the church and cited its lax open-communion policy. Key to the excommunication was the church's affirmation of Pentecostal practices. For decades, Pethrus's congregation was the largest Pentecostal church in the world.

The "Örebro Movement," led by John Ongman, also revealed the tension with holiness and Pentecostal beliefs in international Baptist life. Ongman grew up in Sweden, became Baptist at the age of nineteen, and was baptized in a hole cut out of a frozen lake (1864). After spending some time as pastor of Swedish Baptist churches in the United States (St. Paul and Chicago), he returned to Sweden and became pastor at Örebro. In 1897, he started a new church, the Filadelfia Baptist Assembly. In 1900, he wrote *Kvinnans rätt att förkunna evangelium* (*Women's Right to Preach the Gospel*), a book consistent with Holiness teachings, which promoted views of women's leadership but was too progressive for most Baptists. As the Pentecostal movement spread to Sweden during the first decade of the new century, Ongman affirmed the Pentecostal understanding of the "gifts of the Holy Spirit." Tensions with Pentecostal ideas finally led the Filadelfia Church of Örebro to leave the national union of Swedish Baptists in 1936 and become independent. At the turn of the twenty-first century, the Örebro Mission and the Baptist Union of Sweden remained separate. The Örebro Mission did not participate in the Baptist World Alliance.

The story of Swedish Baptists also revealed how some immigrant groups carried their faith to America. During their temporary stays in America, both Frederick Nilsson and Andreas Wiberg preached and started churches. For example, Nilsson came to America in 1853 with twenty-three other Swedish Baptist immigrants. He helped organize the "Swedish Baptist Church of Village Creek" (now Center Baptist Church), near Lansing, Iowa, the oldest church of Swedish descent in the United States still in existence today.

The first Swedish Baptist Church in the United States, however, was started by Gustaf Palmquist, who is recognized as a third founder of Swedish Baptists. While he was a Lutheran pietistic lay preacher in Sweden, Palmquist had learned about the Baptist faith from Nilsson. Palmquist traveled to America with other Swedish immigrants and decided to become a Baptist after attending a Baptist revival. Subsequently, on 13 August 1852, he organized the first Swedish Baptist church in the United States at Rock Island, Illinois. This is considered the founding date of the Swedish Baptist General Conference in America ("Swedish" was dropped from the title in 1945). For decades Swedish Baptists worked closely with the Northern Baptist Convention, but in 1944 they formed their own foreign mission agency. They have generally been conservative theologically. The best-known congregation in the Baptist General Conference at the turn of the twenty-first century was Bethlehem Church (originally the First

Swedish Baptist Church of Minneapolis, 1871). The church's pastor, John Piper, was considered a key leader of a resurgent Calvinism in Baptist life and was popular with Southern Baptists and evangelical college students.

Denmark. In 1839, Julius Köbner traveled to his native Denmark and preached to a sympathetic group who were gathered around an opponent of infant baptism, Adolph Mönster. With religious renewal already in the air, discussions ensued about the Baptist way. After Mönster led his followers to leave the state church, both Köbner and Johann Oncken traveled to Copenhagen and baptized Mönster and ten other believers. Mönster became the pastor of this first Baptist church in Denmark (and Scandinavia). Persecution began almost immediately and Mönster was imprisoned several times for performing baptisms. In 1842, for example, Oncken attempted to intervene and sent an envoy with a petition signed by hundreds of English Baptists which asked (unsuccessfully) for a cessation of the official repression of the Baptists. On another occasion, American Baptists sent a petition. Religious liberty was granted in 1849, but even late in the twentieth century religious minorities like Baptists were subject to official prejudice. Baptists have remained a small minority in Denmark (about 6,000 at the beginning of the twenty-first century). They participate in the Baptist World Alliance and other ecumenical organizations including the World Council of Churches.

Romania. The influence of Johann Oncken also extended to Eastern Europe. Two illustrative stories are found in the Baptist heritage of Romania and Russia. Baptist beginnings in Romania are rooted in the evangelistic work of Oncken. In 1845, he baptized Karl Johann Scharschmidt, who like other Oncken converts, adhered to his motto and became a missionary. After spending time in Hungary, Scharschmidt settled in Bucharest, Romania in 1856 and initiated mission work with a German-speaking minority. Subsequently, other German Baptists moved to Bucharest and a church was established. Scharschmidt, like Oncken, was commissioned by the church in Hamburg, Germany as a colporteur to distribute Bibles and religious tracts.

When the Bucharest church requested that Oncken provide them a permanent pastor, he sent August Liebig who stayed for four years (1863–1867). During Liebig's pastorate, the church developed tracts in the Romanian language. In 1869, Oncken visited the church as part of a larger tour of Eastern Europe (including Russia, Turkey, Transylvania, Hungary, and Austria).

Baptist work in Romania was difficult because the government restricted evangelization outside the German community. However, growth began slowly amidst some religious toleration and the first indigenous Romanian church was established in 1912. Constantin Adorian, the church's pastor, was the first Romanian graduate of the seminary Oncken started in Hamburg. Adorian was a pivotal figure in the development of Romanian Baptist life. He translated the confession of faith adopted by German Baptists into Romanian, and he served as the first president of the Romanian Baptist Union (1920–1925). The union was organized from Baptist growth in the provinces of Transylvania, Walachia, and Moldova. German and Russian Baptists had aided in these efforts. (Anabaptists were in isolated places earlier than Baptists, but no direct historical link between the two groups has been demonstrated.) Romanian Baptists adhered to a strict moral code: no alcohol or tobacco and conservative dress for women.

The story of Romanian Baptists is often a story of intense persecution. Historians note an almost never-ending persecution (eight episodes) during the two-plus decades between World War I and the end of World War II. For example, churches were closed, Bibles were confiscated, and Baptists serving in the Romanian military were targets of hostility. The Romanian Orthodox Church, unwilling to accept any kind of religious pluralism, pressed for restrictions against Baptists and other religious minorities. Officials of the Baptist World Alliance took special concern in the plight of Romanian Baptists. Their visits with government officials sometimes brought temporary toleration.

Romania was under communist control from 1947 to 1989. Restrictions toward Baptists continued: they were not allowed to teach in a university or serve in the justice department or as a military official. To be accepted, the Romanian Baptist Union acquiesced to support the communist leadership (though not its atheism) and consequently, numerous Baptists objected. In 1959, 540 Baptist pastors were recognized by the government; in 1964, only 140 conformed and were recognized. Dissidents called for the granting of complete religious liberty. One of the leading protestors, Iosif Ton, trumpeted the call for religious liberty in the document, *Doctrina Baptista despre Biserica* (*The Baptist Doctrine of the Church*). Ton criticized the government's involvement in the internal activities of churches. Romania finally sent delegates to the BWA for the first time in 1970.

In 1973, Romania began removing obstacles toward the practice of religion. Iosif Ton was able to develop a radio ministry that was carried on several stations throughout the country. Gains in religious freedom were possible because Western pressure was applied to Romanian ruler Nicolaie Ceausescu who needed Romania to maintain a favorable international economic trade status. However, Baptist calls for religious liberty were not irrelevant. The United States government cited the Ton document for evidence of human-rights violations in Romania.

Baptists in Romania persevered. Religious prejudice was still strong in the post-communist era; however, in the minds of many, to be Romanian was still to be a member of the Orthodox Church. In the midst of this environment of religious nationalism, Baptists and other minorities— Pentecostals, Brethren, and the "Lord's Host" (or Lord's Army)—cooperated in a Romanian Evangelical Alliance that represented churches to the government.

Romanian Baptists' participation in the Baptist World Alliance became an issue in the 1990s. Theologically conservative, the Romanians refused to send delegates to meetings of the European Baptist Federation because the organization had a woman president. At the beginning of the twenty-first century, Romania has one of the largest groups of Baptists in Eastern Europe with more than 100,000 members.

Russia. Russian Baptists came from several roots. Some were heavily influenced by Johann Oncken and German Baptists. Others were more indigenously Russian. Oncken made an evangelistic trip to Russia in 1864. He also worked on behalf of Russian Baptists in the fight for religious toleration. In 1879, he visited a Russian government official and the meeting reportedly gained some temporary relief for persecuted Baptists.

The region of Transcaucasia (or South Caucasus)—specifically modern-day Georgia and its capital city, Tbilisi—was home to the first ethnic Russians to become Baptists. In 1867, Nikita Voronin was baptized in the Kura River by a German Baptist immigrant, Martin Kalweit. Voronin and some other early Baptists came from the Molokans, an indigenous evangelical sect with similarities to Quakerism (for example, sacraments were not literally practiced). He formed the first Russian congregation at Tiflis (modern Tbilisi) and in 1871, baptized two men who later became important Baptist leaders, V. I. Ivanoff and Vasilii Gur'vich Pavlov. While Ivanoff preferred a more independent Russian spirituality, Pavlov studied at Hamburg in 1875 and was baptized by Oncken in 1876. Pavlov advocated the German model of organization and translated Oncken's confession of faith for use in Russia. His missionary work was supported by German-Americans.

Some early Baptists also came from the *Shtundizm* Movement (the Ukraine word for evangelicalism or weekly hours of Bible study, after the German *Stunde*, "hour") in Southern Ukraine. In 1869, Efim Tsymbal became the first South Russian *Shtundist* to claim the Baptist faith. The Russian Baptist Union, founded in 1884, was indebted to the Oncken tradition but its organizational meeting focused on developing Russian missionaries for Russians. Vasilii Pavlov was elected president in 1909 and remained influential for another decade.

Russian Baptists also derived from influences besides Johann Oncken. Baptist work in St. Petersburg benefited from the preaching of a British evangelist, Lord Radstock. One of his converts, Col. Vasili A. Pashkov, was an early leader. These Baptists (including some aristocrats) immersed but did not use the Baptist name; rather, they called themselves *Evangel'skie Khristiane*, "Gospel Christians." In 1888, the Union of Evangelical Christians was formed. Ivan Prokhanoff, who had studied at the English Baptist school, Bristol College, became the dominant leader of this strain of Baptist life.

Before 1905, Baptists in Russia were subject to severe persecution. Several leaders were exiled and hundreds arrested for attending prayer meetings in house churches. Vasilii Pavlov was jailed several times and was exiled twice. Baptists came from different economic levels, but most were common people—peasants, artisans, and from the lower class. In 1881, a leader of the state-supported Russian Orthodox Church said that there must never be any Russian Baptists. Authorities considered them "Damned *Shtundists*."

Dissenting religious groups benefited greatly from a decree of religious toleration issued in 1905 by the tsar, Nicholas II. The era was characterized by industrialization, rapid social changes, urban-worker strikes and agrarian unrest. In this context, the tsar's conciliatory gesture, the "October Manifesto," allowed dissenters who had been persecuted to worship legally and Orthodox believers were no longer punished for joining one of the sects. Yet, dissenters were not to actively proselytize Orthodox believers.

Recent scholarship has suggested that from 1905 to 1929 the role of religion and its relationship to Russian identity was similar to the environment that resulted from the demise of the Soviet Union in 1989. With the decree of religious toleration in 1905, a potential religious pluralism and openness to Western religions seemed to be on the Russian horizon. The grip of the Orthodox Church on society was challenged. Baptists grew faster than any sect: 114,000 by 1912 and then triple that by the late 1920s.

The focus on personal religious experience (Baptist literature was filled with conversion stories which detailed the inadequacy of growing up Orthodox), the right of every believer to read and interpret the Scriptures, the egalitarian quality of congregational church government, and an affirmation of the freedom of conscience appealed to ordinary Russians. While Baptists were not supposed to evangelize Orthodox believers, many did so anyway because of their emphasis on the priesthood of all believers found in Oncken's motto, "Every Baptist a missionary." Baptist women's groups (some Russian women preached, although this was controversial) and youth organizations developed. In 1911, twenty-four Russian Baptists attended the Baptist World Alliance in Philadelphia, where Ivan Prokhanoff was elected a vice-president.

Despite the 1905 decree of religious toleration, the Russian government and the Russian Orthodox Church grew increasingly intolerant of the Baptist movement. Baptist democratic church practices raised suspicions, but more ominously their connections to Germany and the West were considered potentially treasonous. The traditional view that to be Russian was to be Orthodox prevailed in light of World War I, and attacks were leveled against anything tinged with German influence. Baptists appeared to be a foreign and thus an unworthy faith. They were also considered less than patriotic, especially when a good number advocated pacifism during the international conflict.

To demonstrate their Russian identity, Baptists attempted to define their faith in Russian terms. They attempted to affirm their patriotism and spoke of a Russian Reformation. With the fall of the tsar in 1917 and the Bolshevik Revolution, Baptists attempted to offer an alternative perspective to the revolutionary parties who talked of socialistic class conflict. Baptists, as they were prone to do, appealed to the New Testament church. They suggested a biblical socialism—a re-creation of the New Testament model of communism—communal living as found in the Book of Acts. In 1918, Evangelical Christian leader Ivan Prokhanoff published *Gospel Christianity and the Social Question* in which he described three labor collectives that were modeled on early Christianity. In 1919, a Gethsemane commune was formed and eleven families of Evangelical Christians lived together in Tver'. About forty such communes were established among the different Baptist groups in an attempt to duplicate New Testament community and offer and alternative to equating Russian identity with the Orthodox Church or atheism. In 1920, when the two major Baptist groups talked unsuccessfully about merging, Vasilii Pavlov noted that many Baptists wanted to adopt the name, "First Christians."

By the late 1920s, Baptists were accused of fostering a state within a state. Religious opportunity halted with the "law of religious cults" in 1929. The reign of Joseph Stalin imposed severe restrictions on believers which essentially attempted to destroy religious life in the Soviet Union. The Russian Baptist Union dissolved and Evangelical Christians ceased its activity in the 1930s. Optimistic postmillennial language among Baptists gave way to premillennial apocalyptic speculation about an imminent return of Christ.

Baptists and other groups resurfaced after World War II. In 1944, the government pressured all Baptists to unite in the All Union Council of Evangelicals-Baptists (AUCECB). Mennonites and Pentecostals joined later but eventually separated. In 1961, different reactions to the renewed persecution of religious dissent during the era of Soviet dictator Nikita Khrushchev resulted in Baptist internal conflict. Leaders of the AUCECB agreed to abide by new government restrictions on religious activity: no evangelization, no religious instruction to anyone under eighteen years of age, and no baptisms for anyone under thirty years of age. They cited Romans 13 and said they were trying to be good Christian citizens. They were trying to survive.

Dissenters, led by A. F. Prokofiev and Georgi Vins, demanded repentance from leaders of the AUCECB. They accused them of being tools of Satan and clearly not a part of the true church. These "Reform Baptists" formed the Council of Churches of Evangelical Christians-Baptists (CCECB), whose member churches were not allowed to register with the government. Leaders were arrested and an international outcry resulted. In the 1970s, United States President Jimmy Carter worked to free Vins from his imprisonment.

After the collapse of the Soviet Union in 1989, Baptists in Russia organized the Union of Evangelical Christian-Baptists and subsequently the Russian Baptist Union. Baptists in other former Soviet lands also formed Baptist unions. Missionaries from America (for example, Southern Baptists, Conservative Baptists, Baptist General Conference) still did missionary work in Russia. As with the era of the 1905 decree of religious toleration, contemporary Russia is confronting the potential challenges of religious pluralism and renewed episodes of restrictions on religion.

Other Baptists beyond Europe

Johann Oncken's missionary shadow was long and wide, covering Europe and reaching beyond. Yet, Baptist growth internationally is not simply his story. The small beginnings, numerically speaking, of the mission work of William Carey in India have developed into the largest Baptist population outside America (1.5 million). Subsequent missionary activity of the British Baptist Missionary Society spanned the globe. The same can be said of Baptists in America, North and South. Southern Baptists and British Baptists both sent missionaries to Brazil (Brazilian Baptists, especially, have been influenced by Pentecostalism, the largest Protestant group in Brazil). British, Northern, and Southern Baptists all did mission work in Mexico. Cuban and Japanese Baptist history included both Northern Baptist and Southern Baptist missionaries, and like their dealings in the Americas, comity agreements were used to divide the countries into regions of mission activity. The story of Southern Baptist Lottie Moon recalls the American Baptist fascination with China.

Asia. Baptist work in Asian countries met many hardships in an atmosphere of persecution. In 1837, William Dean, appointed by the Triennial Convention of American Baptists, organized the first Baptist and first Protestant Chinese Church in Thailand. China opened up for missionary work, and by 1927 American Baptists had organized 164 churches. In 1845, the year of its birth, the Southern Baptist Convention sent two missionaries to China. The work of Lottie Moon made Chinese work the wonderland of Southern Baptist overseas missions. In 1906, American Baptists and Southern Baptists joined together and started Shanghai Baptist College and Seminary (later University of Shanghai). In 1948, a Chinese Baptist Convention was created to support the ministries and churches initiated by Southern Baptists.

The rise of Communist China meant severe restrictions upon religion. Churches were closed; Christian clergy were imprisoned. "Visible" denominations became extinct. Still, Christianity survived underground in house churches. At the turn of the twenty-first century, churches can openly exist but should be registered with the government. Missionaries are prohibited, but Baptists still go to China as "school teachers" and often share their faith as opportunity arises.

The Philippines is another Asian area to receive extensive Baptist attention. Eric Lund, an American Baptist missionary, established a church at Jaro in 1901. In 1905, the Jaro Industrial School was begun, and in 1953 it became Central Philippine University. In 1935 a Convention of Philippine Baptist Churches was created. At the end of the twentieth century, it was supported by American and Australian Baptists and included about twenty-eight percent of Filipino Baptists.

Southern Baptist work in the Philippines also flourished. The work began in 1948—the Communist difficulties in China necessitated a new focus for missionaries—with an estimated twenty-eight percent of all Filipino Baptists now affiliated with Southern Baptists. In 2006, Robert Nash, the son of former Southern Baptist missionaries to the Philippines, was named Global Missions Coordinator for the Cooperative Baptist Fellowship.

In addition to American and Southern Baptists, other Baptist groups sent missionaries to Asia. For example, in 1847 Seventh Day Baptists sent missionaries to China, followed in 1893 by Swedish Baptists and in 1946 by the Conservative Baptist Foreign Missionary Society. In the Philippines, a plethora of Baptist bodies sent missionaries: Baptist General Conference (1946), Conservative Baptists (1956), Landmark Baptists (1961), Free Will Baptists (1969), Seventh Day Baptists (1971), and Reformed Baptists (1979).

Indigenous work also characterized Asian Baptist bodies. For example, Baptist work in Korea flourished in the last half of the twentieth century. Billy Jang Hwan Kim became pastor of Suwon Central Baptist Church (near Seoul) in 1960, and under his leadership the church grew from ten members to more than 15,000 when Kim retired in 2005. (Kim was president of the BWA, 2000–2005.) In addition, Korean Baptists were one of the fastest growing ethnic churches in America.

Africa. When the future growth of Christianity is projected, observers believe Africa will be the fastest-growing region of Baptist life worldwide. Africa has been a mission post for many Baptist bodies. Africa can serve, then, as a representative picture of the expansion of Baptist missions and the development of indigenous Baptist leadership.

Africa was home to some of the most influential Christians of the "early church" era, for example, Tertullian, Cyprian, and Augustine. In the Middle Ages, Islam came to dominate most of the continent. In the mid-nineteenth century, the missionary adventures of Scottish medical missionary David Livingstone brought attention to African missions. He traveled over one-third of the continent and documented his experiences. Baptists joined others in extending missionary work to Africa. As might be expected, British, American (North, South, and African-American), and German

Baptists were leaders in African missions. Baptists of other countries were participants as well.

Liberia was the earliest focus of the mission work of Baptist groups in America. In 1821, African-Americans Lott Carey and Collin Teague went to Monrovia under the auspices of the Richmond African Baptist Missionary Society. The Triennial Convention of Baptists in America provided support. Northern Baptists and Southern Baptists, after their schism in 1845, continued to make Liberia an area of interest.

Both British Baptists and German Baptists developed the earliest Baptist churches in South Africa. The first English settlers who came to South Africa in 1820 included several Baptists. The Grahamstown Church (Cape Colony), formed by William Miller, is acknowledged as the founding church. Similar to English and American contexts, the church experienced tension over Calvinism and Arminianism.

The influence of Germany's Johann Oncken was felt even in South Africa. German Baptists came to South Africa in the 1850s and in 1861 formed a church at Frankfort. The church asked Oncken for pastoral help and Carl Hugo Gutsche was sent by German Baptists. Gutsche provided stability, and twenty-five churches were built in twenty-five years under his leadership. The Baptist Union of South Africa (including British and German Baptist churches) was created in 1877. It crystallized its own mission efforts in 1892 with the formation of the South African Baptist Missionary Society.

Early Baptist work also occurred in the Congo, an area of interest because of David Livingstone's travels. In 1878, the Baptist Missionary Society of British Baptists sent missionaries. In the 1880s, American Baptists became involved. The story of mission work in this region revealed the challenges of developing and accepting indigenous leadership. Missionaries often maintained control of the mission work. "Western" religious values confronted native social practices with mixed success.

Considered the most-important independent church in Africa, "l'Église de Jésus-christ sur la Terre par le Prophète Simon Kimbangu" ("The Church of Jesus Christ on Earth through the Prophet Simon Kimbangu") traces its roots back to Baptist mission efforts. Simon Kimbangu grew up in the Lower Congo under the influence of the British Baptist Missionary Society and was baptized in 1915. His work in the church focused on preparing candidates for baptism, but the Baptist church at Nkamba chose not to license him to preach. Kimbangu immediately began having visions. He claimed a divine commission from God to be an apostle and divine healer.

According to his followers, he initially rejected the call, but reportedly healed a woman in 1921. He began preaching and attracted large crowds for healing. He was called a prophet (*ngunza*) and many African Baptists were among those who believed in him as a prophet and in his claims of the miraculous.

Church officials gave approval to Kimbangu's ministry and believed that the New Testament church of power was being restored, but senior Baptist missionaries felt that Kimbangu was misguided. After only six months, Belgian authorities concluded that the movement was a threat and arrested Kimbangu. They feared an uprising of anti-European sentiment and African nationalism. Kimbangu was convicted of treason, but his verdict was commuted to a life sentence and he died in prison. His followers developed "Kimbanguism" separate from its Baptist roots. The use of twelve apostles, dependence upon visions and prophetic gifts, and a focus on moral reform (opposition to polygamy and erotic dances) pointed to the power of a gospel of restorationism in an indigenous African context. In 1969, the independent church was accepted into the World Council of Churches.

Zambia. The Baptist movement in Zambia in the early twentieth century serves as a microcosm of an international Baptist mission to Africa. Like many other African missions, the Zambian Baptist mission began with a single work, spread to a spider web of associations and then coalesced into in a centralized union. The Zambia mission is also an example of the convergence of Baptist missions. The work was started by the British and continued by a British colony, South Africa, whose Baptist origins were indebted to Germany's Johann Oncken. Zambian missions were subsequently supported by Australian Baptists, who were originally organized by British Baptists, and by Baptists in America. Indigenous Baptist churches grew as well.

At the turn of the twentieth century, Zambia (formerly Northern Rhodesia) was an English territory administered by the British South African Chartered Company. In 1905 English missionaries W. A. Phillips and H. L Wildey from the Nyasaland Industrial Mission (Malawi) journeyed by foot into the region and founded a mission at Kafulafuta. The mission included a church and a grammar school. In 1913, the South African Baptist Missionary Society provided needed financial support for the mission, and assumed control in an attempt to unify the mission in southern Africa with that in the Congo.

The priority of the mission, besides evangelizing through preaching and education, was the translation of Scripture into the native language. By 1924, South African Baptist missionary Clement Doke had translated the New Testament, and the entire Bible was completed in the latter half of the twentieth century. Much of the Old Testament work was done by Olive Doke; she also taught women's groups and later led a Bible class open to both genders. Education at the mission school focused on reading (for Bible study) and arithmetic. Students, who were imported from various provinces, were trained to assist missionaries in evangelization. Mission travels were originally by foot, then by bicycle, before motorized vehicles were available. Challenges included the practice of polygamy and the worship of ancestral spirits by the native peoples.

In the 1930s, the Zambian mission work expanded significantly. The Scandinavian Independent Baptist Union, in consultation with the South African Baptist Missionary Society, founded a mission at Mpongwe. The South Africans also founded the Fiwale Hill Mission. A growing number of native ministers assisted the European ministers. For several years "Paul, the Apostle to the Lambas," was the only chief guide of missionaries and nationals in his region. Gradually a number of indigenous churches were founded in mining compounds. The successful mission at the Ndola Compound, under the guidance of South African missionary Arthur Cross, attracted the interest of other denominations and became ecumenical.

In the 1960s, another wave of significant organizational changes took place among Zambian Baptists. The South African Baptist Missionary Society concluded its work and the Australian Baptist Missionary Society became, for twenty-nine years (1969–1998), the primary support system for Zambian nationals. Southern Baptists began their mission work in 1959. In the early 1970s, three Zambian Baptist associations were formed, and in 1975 they joined together to create the Baptist Union of Zambia. The Union has supported education (Fiwale Hill Bible College), women's evangelistic work (they raised funds for church planters), and evangelization. The indigenous Baptist church in Zambia became established in almost all areas of Zambia.

One of the regions of the Baptist World Alliance also calls Zambia its home. The office of the All-Africa Baptist Fellowship is located in Lusaka, Zambia. It represents thirty-seven Baptist unions in twenty-two African countries.

The Baptist World Alliance

Origins. The "honor" of who is primarily responsible for envisioning an organization of the world's Baptists is disputed, even among some of the earliest participants. Very early voices for international relationships were seventeenth-century English General Baptist leader, Thomas Grantham, and John Rippon, late-eighteenth-century English Baptist who developed the publication, *The Annual Baptist Register*. In 1806, missionary pioneer William Carey even hoped for an ecumenical association of all Christians. Foreign mission work ultimately made Baptists realize the need for cooperation. Improvements in transportation and international communication made correspondence easier. Other denominations also had begun international meetings (for example, Anglicans and American Episcopalians, 1867).

A precursor in Baptist life to a world organization was the "Baptist Congress" movement. These "congresses" were discussion forums held in major American cities which attracted Baptist intellectuals from the United States (North and South), Canada, and a few participants from Britain. The first was held in 1881. At the 1903 gathering, Russell Conwell of Philadelphia called for a national or international Baptist meeting. In 1895, R. H. Pitt of Virginia wrote editorials in the *Religious Herald* calling for a meeting and J. N. Prestridge of Kentucky followed suit in the *Baptist Argus* from 1902 to 1904. Professor A. T. Robertson of Southern Baptist Theological Seminary claimed his writings published in the *Baptist Argus* in 1902 were responsible for the call of an international Baptist meeting. In 1904, British Baptists issued the invitation.

The First Baptist World Congress was held in London in 1905. According to J. N. Prestridge, Baptists had achieved a "world consciousness." Delegates numbered 3,000 and came from twenty-six countries. A committee to develop an ongoing structure was appointed that underscored the Anglo-centric leadership in Baptist life at the turn of the century. The committee included eight delegates from the United States and four British Baptists. E. C. Morris of the National Baptist Convention was the only African-American; no women served. Never shy about touting their Baptist identity, denominational uniqueness was clearly heard in those initial meetings of what we now call the Baptist World Alliance.

Religious liberty. From its origins, the Baptist World Alliance strongly supported complete religious liberty. The historical backdrop for the 1905 First World Congress was a conflict over the role of government in English schools. The educational system had been providing nonsectarian teaching of religion in schools, but with the passage of the Education Acts of 1902–1903, English elementary and secondary schools were placed under government control. Religious tests for teachers were enacted and religious schools were afforded support through local taxes.

Preeminent English Baptist leader John Clifford led the "Free Church" protest. At the First Baptist Congress he chastised the discriminatory taxation to support sectarian religion in schools. He declared that the Baptist belief in an individual's "soul liberty"—a believer must be free from others to follow the absolute authority of Christ—led to the doctrine of religious liberty. Baptists from America joined in the fray and were not shy in trumpeting the call for religious freedom and the separation of church and state. William Whitsitt, former president of Southern Baptist Theological Seminary, declared that the state's function was to teach citizenship, not churchmanship. E. Y. Mullins, in his sixth year as Whitsitt's successor as president of the Louisville seminary, preached about Baptist distinctives and explained his now-famous "axioms of religion" which included the religious-civic axiom, "A free church in a free state." In a keynote address, American Baptist theologian Augustus H. Strong focused on the necessity of religious liberty. If speeches were not enough, the presence of Russian Baptists drew attention to the cause. Russian leader Vasilii Pavlov testified about being persecuted on behalf of Christ. The message was loud and clear: Baptists were committed to religious liberty.

BWA officials consistently worked for religious liberty. In 1928, J. H. Rushbrooke of England was elected the first general secretary. Rushbrooke was indefatigable in support of religious freedom, and pleaded his case with totalitarian government officials in countries like Romania. Upon his election as general secretary, Rushbrooke reminded BWA delegates in Toronto that the Alliance stood for "the message of Roger Williams uttered to the ends of the earth."

At the 1934 BWA meeting in Berlin, the flag of Hitler's Third Reich hung ominously in the meeting hall. Some observers noted with approval Hitler's stand against smoking and drinking and welcomed his anticommunism. Paul Schmidt, editor of a German Baptist paper, reflected the anti-Semitism prevalent in Germany when he told BWA delegates that Jesus would not stop stronger races from overwhelming weaker ones in the natural course of history. Still, most Baptists at the BWA opposed the racist, militaristic nationalism engulfing Germany. The BWA passed a strongly worded resolution promoting the separation of church and state.

At the 1955 Golden Jubilee Congress in London, the political tensions of the era reminded Baptists of the importance of their historic focus on religious liberty. British and American missionaries had recently been excluded from China. Baptists in Spain and Columbia were hampered by repressive edicts or persecution. The Communist threat raged internationally. In 1950, no delegates from communist countries had attended in Cleveland, Ohio, but in 1955 all but two Baptist national unions were represented. The meeting halls of the BWA celebration buzzed with the news that Russian Baptists were in attendance. Many participants were excited by their courage, but some observers wondered aloud whether the Russian interpreter was a communist "plant" and if the real Russian Baptists were those persecuted ones not free to attend the Congress.

Delegates approved a "Golden Jubilee Declaration on Religious Liberty" as an "essential part" of the Baptist contribution to the worldwide church. Speakers also reiterated the clarion call for religious liberty, but offered no simplistic litany of verbiage void of serious commitment. Gunnar Westin of the University of Uppsala in Sweden said it was easy to take a stand for religious liberty when your own group would be the benefactor, but the real test was the willingness to fight a disinterested battle for liberty. Norwegian Arnold T. Ohrn, BWA general secretary at the time, declared that Baptists might find it is easy to publish protests against the perpetuators of religious persecution, but these protests must not make matters more difficult for the persecuted. Baptists worldwide understood what it meant to be a persecuted minority.

Religious liberty remained a concern for the BWA at the turn of the twenty-first century. Beginning in 1965, the BWA officially added human rights to its religious-liberty platform. The BWA articulated a growing social awareness, for example, speaking out against apartheid in South Africa. The first decade of the twenty-first century was named "Decade of Racial Injustice" to highlight the relationship between human rights and racial and ethnic conflict.

Confessions. Confessions have been widely used in European Baptist life. Similar to their roles in early English contexts, confessions expressed Baptist identity to assert commonalities with other Protestant bodies. In addition, European Baptists who struggled to survive in countries with state-supported churches had to write confessions in order to receive government toleration. A few countries (Spain, Portugal, and Greece) adopted the "1963 Baptist Faith and Message" of the Southern Baptist Convention. At the same time, European Baptists have strongly resisted creeds, especially since state-supported churches had used their creeds to inflict persecution upon minority religious groups. The German Baptist confession, for example, insisted that it was a voluntary statement of faith and had no compulsory powers. Baptists in some regions (for example, Britain, Sweden, and Norway) only used brief general statements of principles. Commenting upon British Baptists' detachment from creeds, In 1927, English biblical scholar H. Wheeler Robinson commented that they held to the contents of the historic Christian confessions as loyally as other Christian bodies, but they felt confessions substituted formal intellectual assent for the personal experience of faith.

Throughout the history of the Baptist World Alliance, international Baptist leaders affirmed the use of confessions but opposed creedalism. At the opening Baptist World Congress in 1905, British leader Alexander MacLaren invited the delegates to stand and repeat the ancient Apostles' Creed. No attempt was made to adopt a Baptist creed, however. MacLaren thought a demonstration to the world that Baptists were doctrinally orthodox within the larger Christian community was appropriate at the founding assembly of the BWA. His use of the Apostles' Creed, however, also revealed that Baptists had never had a consensus statement of faith beyond the Bible.

Subsequent world Baptist congresses clearly opposed creedalism. At the second BWA gathering in 1911, English minister J. Moffatt Logan said that the world would not be Christianized through the use of creeds. Ancient creeds had been used cruelly to enforce conformity, Logan declared, and Christ's message should be trusted to an environment of freedom. To a BWA audience of European Baptists in 1913, the most influential British Baptist of the era, John Clifford, preached that no confessional statement was absolute because openness to the Holy Spirit always led to fresh understandings of the Scriptures.

As the BWA matured and gained greater representation beyond its early British/American dominance, international voices also denounced creedalism. At the tenth Baptist World Congress in 1960 in Rio de Janeiro, Alfonso Olmedo, a pastor and missionary from Argentina, emphasized that Baptist unity across the world could not be based on a type of organization or adherence to a creed, but a common commitment to "deeds" and "subjection" to God. Denton Lotz, general secretary of the BWA, 1988–2007, continued the BWA's commitment to a noncreedal Baptist witness. Lotz acknowledged that Baptists had "core doctrines," but the Bible rather than imposed creeds was the final authority for faith. Southern Baptists, with their recent insistence on creedalism, withdrew from the BWA in 2004.

Internationalization. The 1960s, known for rapid cultural changes in American society, also witnessed the beginnings of the internationalization of the structure of the BWA. In 1960, the BWA met in Rio de Janeiro, the first world congress convened outside of North America or Europe. In 1965, William R. Tolbert, Jr. of Liberia, a vice-president in the government of Liberia, was the first African elected president of the BWA. Since 1960, other presidents have come from Brazil, Hong Kong, Australia, Denmark, and Korea. The election of Billy Jang Hwan Kim, Korean, president from 2000 to 2005, pointed to the global spread of the "megachurch" phenomenon. Kim led his church, Suwon Central Baptist Church near Seoul, South Korea, from a membership of ten in 1960 to more than 15,000 when he retired from the pastorate in 2005. The internationalization of BWA participation was institutionalized with the creation of six regions after 1980: European Baptist Federation, All-Africa Baptist Fellowship, Asian Baptist Federation, Caribbean Baptist Fellowship, Union of Baptists in Latin America, and North American Baptist Fellowship. Baptists from these different regions serve on committees and in elected posts. In 2006, the BWA reported a membership of 214 different Baptist groups totaling more than thirty million Baptists.

Women. The role of women in the life of the BWA mirrored that of Baptist life in general. Opportunities for women increased gradually during the twentieth century, but ministerial equality was not widely accepted. At the initial meeting in 1905, Lucy Waterbury, secretary of the Woman's Baptist Foreign Missionary Society of the Northern Baptist Convention, was the first woman to address the Congress. A second woman to address the world's Baptists was Nannie Helen Burroughs, secretary of the Woman's Auxiliary of the National Baptist Convention. Burroughs's presence was noteworthy: an African-American woman who spoke on the needs of Africa. Hailed as a popular speaker, her audience was captivated by her story about a beggar who asked a deacon for bread. After praying the Lord's Prayer, the beggar, who had noticed how thin the slice of bread was, said, "Deacon, did you say 'Our Father'? Then that means you are my brother. Then if that is so, will you please cut it thick since we are kin. . . . And so for hungry and starving Africa . . . I ask you to cut the slice a little thicker."

Baptist women did not use the BWA as a platform to push for women's rights. As they did in their specific denominations, most Baptist women focused on supporting missions. A few progressive voices were heard, however, in the first decades of the BWA on the issue of women's involvement in Baptist life. The Second World Congress in 1911 featured a special afternoon session for women. Isabel James of the British Women's League argued that the future of Baptists depended on the loyalty of Baptist women, and said women's gifts should be fully utilized. At the same meeting, progressive Southern Baptist Fannie E. S. Heck did not push for women's equality, but voiced an ecumenical vision when she confessed that Baptists in America unfortunately often equated Baptist truth with American truth. In 1923, Helen Barrett Montgomery, then the first woman president of the Northern Baptist Convention, said that Christ was the "emancipator" of women and that "no area of religious privilege" was reserved for men. British leader J. H. Shakespeare (a friend of Isabel James) was a key reason women had the limited opportunities that were extended to them in the early years of the BWA.

Since the mid-twentieth century, women have been more visible in BWA leadership. Marion Bates of Canada was the first woman to serve as a vice-president (1995–2000). The BWA Women's Department has thrived since the 1960s. Since 1985, some women have addressed (that is, preached at) BWA meetings on subjects other than missions. At the turn of the twenty-first century, however, the most-accepted ministerial role in international Baptist life for a woman was still that of a missionary.

New Testament Christianity. As Baptists in America have emphasized their identity as a New Testament church, Baptists internationally have followed suit. In the 1920s, the growing ecumenical movement posed the issue: emphasize cooperation between denominations or develop a strong international Baptist fellowship. In 1922, Swedish Baptist C. E. Benander spoke to the BWA to support the Baptist way because Baptists, with their commitment to believer's baptism and regenerate church membership, freedom of conscience and soul competency, were followers of the apostolic New Testament pattern. In 1929, John MacNeill, the BWA's only Canadian president in its history, concurred that a Baptist witness was paramount for the world because Baptists are "New Testament people." International Baptist groups also have relied on their New Testament identity in light of their minority status in their country. In the 1960s, A. V. Karev, one of the general secretaries of Russia's All Union Council of Evangelical Christian-Baptists, contended that Baptists alone faithfully adhered to "apostolic Christianity."

Conclusion

At the outset of the twenty-first century, Baptists continued to grow internationally. The contribution of Johann Oncken was immeasurable, but Baptists had developed even beyond the German Baptist's extensive influence. Missionary work was a contributing factor, but indigenous Baptist work increased dramatically. Baptist diversity flourished, of course, but cooperative work was found in the ministry of the Baptist World Alliance. International Baptists affirmed many of the historic Baptist distinctives found in English and American Baptist history, but a deep common bond was their existence in the midst of state-sponsored persecution. Religious liberty was the clarion call for these Baptist minorities. Charismatic influences made significant impact upon Baptists worldwide, and most observers believe the trend will continue. Whatever the stifling environment, Baptists internationally believed that faithfulness to the New Testament was imperative. The search for the New Testament church was an international journey.

Epilogue

At the beginning of the twenty-first century, Baptists totaled 43,000,000 baptized members in approximately 160,000 churches scattered across the globe. Growth was fastest in the regions of Africa, Asia, and Latin America. The Baptist future, at least in terms of population and church growth, appeared bright. Challenges remained, however. Will the Southern Baptist Convention resist the tides of postmodernism? Will it continue to fragment? Will the centuries-old battle between Calvinism and Arminianism erupt again? Will the former moderates of the Southern Baptist Convention sustain their identity in the Cooperative Baptist Fellowship? Will American Baptists reverse the numerical decline that has adversely affected many mainline denominations in America? Will the Baptist World Alliance continue to be common ground for international Baptists? Will Pentecostal influences continue to make inroads in Baptist life? How will Baptist ecumenical involvement take shape in future years? What cultural influences, as they always have, will affect or mold the nature of the future Baptist witness?

As Baptists confront an ever-changing future, especially one in which denominational affiliation seems to be lessening in importance for some adherents, what role will Baptist distinctives play? Perhaps that is the key question that scholars and observers continue to grapple with and disagree about. Can the essence of being Baptist even be described?

Baptist diversity prohibits the delineation of one definitive answer about the Baptist identity. The Baptist story/stories described in this historical overview, nevertheless, point to several historic distinctives that have played prominent roles in the shaping of the Baptist heritage. While held with varying degrees of intensity, where the Baptist way of being Christian was described, the insistence was upon a believer's church: believer's baptism and regenerate church membership. As the eighteenth-century chronicler, Morgan Edwards declared, *baptism* was the denominating article.

At the root of the call for a believer's church was the necessity of freedom. In Baptist life, freedom has been seen in the centrality of voluntary personal faith and the sacred nature of the individual conscience. This freedom formed the foundation for religious liberty. For most Baptists, this meant the separation of church and state and guaranteed the right to dissent in opposition to forced conformity. Freedom also formed the foundation for the independence of the local church. From early in their history, Baptists cooperated with others in associations, but the local church remained autonomous. At the same time, as Baptists formed larger denominational entities, they increasingly centralized to the point that freedom was diminished or even lost.

Throughout their history Baptists were individualists: salvation was personal, and the believer had to be free to follow the dictates of his or her conscience because each person would meet God in the judgment. Could a Baptist abuse freedom of belief, this "soul liberty"? Of course, but Baptist individualism was never simply freedom run amok. If it tried to, the local church with its democratic congregational church polity could function as a Baptist bishop-like safeguard. The autonomous local church, while it usually associated with other churches, handled its own affairs and disciplined its members if freedom got out of hand. In twenty-first-century language, the local church was the "community" where voluntary covenant relationships between individuals were nurtured.

Whatever the century or decade, Baptists claimed to be people who believed the Bible. It was the sole authority for their faith and they attempted to live their lives in light of the Bible. New Testament faith had to be practiced freely to be genuine. Creeds—though not confessions—were usually avoided. At least when battle lines were drawn, the Bible became the stated judge of orthodoxy. The role of creeds in the Southern Baptist controversy of the late-twentieth century muddied the waters when it came to the Baptist distinctive of the authority of the Bible.

Of course cultural, economic, social, and political factors influenced Baptist faith, perhaps in ways Baptists did not recognize or refused to understand. For example, on matters of race, different Baptists read different Bibles and lived radically different expressions of Christianity. The same could be said for other issues. An apparent or implied common set of Baptist distinctives often did not produce unity of perspective.

Why? Baptist history has often been a journey in search of the New Testament church. Many Baptists assumed that the New Testament only had one type of church structure and they embodied it. However, this restorationism, this constant quest for the pure church, produced an ever-flowing stream of different readings of the Bible. One distinctive would be emphasized by one group, and then another group would emphasize something else. For example, one group said that footwashing had to be duplicated, one group said that laying on of hands after baptism had to be duplicated, one group said that the theory of inerrancy had to be creedalized, and on and on. In all cases, the Bible was the justification. Add in the mix of cultural factors and the unique circumstances of a particular era, and Baptists produced, and will no doubt continue to produce, a wide variety of Baptist stories. Where there was uniformity or a sense of finality, coercion was often close behind.

In the end, a freedom based on some "informal" Baptist distinctives has dotted the Baptist landscape with surprising regularity. However, they were never understood or even accepted in the same way by every group of Baptists. Diversity is simply what messy freedom allows. Baptists attuned to their history, however, will note that one of the most common and radical distinctives—an unfettered conscience—is worth the risk. A Baptist cannot choose to be a Baptist, or refuse to remain one, without it.

A Bibliographical Note

Selected resources for further reading in Baptist history.

Abbreviations for frequently cited journals:
ABQ, American Baptist Quarterly
BHH, Baptist History and Heritage
BQ, Baptist Quarterly (English Baptists)
Chr, Chronicle (superseded by *Foundations*)
Foun, Foundations (superseded by ABQ)
PRS, Perspectives in Religious Studies
RE, Review and Expositor

Abbreviations for frequently cited book publishers:
ABPS: Philadelphia: American Baptist Publication Society
Arno: New York: Arno Press
BP: Nashville: Broadman Press
BHP: Nashville: Broadman and Holman Press
Duke: Durham: Duke University Press
Eerdmans: Grand Rapids MI: Wm B. Eerdmans Publishing Co.
JP: Valley Forge PA: Judson Press
MUP: Macon GA: Mercer University Press
UGAP: Athens: University of Georgia Press
UKP: Lexington: University of Kentucky Press
UAP: Tuscaloosa: University of Alabama Press
UNCP: Chapel Hill: University of North Carolina Press
UTP: Knoxville: University of Tennessee Press

General Works

Numerous histories of Baptists have been written. Well-known comprehensive histories that cover Baptists in America, England, and internationally include
Bill J. Leonard, *Baptist Ways* (JP, 2003)
H. Leon McBeth, *The Baptist Heritage. Four Centuries of Baptist Witness* (BP, 1987)
Robert G. Torbet, *A History of the Baptists*, 3rd ed. (JP, 1973)

Primary sources are pivotal for understanding Baptist history. In addition to full texts, some of which are cited in this note, good collections of excerpts include
Robert A. Baker, *A Baptist Source Book* (BP, 1966)

William H. Brackney, ed., *Baptist Life and Thought: A Source Book* (JP, 1998)
H. Leon. McBeth, *A Sourcebook for Baptist Heritage* (BP, 1990; reprints, BHP).

Dictionaries of Baptists are also useful for general information, including
William H. Brackney, *Historical Dictionary of the Baptists* (Lanham MD: The Scarecrow Press, 1999)
Encyclopedia of Southern Baptists, 2 vols. + 2 suppl. vols. + index vol. (BP and BHP, 1958, 1958, 1962, 1984)
Bill J. Leonard, ed,. *Dictionary of Baptists in America* (Downer's Grove IL: Intervarsity Press, 1994)

General surveys of the various Baptist conventions in America are voluminous. Standard histories of the Southern Baptist Convention include
W. W. Barnes, *The Southern Baptist Convention, 1845–1953* (BP, 1954)
Robert A. Baker, *The Southern Baptist Convention and Its People, 1607–1972* (BP, 1974)
Jesse Fletcher, *The Southern Baptist Convention: A Sesquicentennial History* (BHP, 1994)

See also
Walter B. Shurden, *Not A Silent People; Controversies That Have Shaped Southern Baptists* (Macon: Smyth & Helwys, 1995)
Albert W. Wardin, Jr., *Baptist Atlas* (BP, 1980)

For a one-chapter summary of Southern Baptists, see
C. Douglas Weaver, "Southern Baptists," in Glenn Jonas, ed., *The Baptist River: Essays on Many Tributaries of a Diverse Tradition* (MUP, 2006)

Beyond the work of Robert Torbet, for American Baptists, see
Everett Goodwin, *Down By the Riverside: A Brief History of the Baptists* (JP, 2002)
Warren Mild, *The Story of American Baptists: The Role of a Remnant* (JP, 1976)
Henry C. Vedder, *A Short History of the Baptists* (1892), rev. ed. (JP, 1907; reprint, 1969)

For recent accounts of the broad Baptist story in America, see
Bill J. Leonard, *Baptists in America* (NY: Columbia University Press, 2005)
William H. Brackney, *Baptists in America: An Historical Perspective* (Williston VT: Blackwell, 2006)

Pamela and Keith Durso, *The Story of Baptists in the United States* (BHH Society, 2006)

In addition to American and Southern Baptists, histories of smaller Baptist groups give important witness to Baptist diversity. For example, see

John Crowley, *Primitive Baptists of the Wiregrass South: 1815 to the Present* (Gainesville: University of Florida Press, 1998)

William F. Davidson, *The Free Will Baptists in History* (Nashville: Randall House Publications, 2001)

Richard Knight, *History of the General or Six-Principle Baptists in Europe and America* (Arno, 1980; reprint of 1827 ed.)

Ollie Latch, *History of the General Baptists* (Poplar Bluff MO: General Baptist Press, 1954)

Don A. Sanford, *A Choosing People: The History of the Seventh Day Baptists* (BP, 1992)

Bruce L. Shelley, *A History of Conservative Baptists* (Wheaton IL: Conservative Baptists Press, 1971)

Glenn Jonas, editor, *The Baptist River* (MUP, 2006) has essays on several smaller Baptist groups.

Classic texts are cited throughout the book. To highlight a few overviews, see the following on Baptists in America:

David Benedict, *A General History of the Baptist Denomination* (NY: Colby, 1948)

William Cathcart, ed., *The Baptist Encyclopaedia*, 2 vols. (Philadelphia: Louis H. Everts, 1881)

Classic surveys of English Baptist history include

Thomas Crosby, *The History of the English Baptists*, 4 vols. (London: n.p. 1738–1740)

Joseph Ivimey, *A History of the English Baptists*. 4 vols. (London: printed for Ivimey, 1811)

A. C. Underwood, *A History of the English Baptists* (London: Baptist Union Publishing, 1947)

W. T. Whitley, *A History of British Baptists* (London: Charles Griffin and Co., 1923)

In addition to telling the Baptist story at the national level, Baptist history is studied at the regional level. State Baptist histories vary in quality and, in the past, like some older broader Baptist histories, were plagued with denominational triumphalism. Some recent works of scholarly note are

H. Leon McBeth, *Texas Baptists: A Sesquicentennial History* (Dallas: Baptistway Press, 1998)

E. Glenn Hinson, *A History of Baptists in Arkansas* (Little Rock, AR: Arkansas Baptist State Convention, 1979)

Wm. Loyd Allen, *You Are a Great People: Maryland/Delaware Baptists, 1742–1998* (Franklin TN: Providence House Publishers, 2000)

Wayne Flynt, *Alabama Baptists: Southern Baptists in the Heart of Dixie* (UAP, 1998) (Flynt, a Southern historian, gives excellent attention to larger social and economic issues.)

In recent years, scholarly attention has been given to local church histories and how these stories illustrate broader Baptist themes. For example, see

Charles W. Deweese, *The Power of Freedom: First Baptist Church, Asheville, North Carolina, 1829–1997* (Franklin TN: Providence House, 1997)

George Shriver, *Pilgrims through the Years: A Bicentennial History of First Baptist Church, Savannah, Georgia* (Franklin TN: Providence House, 1999)

C. Douglas Weaver, *Every Town Needs a Downtown Church: A History of First Baptist Church, Gainesville, Florida* (BHH Society, 2000)

Second to None: A History of Second-Ponce de Leon Baptist Church, Atlanta, Georgia (BHH Society, 2004)

Analyses of Baptist theology are found in numerous journal articles. Important books include the work of William H. Brackney:

The Baptists (Westport CT: Praeger, 1994)

A Genetic History of Baptist Thought (MUP, 2004)

See also

Timothy George and David Dockery, eds., *Baptist Theologians* (BP, 1990)

James E. Tull, *Shapers of Baptist Thought* (MUP, 1984)

* * *

Chapter 1

Early English Baptists:
The Search for the New Testament Church Begins

The English Baptist story begins with John Smyth. For his writings see W. T. Whitley, *The Works of John Smyth*, 2 vols. (Cambridge: Cambridge Univ. Press, 1915). For example, see "The Character of the Beast" for Smyth's criticism of infant baptism.

Two monographs about Smyth are James Robert Coggin, *John Smyth's Congregation: English Separatist, Mennonite Influence, and the Elect Nation*

(Waterloo ON: Herald Press, 1991); and Jason Lee, *The Theology of John Smyth. Puritan, Separatist, Baptist, Mennonite* (MUP, 2003).

The important ideas on religious liberty of Thomas Helwys are found in his influential *A Short Declaration of the Mystery of Iniquity (1611/1612)*, Richard Groves, ed. (MUP, 1998).

Other important primary sources include the works of the influential General Baptist, Thomas Grantham, who vividly illustrated the search for New Testament Christianity: *Christianismus Primitivus* (London: n.p., 1678); and *The Successors of the Apostles* (London: n.p., 1674). An early Particular Baptist writing was John Spilsbury, *God's Ordinance, the Saints Priviledge* (London: M. Simmons, 1646). Confessions of faith are one of the most important primary sources for Baptist theology. Pivotal confessions penned by Smyth, Helwys and General and Particular Baptist bodies (as well as later important confessions in Baptist life) are found in William Lumpkin, *Baptist Confessions of Faith* (JP, 1959). See also "The Reformed Reader: Historic Baptist Documents," online at <http://www.reformedreader.org/ccc/hbd.htm>.

One of the most popular figures in early English Baptist life was John Bunyan. For his advocacy of open membership, see *Differences in Judgment about Water-Baptism; No Bar to Communion* (London, 1673). His most popular work was the devotional classic: *Pilgrim's Progress*, in E. Glenn Hinson, ed., The Doubleday Devotional Classics 1 (Garden City NY: Doubleday, 1978). See also: Harry L. Poe, "John Bunyan's Controversy with the Baptists," *BHH* 23 (April 1988): 25-35.

One of the biggest controversies in the study of Baptist history centers upon Baptist origins and the role of Anabaptist influence. Historians who favor Anabaptist influence upon John Smyth and the first Baptists include William Estep, "On the Origins of English Baptists," *BHH* 22 (April 1987): 19-26; and Glenn Stassen, "Anabaptist Influence in the Origin of the Particular Baptists," *The Mennonite Quarterly Review* 36 (October 1962): 324-33. Those who focus upon Puritan-Separatist roots and question Anabaptist influence include Winthrop Hudson, "Baptists Were Not Anabaptists," *Chr* 16 (October 1953): 171-79; Lonnie D. Kliever, *Mennonite Quarterly Review* 36 (October 1962); and the writings of B. R. White. The "origins debate" has received renewed attention in recent years. Stephen Wright has strongly questioned Anabaptist influence, but has also called into question the traditional account of the development of General and Particular Baptists as separate traditions from the outset. See Stephen Wright, "Baptist Alignments and the Restoration of Immersion, 1638–1644, Part I," *BQ* (January 2004): 260-83; "Baptist Alignments and the Restoration of Immersion, 1638–1644, Part 2," *BQ* (April 2004): 346-68; and The *Early English Baptists, 1603–1649* (Woodbridge UK: Boydell Press, 2006).

B. R. White was one of the most influential twentieth-century historians of seventeenth-century Baptist life. His important works include *The English Separatist Tradition* (London: Oxford, 1997), and the best survey of this era of

English Baptist history, *The English Baptists of the Seventeenth Century,* rev. ed. (Didco: Baptist Historical Society, 1996). See also "The Frontiers of Fellowship between English Baptists, 1609–1660." *Foun* 11 (July 1968): 244-56.

Specific topics in early English Baptist life are covered in monographs and articles. The stories of women like Dorothy Hazzard are told in John H. Briggs, "She-Preachers, Widows, and Other Women: The Feminine Dimension in Baptist Life Since 1600," *BQ,* 31 (July 1986), 346-47; and H. Leon McBeth, *Women in Baptist Life* (BP, 1979). The relationship of English Baptists and earlier Christian tradition was analyzed in Michael A. Smith, "The Early English Baptists and the Church Fathers" (Ph.D. diss., Southern Baptist Theological Seminary, Louisville KY, 1982). Several recent theologians like Philip Thompson are searching the sources for an emphasis on community and connections to the Catholic tradition. For a sample of Thompson's writings, see "Seventeenth-Century Baptist Confessions in Context." *PRS* 29/4 (2002): 335-48; and "People of the Free God: The Passion of Seventeenth-Century Baptists," *ABQ* 15 (1996): 223-41. Some theologians contend that seventeenth-century English Baptists were sacramental in their view of the ordinances: Anthony Cross, "The Myth of Baptist Anti-Sacramentalism," in Philip Thompson and Anthony Cross, eds., *Recycling the Past or Researching History? Studies in Baptist Historiography and Myths,* Studies in Baptist History and Thought 11 (Waynesboro GA: Paternoster, 2005).

Helpful representative articles of seventeenth century English Baptist life include: J. M. Givens, Jr., "'And They Sung a New Song': The Theology of Benjamin Keach and the Introduction of Congregational Hymn Singing to English Worship," *ABQ* 22 (December 2003): 406-20; Raymond Irwin, "A Study in Schism: Sabbatarian Baptists in England and America, 1665–1672," *ABQ* 13 (1994): 237-48; James Lynch, "English Baptist Church Discipline to 1740," *Foun* 18/2 (1975): 121-35; and J. Nicholson, "The Office of 'Messenger' amongst British Baptists in the Seventeenth and Eighteenth Centuries," *BQ* 17 (January 1958): 206-25. Additional articles about early English Baptists can be found in the *Baptist Quarterly.*

Chapter 2

Baptist Origins in America:
The Search for the New Testament Church Begins Again

In the colonial era the legacies of Roger Williams, John Clarke, and Obadiah Holmes are important to Baptist identity. For the writings of Williams and an introduction by the prominent Puritan scholar, Perry Miller, see Perry Miller, ed., *The Complete Writings of Roger Williams,* 7 vols. (New York: Russell and Russell, 1963). See also Roger Williams, *The Bloudy Tenent of Persecution, For Cause of Conscience Discussed in a Conference Between Truth and Peace* (MUP, 2001). Important secondary treatments of Williams include James P. Bryd, Jr., The *Challenge of Roger Williams: Religious Liberty, Violent Persecution, and the Bible*

(MUP, 2002); and Edwin S. Gaustad, *Liberty of Conscience: Roger Williams in America* (Eerdmans, 1991). Byrd highlights Williams's dependence upon the Bible. Gaustad's book is the best biography of Williams.

John Clarke's important work on religious persecution and the call for religious liberty, *Ill Newes from New England,* is located in Edwin S. Gaustad, ed., *Colonial Baptists: Massachusetts and Rhode Island* (Arno, 1980). Examinations of Clarke's views of religion and politics include: Edwin S. Gaustad, "John Clarke: 'Good News' from Rhode Island," *BHH* 24 (October 1989): 20-28; Bryant Nobles, "John Clarke's Political Theory." *Foun* 13 (1970): 221-36; and George Selement, "John Clarke and the Struggle for Separation of Church and State." *Foun* 15 (1972): 111-25. A recent article has questioned Clarke's commitment to complete religious liberty during his time in England in the 1650s. See Theodore Dwight Bozeman, "John Clarke and the Complications of Liberty," *Church History* 75 (March 2006): 69-93. The key primary and secondary source for the study of Obadiah Holmes is Edwin S. Gaustad, *Baptist Piety; The Last Will and Testimony of Obadiah Holmes* (JP, 1994).

Two extremely important authors for understanding colonial religion and particularly the role of Baptists are Edwin S. Gaustad and William L. McLoughlin. In addition to the Gaustad material already listed, see his *The Great Awakening in New England* (San Francisco: Harper & Row, 1957); *Baptists, The Bible, Church Order, and the Churches: Essays from Foundations, a Baptist Journal of History and Theology* (Arno, 1980); "New Light on the Six-Principle Controversy in the First Baptist Church, Providence, R.I." *Chr* 12 (October 1949): 183-86; and "The Public Role of Baptists in Colonial America," *RE* 97 (Winter 2000): 11-23. McLoughlin is especially important for understanding Thomas Goold and the diversity of Baptist views on religious liberty among Boston Baptists. See *New England Dissent, 1630–1833: The Baptists and the Separation of Church and State* (Cambridge MA: Harvard University Press, 1971); and *Soul Liberty: The Baptists' Struggle in New England, 1630–1833* (Hanover NH: University Press of New England, 1991).

Other helpful books in the study of colonial Baptists include Robert Gardner, *Baptists in Early America: A Statistical History, 1639–1790* (Atlanta: Georgia Baptist Historical Society, 1983); Thomas McKibbens, *The Forgotten Heritage: A Lineage of Great Baptist Preaching* (MUP, 1986) (with a concise examination of Henry Dunster); and Nathan Wood, *The History of the First Baptist Church of Boston, 1665–1899* (ABPS, 1899). See esp. chap. 8, "John Russell's Narrative" about the 1600s.

Chapter 3

Baptists in America during the Eighteenth Century:
The Quest for New Testament Faith
through Revivalism and Religious Liberty

The 1700s in American Baptist life has grabbed the attention of both Baptists and other historians of American religion. Primary sources are plentiful and rich in substance. The observations of Morgan Edwards of Philadelphia are the starting point for many researchers. See *Materials Toward a History of American Baptists*, 6 vols. (Philadelphia: Joseph Crukshank and Isaac Collins, 1770). Another important work for the early eighteenth century is *The Diary of John Comer,* C. Edwin Barrows, ed. (ABPS, 1892).

The story of colonial Baptists of Virginia, so important to the Baptist commitment to religious liberty, has received extensive treatment. Important primary sources include Robert Semple, *History of the Rise and Progress of Baptists in Virginia* (Richmond: Robert Semple, 1810); William Fristoe, *History of the Ketoctin Baptist Association, 1766–1808* (Staunton VA: William Lyford, 1808); and the theology of David Thomas in *The Virginia Baptist; or, A View of Defense of the Christian Religion as It Is Professed by the Baptists of Virginia* (Baltimore: Enoch Story, 1774). An analysis of David Thomas is found in C. Douglas Weaver, "David Thomas and the Regular Baptists in Colonial Virginia." *BHH* 18 (October 1983): 3-19. Social historians have also examined Virginia Baptists. See: Rhys Isaac, *The Transformation of Virginia 1740–1790* (UNCP, 1982). See also Charles Irons, "Believing in America: Faith and Politics in Early National Virginia," *ABQ* 21 (December 2002): 396-412.

For a discussion of church and state in colonial Virginia, see Thomas Buckley: "Keeping Faith: Virginia Baptists and Religious Liberty." *ABQ* 22 (December 2003): 421-33; and *Church and State in Revolutionary Virginia, 1776–1787* (Charlottesville: University Press of Virginia, 1977). The writings of radical religious liberty advocate, John Leland, are indispensable. See L. F. Greene, ed., *The Writings of Elder John Leland* (Arno, 1969, reprint of 1845 ed.). For example, see "Events in the Life of John Leland," "Further Sketches of the Life of John Leland," and "The Rights of Conscience Inalienable."

Leland was a part of the important "Sandy Creek" tradition of Separate Baptists in the South. See William Lumpkin, *Baptist Foundations in the South* (BP, 1961). For a study of the "founder" of Southern Separates see John Sparks, *The Roots of Appalachian Christianity; The Life & Legacy of Elder Shubal Stearns* (UKP, 2001). See also Gregory Hunt, "Daniel Marshall: Energetic Evangelist for the Separate Baptist Cause," *BHH* 21 (April 1986): 5-18; and Wesley Gewehr, *The Great Awakening in Virginia, 1740–1790* (Duke, 1930).

Isaac Backus is key to studying Separate Baptists and the fight for religious liberty in the North. His important primary sources include: *Your Baptist Heritage,*

1620–1804 (Emmaus, PA: Challenge Press, 2001); *Church History of New England from 1620 to 1804* (ABPS, 1844); A *History of New England with Particular Reference to the Baptists* (Arno, 1969); *The Diary of Isaac Backus*, 3 vols., William G. McLoughlin, ed. (Providence RI: Brown University Press, 1979); and *Isaac Backus on Church, State, and Calvinism: Pamphlets, 1754–1789*, William G. McLoughlin, ed. (Cambridge MA: Belknap Press, 1968). See esp. Pamphlet 3, "A Fish Caught in his Own Net," a diatribe against the views of Joseph Fish of Connecticut. Backus's views of church and state, considered less radical than Leland, have received scholarly attention: Joe L. Coker, "Sweet Harmony vs. Strict Separation: Recognizing the Distinctions between Isaac Backus and John Leland," *ABQ* 16 (1997): 241-50; Edwin S. Gaustad, "The Backus-Leland Tradition," *Foun* 2/2 (1959): 131-52; and Stanley J. Grenz, "Isaac Backus: Eighteenth-Century Light on the Contemporary School Prayer Issue," *PRS* 13/4 (1986): 35-45.

The important Philadelphia Baptist tradition is chronicled in A. D. Gillette, ed., *Minutes of the Philadelphia Baptist Association* (ABPS, 1851). Other primary sources include: Isaac Eaton, *The Qualifications, Characters, And Duties of a Good Minister of Jesus Christ Considered, A Sermon Preached at the Ordination of Rev. Mr. John Gano* (Philadelphia: Ben Franklin, 1755); Samuel Jones, A *Treatise of Church Discipline* (Lexington KY: T. Anderson, 1805); and John Gano, *Biographical Memoirs of the Late Rev. John Gano* (NY: Southwick and Hardcastle, 1806). Helpful secondary works include: Dean Ashton, "Isaac Eaton—Neglected Baptist Educator." *Chr* 20 (April 1957): 67-79; Edward Hartman, "The Welsh Baptists in America," *Chr* 10 (April 1956): 90-96; E. Glenn Hinson, "Baptist Approaches to Spirituality," *BHH* 37 (Spring 2002): 6-31 (Hinson examines John Gano); Joseph Sweeney, "Elhanan Winchester and the Making of American Baptist Theological Identity," *ABQ* 4 (1985): 146-64; and Robert C Torbet, *A Social History of the Philadelphia Baptist Association: 1797–1940* (Philadelphia: Westbrook Publishing, 1944). The Baptist use of associations is surveyed in Walter B. Shurden, "The Baptist Association in Colonial America, 1707–1814." *PRS* 13/4 (1986): 105-20. A look at the founder of the Free Will Baptist movement in the north is found in John Buzzell, *The Life of Elder Benjamin Randall; And the Early Growth of the Free Will Baptist Movement.* (Hampton NB: Atlantic Press, 1970).

For a discussion of Baptists and varying responses to the American Revolution, see William R. Estep, *Revolution Within the Revolution; The First Amendment in Historical Context 1612–1789* (Eerdmans, 1990); and the writings of William G. McLoughlin, including "Mob Violence against Dissent in Revolutionary Massachusetts," *Foun* 14 (1971): 294-317; and "Patriotism and Pietism, the Dissenting Dilemma: Massachusetts Rural Baptists and the American Revolution." *Foun* 19 (1976): 121-41. A field receiving increased attention in contemporary scholarship is the role of women in American religion. Baptist women receive extensive discussion in Catherine A. Brekus, *Strangers & Pilgrims; Female Preaching in America, 1740–1845* (UNCP, 1998); and Susan Juster, *Disorderly Women: Sexual*

Politics and Evangelical Women in Revolutionary New England (Ithaca NY: Cornell University Press, 1994).

Chapter 4

Antebellum America—Baptist Democratization, Denominational Centralization, and Slavery, or, Baptists and Their Different Bibles

As Baptists grew rapidly in the early nineteenth century, they participated in the "democratization of American Christianity." This theme is highlighted by Nathan Hatch, *The Democratization of American Christianity* (New Haven: Yale University Press, 1989). Important primary sources about Baptist ministry and distinctives and how Baptists adapted to cultural progress and centralization include David Benedict, *Fifty Years among the Baptists* (New York: Sheldon and Company, 1860); and Francis Wayland, *Notes on the Principles and Practices of Baptist Churches* (New York: Sheldon, Blakeman, 1857). A developing missionary identity—seen in the creation of the Triennial Convention and the overseas work of missionary icons like Adoniram and Ann Judson, can be explored in Thomas Halbrooks: "Francis Wayland and the Great Reversal," *Foun* 20 (July 1977): 196-214; and Rosalie Hall Hunt, *Bless God and Take Courage: The Judson History and Legacy* (JP, 2005).

Religious fervor on the western frontier is discussed in Southern historian John Boles's *The Great Revival, 1787–1805* (UKP, 1972). See also the sometimes humorous Ross Phares, *Bible in Pocket, Gun in Hand; The Story of Frontier Religion* (Lincoln: University of Nebraska Press, 1964). The impact of William Miller's Adventism on Baptists is revealed in David L. Rowe, "Elon Galusha and the Millerite Movement," *Foun* 18/3 (1975): 252-60. Church discipline, especially strong in rural areas, is discussed in Gregory Wills, *Democratic Religion: Freedom, Authority, and Church Discipline in the Baptist South, 1785–1900* (New York: Oxford University Press, 1997).

Important primary sources that illustrate the biblical primitivism and rural localism of the antimissions movement include the "Black Rock Address, Black Rock Church, Maryland, 1832." <http://www.carthage.lib.il.us/community/churches/primbap/pbl.html>; and the writings of Kentuckian John Taylor: *Baptists on the American Frontier; A History of Ten Baptist Churches of Which the Author Has Been Alternately a Member* (MUP, 1995); and *Thoughts on Missions* (Frankfort KY, 1819). An influential secondary article is Southern historian Bertram Wyatt-Brown's "The Antimission Movement in the Jacksonian South: A Study in Regional Folk Culture," *Journal of Southern History* 36 (November 1970): 501-29. The antimissions movement helped give birth to "primitive Baptist groups" in Appalachia. One scholar of this region is Howard Dorgan: *Giving Glory to God in Appalachia: Worship Practices of Six Baptist Subdenominations* (UTP, 1987); and *The Old Regular Baptists of Central Appalachia: Brothers and Sisters in Hope*

(UTP, 1989). See also: Jeffrey Wayne Taylor, *The Formation of the Primitive Baptist Movement* (Kitchener ON: Pandora Press, 2004).

The study of the antebellum South, especially the culture of slavery, is a major field of study in American religion. A few important secondary works include Christine Leigh Heyrman, *Southern Cross: The Beginnings of the Bible Belt* (UNCP, 1997); Donald Mathews, *Religion in the Old South* (Chicago: University of Chicago Press, 1977); and H. Shelton Smith, *In His Image, But: . . . Racism in Southern Religion, 1790–1810* (Duke, 1972). Two important primary sources about slavery are Richard Furman's 1823 classic proslavery defense, found in James A. Rogers, *Richard Furman: Life and Legacy* (MUP, 2001); and David Walker's vitriolic warning against slavery in *Walker's Appeal, in Four Articles; Together with a Preamble, to the Coloured Citizens of the World, but in Particular, and Very Expressly, to Those of the United States of America, Written in Boston, State of Massachusetts, September 28, 1829* (Boston: David Walker, 1830). Southern activism was seen in David Barrow: Vivien Sandlund, "A Devilish and Unnatural Usurpation: Baptist Evangelical Ministers and Antislavery in the Early Nineteenth Century, A Study of the Ideas and Activism of David Barrow," *ABQ* 13 (1994): 262-77.

A now-classic look at slave religion is Albert J. Raboteau, *Slave Religion; The "Invisible Institution" in the Antebellum South* (New York: Oxford University Press, 1978). The popular antebellum African-American Baptist John Jasper received the attention of Virginian William Hatcher in *John Jasper: The Unmatched Negro Philosopher and Preacher* (New York: Fleming H. Revell, 1908). More recently, Samuel Roberts suggested that Jasper's preaching spoke different messages to whites and African-Americans. See "John Jasper—Offstage." *ABQ* 22 (June 2003): 129-41. Disagreement exists over the first African-American Baptist church. See the older claims about Savannah, Georgia in James M. Simms, *The First Colored Baptist Church in America* (Philadelphia: J. B. Lippincott, 1888). For early African-American missions, see Clement Gayle, *George Liele: Pioneer Missionary to Jamaica* (Nashville: Bethlehem Book Publishers, 2002).

The typical northern Baptist gradual abolitionist response to slavery was seen in the views of Francis Wayland: Thomas Halbrooks, "Francis Wayland: Influential Mediator in the Baptist Controversy Over Slavery," *BHH* 13 (October 1978): 21-35; and Deborah Van Broekhoven, "Suffering with Slaveholders: The Limits of Francis Wayland's Antislavery Witness" in *Religion and the Antebellum Debates over Slavery*, Mitchell Snay and John McKivigan, eds. (UGAP, 1998).

Other helpful articles about slavery and Baptists in the North include Bruce Dahlberg, "Before Emancipation: Massachusetts Baptists and the Nineteenth-Century Antislavery Struggle," *ABQ* 21 (2002): 51-64; and two articles from William G. McLoughlin, "First Antislavery Church in New England," *Foun* 15 (1972): 103-10; and "The Cherokee Baptist Preacher and the Great Schism of 1844–1845: A Footnote to Baptist History." *Foun* 24 (1981): 137-47.

Primary sources about the formation of the Southern Baptist Convention include the "debate" between Francis Wayland and Richard Fuller. Some excellent documents can be found in source books (for example, William B. Johnson's apology for the formation of the SBC, the "Address to the Public," in Robert Baker's *Sourcebook*). Two important monographs that deal with Baptists, slavery, and the formation of the SBC include E. Luther Copeland, *The Southern Baptist Convention and the Judgment of History: The Taint of Original Sin* (Lanham MD: University Press of America, 1995); and Robert Gardner, *A Decade of Debate and Division: Georgia Baptists and the Formation of the Southern Baptist Convention* (MUP, 1995). Gardner reveals that most Georgians who attended the organizational meeting of the SBC were slave owners. Baptist distinctives in this era can be seen in the writings of the first SBC president: William B. Johnson, *The Gospel Developed through the Government and Order of the Churches of Jesus Christ* (Richmond: H. K. Ellyson, 1846). Broader important studies of how the slavery conflict in churches foreshadowed the "broken" nation of the Civil War are: C. C. Goen, *Broken Churches, Broken Nation; Denominational Schisms and the Coming of the Civil War* (MUP, 1985); and Mitchell Snay, *Gospel of Disunion: Religion and Separation in the Antebellum South* (UNCP, 1997).

Chapter 5

1850–1950 and Baptists in the North:
The Strength of Denominational Efficiency,
the Challenges of Rapid Change and Conflict

Evangelical historian George Marsden is a recognized expert in the study of the emergence of fundamentalism in the late nineteenth century. See his several books on American evangelicalism, particularly *Fundamentalism and American Culture; The Shaping of Twentieth Century Evangelicalism 1870–1925* (New York: Oxford University Press, 1980). Ernest Sandeen emphasized the relationship of millenniarism and fundamentalism. For his comments on Baptists: "Baptists and Millenarianism." *Foun* 13 (1970): 18-25.

Allyn Russell has given special attention to biographical sketches of Northern Baptist fundamentalist leaders. For example, see "Adoniram Judson Gordon: nineteenth-Century Fundamentalist." *ABQ* 4 (1985): 61-89; and *Voices of American Fundamentalism* (Philadelphia: Westminister Press, 1976). For other leaders, see John W. Bradbury, "Curtis Lee Laws and the Fundamentalist Movement," *Foun* 5 (1962): 52-58; Brenda Meehan, "A. C. Dixon: An Early Fundamentalist," *Foun* 10 (January 1967): 50-63; and Joseph Ban, "Two Views of One Age: Fosdick and Straton," *Foun* 14 (April 1971): 153-71.

Liberal/Modernist trends in Baptist life can be seen in the writings of William Newton Clarke, Harry Emerson Fosdick and the "Chicago School." For example, see William Newton Clarke, *Sixty Years with the Bible* (New York: Scribner's, 1909); Shailer Mathews, *The Faith of Modernism* (New York: AMS Press, 1924);

and Harry Emerson Fosdick, "Shall the Fundamentalists Win?" *Christian Work* 102 (10 June 1922): 716–22. The classic autobiography of Fosdick is *For the Living of These Days: An Autobiography* (New York: Harper & Row, 1956). See also Robert M. Miller, "Harry Emerson Fosdick and John D. Rockefeller, Jr." *Foun* 21 (October 1978): 292-304. For an excellent synopsis of the theology of the Chicago School and individual theologians of this era, see William H. Brackney, *A Genetic History of Baptist Thought* (MUP, 2004).

One "sub area" of the liberal movement was the social gospel. Of the many books on American social Christianity, see: Roland White, Jr. and C. Howard Hopkins, *The Social Gospel; Religion and Reform in Changing America* (Philadelphia: Temple University Press, 1976). The writings of the most prominent social gospel advocate, Baptist Walter Rauschenbusch, include *A Theology for the Social Gospel* (Louisville: Westminster/John Knox Press, 1945); *Christianizing the Social Order* (New York: MacMillan, 1907); *Christianity and the Social Crisis* (New York: MacMillan, 1907); and "Why I Am a Baptist," *Christian Ethics Today* (April 1995): 23. An important new work on Rauschenbusch's life and thought which demonstrates his desire to recover the social thrust of a New Testament church is Christopher H. Evans, *The Kingdom Is Always but Coming; A Life of Walter Rauschenbusch* (Eerdmans, 2004). Some Baptists like Russell Conwell had a message of social "uplift" more like Andrew Carnegie's "gospel of wealth." See Conwell's *Acre of Diamonds* (Westwood NJ: Revell, 1960); and Clyde K. Nelson, "Russell H. Conwell and the Gospel of Wealth," *Foun* 5 (January 1962): 39-51. Other expressions of progressive concerns can be seen in William Brackney's "The Frontier of Free Exchange of Ideas: The Baptist Congress as a Forum for Baptist Concerns, 1880–1912," *BHH* 38 (Summer 2003): 8-27.

Northern Baptists provided leadership in ecumenical efforts and opportunities for women in ministry. Not all were in favor. See Eldon Ernst, "American Baptists and the New World Movement, 1918–1924," *Foun* 8 (1965): 161-71. Often, women were ecumenical leaders. For an analysis of the first president of the Northern Baptist Convention, see Conda Delite Hitch, *Envoy of Grace: The Life of Helen Barrett Montgomery* (Valley Forge: ABHS, 1997). For the broader story of women in ministry, see James R. Lynch, "Baptist Women in Ministry through 1920," *ABQ* 4 (1994): 304-18; Mary L. Mild, "Whom Shall I Send?": An Overview of the American Baptist Women's Foreign Missionary Movement from 1873 to 1913," *ABQ* 3 (1993): 194-209; Wendy J. Deichmann, "Domesticity with a Difference: Woman's Sphere, Women's Leadership, and the Founding of the Baptist Missionary Training School in Chicago, 1881," *ABQ* 9 (September 1990): 141-57; and Olive M. Tiller, "Baptist Women as Ecumenical Pioneers and Leaders," *ABQ* 4 (1997): 292-302.

Throughout the nineteenth century, Northern Baptists did ministry via the societal method. In the early twentieth century, like other denominational groups, they focused on business "efficiency" and centralization. They also confronted issues such as immigration, ministry to African-Americans and relations with Southern Baptists. Representative secondary readings on these topics include: Robert A. Baker, *Relations between Northern and Southern Baptists,* 2nd ed. (1954; Arno, 1980); Robert T. Handy, "American Baptist Leadership in Cooperative Home Missions: 1900–1950," *Foun* 24 (1981): 343-57; David A. Jalovick, "For Country and God: Baptists and the Evangelization of Immigrants in the Late Nineteenth Century," *ABQ* 3 (1990): 184-96; Norman A Maring, "New Jersey Baptists Enter the Age of Big Business, 1890–1920," *Foun* 7 (1964): 341-70; Sandy D. Martin, "The American Baptist Home Mission Society and Black Higher Education in the South, 1865–1920," *Foun* 24 (1981): 310-27; Natalie N. Ogle, "Brother Against Brother: Baptists and Race in the Aftermath of the Civil War," *ABQ* 23 (June 2004): 137-54; and Allyn Russell, "Rhode Island Baptists, 1825–1931," *Foun* 14 (1971): 33-49.

Resources on Baptist distinctives and the idea of the New Testament church include Thomas Armitage, *A History of the Baptists: Traced by Their Vital Principles and Practices from the Time of Our Lord and Savior Jesus Christ to the Year 1886* (New York: Bryan, Taylor, and Co., 1887); and Charles A. Jenkins, ed., *Doctrines: Being an Exposition, in a Series of Essays by Representative Baptist Ministers, of the Distinctive Points of Baptist Faith and Practice* (St. Louis: C R. Barns, 1892). In Jenkins, see esp. Thomas Armitage, "Baptist Faith and Practice," and Albert H. Newman, "Baptist Churches Apostolical."

Chapter 6

In Search of a New Testament Church, Southern Style

As with the antebellum period, numerous historians of Southern religion have pointed to the determining factor of race for Southern society. For example, Southern historian Charles R. Wilson revealed how Southerners maintained their spiritual innocence and adjusted to post-Civil War realities in *Baptized in Blood; Religion and the Myth of the Lost Cause, 1865–1920* (UGAP, 1980). Paul Harvey focused on Southern Baptists, New South culture, and, among other insights, revealed tensions between rural and urban Southern Baptists in his *Redeeming the South; Religious Cultures and Racial Identities among Southern Baptists 1865–1925* (UNCP, 1997). Michael Williams demonstrated the relationship of the economic New South and Southern Baptist development in *Isaac Taylor Tichenor: The Creation of the Baptist New South* (UAP, 2005). How attitudes of racial superiority helped determine missionary praxis is explored by Robert Nash, "Anglo-Saxon Supremacy and the Foreign Mission Board of the SBC," in *Festschrift Walter B. Shurden: Distinctively Baptist, Essays on Baptist History,* Marc A. Jolley and John Pierce, eds. (MUP, 2005). This volume also describes how Baptists became "business Baptists" marked by efficiency and centralization: E. Glenn Hinson, "O Baptist, How Your Corporation Has Grown." See also an earlier Hinson article: "The Baptist Experience in the United States." *RE* 78 (Fall 1981):

190-204. To view Baptist identity through the lenses of race and a growing denominational loyalty, see Bill J. Leonard, *God's Last and Only Hope: The Fragmentation of the Southern Baptist Convention* (Eerdmans, 1990).

Biblical primitivism (and rural response to the New South) was most embodied in Landmarkism. Key primary sources for the study of Landmarkism include J. R. Graves, *Old Landmarkism: What Is It?* (Texarkana TX: Bogard Press, 1880); J. M. Pendleton, An *Old Landmark Reset* (Fulton KS: National Baptist Publishing House, 1899); and A. C. Dayton, *Theodosia Ernest, or, The Heroine of Faith* (ABPS, 1903). The influence of Landmarkism on later twentieth-century Southern Baptist literature can be seen in Joe T. Odle, *Church Member's Handbook* rev. ed. (BP, 1962; original, 1941); and J. M. Carroll, *The Trail of Blood* (Lexington KY: Ashland Avenue Baptist Church, 1931). Important secondary works include Marty Bell, "James Robinson Graves and the Rhetoric of Demagogy: Primitivism and Democracy in old Landmarkism" (Ph.D. diss., Vanderbilt University, 1991); James E. Tull, "A Study of Southern Baptist Landmarkism in the Light of Historical Baptist Ecclesiology" (Ph.D. diss., Columbia University, New York, 1960), published as *A History of Southern Baptist Landmarkism in the Light of Historical Baptist Ecclesiology* (New York: Arno Press, 1980), now revised as *High-Church Baptists in the South. The Origin, Nature, and Influence of Landmarkism*, ed. Morris Ashcraft (MUP, 2000). An overview of the related Gospel Mission Movement is given in Adrian Lampkin, Jr., "The Gospel Mission Movement within the Southern Baptist Convention" (Ph.D. diss., Southern Baptist Theological Seminary, 1980).

The Whitsitt controversy, also a legacy of Landmarkism, was the result of Whitsitt's publication of *A Question in Baptist History. Whether the Anabaptists in England Practiced Immersion before the Year 1641?* (Louisville: Chas. T. Dearing, 1896). See Rosalie Beck, "The Whitsitt Controversy: A Denomination in Crisis," (Ph.D. diss., Baylor University, 1984) and William E. Hull, "William Heth Whitsitt: Martyrdom of a Moderate," in *Festschrift Walter B. Shurden.*

Another Landmark legacy was antiecumenism. See: Timothy George, "Southern Baptist Relationships with other Protestants," *BHH* 25 (July 1990): 24-34; G. Thomas Halbrooks, "The Roots of Southern Baptist Relationships with Other Denominations," *BHH* 25 (July 1990): 3-13; and Glenn Igleheart, "Southern Baptist Relationships with Roman Catholics," *BHH* 25 (July 1990): 35-42.

The study of Southern Baptist women has largely focused on their field of opportunity: missions. For missionary correspondence of the two missionary "saints," see Keith Harper, ed., *Send the Light: Lottie Moon's Letters and Other Selected Writings* (MUP, 2002); and Harper's *Rescue the Perishing: Selected Correspondence of Annie W. Armstrong* (MUP, 2004). Martha Wilson, another early leader, who had conflict with Armstrong, is discussed in C. Douglas Weaver, "From Saint to Sinner: Missionary Pioneer to Gospel Mission Convert—The

Legacy of Martha Loftin Wilson," *Viewpoints: Georgia Baptist History* (2002): 71-85.
Catherine Allen wrote a comprehensive account of the WMU: *A Century to Celebrate: History of Woman's Missionary Union* (Birmingham: WMU, 1987). The WMU's involvement in social ministry is discussed in Betsy Flowers, "Southern Baptist Evangelicals or Social Gospel Liberals? The Woman's Missionary Union and Social Reform, 1888 to 1928," *ABQ* 19 (2000): 106-28; and Carol Holcomb, "Mothering the South: The Influence of Gender and the Social Gospel on the Social Views of the Leadership of the WMU, Auxiliary to SBC, 1888–1920" (Ph.D. diss., Baylor University, 1999). Dissertations will continue to be an excellent source of new studies about Baptist women: Sally Dean Smith Holt, "The SBC and the WMU: Issues of Power and Authority Relating to Organization and Structure," (Ph.D. diss., Vanderbilt University, 2001) and C. Delane Tew's "From Local Society to Para-Denomination: Woman's Missionary Union, 1890–1930" (diss., Auburn University, 2003). For additional study of women's issues, see David Morgan, *Southern Baptist Sisters: In Search of Status, 1845–2000* (MUP, 2003) and T. Laine Scales, *"All That Fits a Woman": Training Southern Baptist Women for Charity and Mission, 1907–1926* (MUP, 2000).
The Southern version of the fundamentalist conflict actually started with the dismissal of Crawford Toy from the faculty of Southern Baptist Theological Seminary. See W. H. Bellinger and Phyliss R. Tippitt, "Repeating Baptist History: The Story of C. H. Toy," *BHH* 38 (Winter 2003): 19-35; and Dan G. Kent, "The Saint's Suitor: Crawford H. Toy," *BHH* 38 (Winter 2003): 6-18. The fundamentalist conflict of the 1920s and anti-Catholicism are discussed in James Thompson, Jr., *Tried as by Fire; Southern Baptists and the Religious Controversies of the 1920s* (MUP, 1982). J. Frank Norris was the focus of Southern fundamentalism. See the work of Barry Hankins: "The Fundamentalist Style in American Politics: J. Frank Norris and Presidential Elections, 1928–1952," *ABQ* 11 (1992): 76-95; and *God's Rascal: J. Frank Norris and the Beginnings of Southern Fundamentalism* (UKP, 1996). See also: Mark Toulouse, "A Case Study in Schism: J. Frank Norris and the Southern Baptist Convention." *Foun* 24 (1981): 32-53.
The moderate anticreedal perspective was seen in E. Y. Mullins who wrote about "soul competency" and other Baptist distinctives in *The Axioms of Religion* (ABPS, 1908); and *Baptist Beliefs* (JP, 1925). See also E. Y. Mullins, "The Baptist Conception of Religious Liberty," in Walter B. Shurden, ed., *The Life of Baptists in the Life of the World* (BP, 1985); and the biography by William E. Ellis, *"A Man of Books and A Man of the People"; E. Y. Mullins and the Crisis of Moderate Southern Baptist Leadership* (MUP, 1985). For similar perspectives on Baptist distinctives that preceded Mullins, see J. L. Burrow, "Centennial Discourse, Dover Baptist Association—1783–1883," *Chr* 3 (April 1940): 70-81; H. G. Hillyer, *Reminiscences of Georgia Baptists* (Atlanta: Fotte and Davies, 1902); and William H. Whitsitt, "Position of the Baptists in the History of American Culture; Inaugural Professorial Address, Greenville, South Carolina, 1872," *The Whitsitt Journal* 13

(Fall 2005): 1, 4-15. For the religious liberty views of influential George W. Truett, see Lee Canipe, "The Echoes of Baptist Democracy: George Truett's Sermon at the U.S. Capitol as Patriotic Apology," *ABQ* 21 (December 2002): 415-31.

The question of whether Southern Baptists had a "social gospel" and what kind has been a topic of scholarly interest. Influential studies include the work of John Lee Eighmy, *Churches in Cultural Captivity; A History of the Social Attitudes of Southern Baptists* (UTP, 1972); "Religious Liberalism in the South during the Progressive Era," *Church History* 38 (1969): 359-72; and Rufus Spain, At *Ease in Zion: A Social History of Southern Baptists, 1865–1900* (Nashville: Vanderbilt University Press, 1961). A recent work that emphasized a social Christianity among Southern Baptists, calling them more "passive reformers," is Keith Harper, *The Quality of Mercy: Southern Baptists and Social Christianity, 1890–1920* (UAP, 1996). Southern historian Wayne Flynt has emphasized the social and economic context in his work: "Southern Baptists: Rural to Urban Transition," *BHH 16* (January 1981): 24-34; and "The Impact of Social Factors on Southern Baptist Expansion, 1800–1914." *BHH* 17 (July 1982): 20-31. See also John M. Heffron, "To Form a More Perfect Union": The Moral Example of Southern Baptist Thought and Education, 1890–1920," *Religion and American Culture* 8 (1998): 179-204.

Chapter 7

1950 to the Present:
American Baptists Confront the Future

In the latter half of the twentieth century, American Baptists remained strongly ecumenical. See Eldon Ernst, "The American Baptists and the Ecumenical Movement after 50 Years," *Foun 4* (April 1961): 112-19; and Olive Tiller, "Baptist Women as Ecumenical Pioneers and Leaders," *ABQ* 16 (December 1997): 292-302. There was also some progressive response to the Civil Rights Movement: Dana Martin, "The American Baptist Convention and the Civil Rights Movement: Rhetoric and Response," *BHH* 34 (Winter 1999): 21-32. Baptist progressives, especially among American Baptists, became involved in peacemaking. See Paul Dekar, *For the Healing of the Nations: Baptist Peacemakers* (Macon GA: Smyth & Helwys, 1993); E. Glenn Hinson, "Baptist Attitudes toward War and Peace since 1914," BHH 39 (Winter 2004): 98-116; and Reid Trulson, "Baptist Pacifism: A Heritage of Nonviolence," *ABQ* 10 (September 1991): 199-217.

The charismatic movement brought a Pentecostal emphasis into church life in the 1960s. For an overview, see Stanley M. Burgess and Gary B. McGee, eds, *Dictionary of Pentecostal and Charismatic Movements* (Grand Rapids: Zondervan, 1988). For Baptist involvement, see Vinson Synan, "Baptists Ride the Third Wave," *Charisma* (December 1986): 52-55. More American Baptists were open than Southern Baptists. See the biblical defense offered by American Baptist Howard Ervin: *Spirit Baptist: A Biblical Investigation* (Peabody MA: Hendrickson, 1987).

American Baptists also reorganized and faced theological and structural challenges and debated their future. See Philip Jenks, "In SCODS We Trusted," *ABQ* 2 (December 1983): 292-303. Some evangelicals were upset because they believed liberalism dominated the convention: Scott Gibson, "American Baptist Evangelicals: Holding On to the Gospel and Each Other," *ABQ* 16 (June 1997): 140-44. See this whole issue on American Baptists and their future. The journey of schism from American Baptists is explored in: Mark Marchak, "In Previews: Conservative Baptists and the New Song," *ABQ* 19 (2000): 222-31; and Joseph Stowell, *Background and History of the General Association of Regular Baptists* (Hayward CA: Gospel Tracts Unlimited, 1949). See also Everett Goodwin's *Down by the Riverside: A Brief History of the Baptists* (JP, 2002).

Chapter 8

1950 to the Present:
Baptists in the South Battle for Denominational Identity

Numerous books on "The Controversy" that began in 1979 have been written. For a moderate perspective, consult Bill J. Leonard, *God's Last and Only Hope: The Fragmentation of the Southern Baptist Convention* (Eerdmans, 1990); Walter B. Shurden, *Not A Silent People: Controversies that Have Shaped Southern Baptists* (Macon: Smyth and Helwys, 1995); and Nancy Ammerman, *Baptist Battles: Social Change and Religious Conflict in the Southern Baptist Convention* (New Brunswick NJ: Rutgers University Press, 1990). The most detailed "blow-by-blow" account is David T. Morgan, *The New Crusades: The New Holy Land; Conflict in the Southern Baptist Convention, 1969–1991* (UAP, 1996). An excellent collection of primary sources is Walter B. Shurden and Randy Shepley, eds., *Going for the Jugular: A Documentary History of the SBC Holy War* (MUP, 1996). To view the conflict at the local church level, see C. Douglas Weaver, " 'I Don't Let Nobody Blow Smoke on My Blue Skies': A Study of the 'SBC Controversy' in a Local Church," *BHH* 42 (Spring 2007).

For an important analysis of Baptist progressives who worked outside the SBC or on its fringes, see David Stricklin, *A Genealogy of Dissenters: Southern Baptist Protest in the Twentieth Century* (UKP, 2000). The difficulties for women in ministry are told through autobiographical stories in Pamela and Keith Durso, eds., *Courage and Hope: Stories of Ten Baptist Women Ministers* (MUP, 2005). For other changes in the Baptist landscape, see Nancy Ammerman, ed., *Southern Baptists Observed: Multiple Perspectives on a Changing Denomination* (UTP, 1993). A helpful look at Baptists at mid-century is found in Sam Hill's article in Ammerman: "The Story before the Story: Southern Baptists since World War II."

For the conservative viewpoint of the SBC "controversy," see James Hefley, *The Conservative Resurgence of the Southern Baptist Convention* (Hannibal MO: Hannibal Books, 1991); James Hefley, *Truth in Crisis*, vols. 1-5 (Hannibal MO: Hannibal Books, 1986–1989); and Jerry Sutton, *The Baptist Reformation: The*

Conservative Resurgence in the Southern Baptist Convention (BHP, 2000). For the memories of one of the two main conservative leaders, see Paul Pressler, *A Hill on Which to Die* (BHP, 1999). American historian Barry Hankins did interviews with conservatives to tell their story: *Uneasy in Babylon: Southern Baptists and American Culture* (UAP, 2003).

Ralph Elliott's Genesis commentary was actually the trigger for the later controversy of the 1980s. See his *The Message of Genesis* (BP, 1961) and Elliott's reflections in his *The "Genesis Controversy" and Continuity in Southern Baptist Chaos: A Eulogy for a Great Tradition* (MUP, 1992). For the second skirmish of the 1960s, see Jerry Faught, "Round Two, Volume One. The Broadman Commentary," *BHH* 38 (Winter 2003): 94-114. An important article written early in the controversy was Walter B. Shurden, "The Southern Baptist Synthesis: Is It Cracking?" *BHH* 16 (April 1981): 2-11.

Charismatic impulses and Calvinistic orthodoxy, though not without conflict, have accompanied the "conservative resurgence" among some Southern Baptists. Edith Blumhofer, ed., includes studies of Baptists in *Pentecostal Currents in American Protestantism* (Urbana: University of Illinois Press, 1999). Ron Phillips is a charismatic Southern Baptist: *Awakened by the Spirit* (Nashville: Nelson Books, 1999). On Calvinism, see C. Douglas Weaver and Nathan Finn. "Youth for Calvin: Reformed Theology and Baptist Collegians," *BHH* 39 (Spring 2004): 40-55. For a look at contemporary issues in Baptist life, see Bill J. Leonard, *Baptists in America* (New York: Columbia University Press, 2005).

The standard account of independent fundamentalism by an "insider" is George W. Dollar, A *History of Fundamentalism in America* (Greenville: Bob Jones University Press, 1973). A representative book by leading Independent Baptist John R. Rice was *Bobbed Hair, Bossy Wives, and Women Preachers* (Murfreesboro TN: Sword of the Lord, 1990, reprint). Sociologist Nancy Ammerman contributed *Bible Believers: Fundamentalists in the Modern World* (New Brunswick NJ: Rutgers, 1987). Historian Bill J. Leonard has written about Independent Baptists: "Independent Baptists: From Sectarian Minority to 'Moral Majority,' " *Church History* 56 (December 1987): 504-17; and "Southern Baptist Relationships with Independent Baptists," *BHH* 25 (July 1990): 43-51.

Southern Baptists and race continues to be an area of study: For example, see Bill J. Leonard, "A Theology of Racism: Southern Fundamentalists and the Civil Rights Movement," *BHH* 34 (Winter 1999): 49-68; H. Leon McBeth, "Southern Baptists and Race since 1947," *BHH* 7 (July 1972): 159-68; and Mark Newman, *Getting Right with God: Southern Baptists and Desegregation, 1945–1995* (UAP, 2001).

Chapter 9

African-American Baptists:
From the Slave Cabin to a National Podium

General histories of African-American Christianity provide helpful material for the study of African-American Baptists. See Eric C. Lincoln and Lawrence H. Mamiya, *The Black Church in the African American Experience* (Duke, 1990); Wardell Payne, *Directory of African American Religious Bodies: A Compendium by the Howard University School of Divinity* (Washington DC: Howard University Press, 1991); and Milton C. Sernet, *African American Religious History: A Documentary History* (Duke, 1999). General surveys of African-American Baptists include Leroy Fitts, *A History of Black Baptists* (BP, 1985); John W. Kinney, "The National Baptist Convention of the United States of America: "Give Us Free," *ABQ* 19 (2000): 232-44; Owen Pelt and Ralph Smith, *The Story of the National Baptists* (New York: Vantage Press, 1960); William D. Booth, *The Progressive Story: New Baptist Roots* (St. Paul MN: Braun Press, 1981) and Lawrence Williams, "The Progressive National Baptist Convention," *BHH, 40* (December 2005): 24-33.

In the late-nineteenth century African-American Baptists formed independent churches and organized at the national level. A sometimes gripping account of slave life followed by an influential ministry is Peter Randolph's *From Slave Cabin to the Pulpit: The Autobiography of Rev. Peter Randolph* (Boston: J. H. Earle, 1893). The organization of the National Baptist Convention and African-Americans' passion for missions is analyzed in Sandy Martin's *Black Baptists and African Missions: The Origins of a Movement* (MUP, 1989). See also James M. Washington, *Frustrated Fellowship; The Black Baptist Quest for Social Power* (MUP, 1986). For more on missions and the involvement of whites, see William C. Turner, Jr. "African-American Education in Eastern North Carolina: American Baptist Mission Work," *ABQ* 11 (1992), 290-308. The writings of E. C. Morris, the first president of the National Baptist Convention, are invaluable for understanding African-American Baptist life at the beginning of the twentieth century: *Sermons, Addresses, and Reminiscences* (Nashville: National Baptist Publication Board, 1901).

Nannie Helen Burroughs was one of the most colorful and influential women in African-American Baptist life. See Dormetria la Sharne Robinson, "Nannie Helen Burroughs: The Trailblazer," *ABQ* 23 (June 2004): 155-78. For a larger discussion of African-American Baptist women at the turn of the century, see Evelyn Brooks Higginbotham, *Righteous Discontent: The Women's Movement in the Black Baptist Church, 1880–1920* (Cambridge: Harvard University Press, 1993). Charismatic influences in African-American Baptist life are readily found on the internet. See, for example, <http://www.newbirth.org/> (Eddie Long ministries); and <http://www.paulmorton.org/> (Paul Morton Ministries, Full Gospel Baptist Churches).

Studies of the civil rights movement continue to be produced. The work of Charles Marsh includes some material on Baptists: *God's Long Summer; Stories of Faith and Civil Rights* (Princeton NJ: Princeton University Press, 1997). Andrew Manis has written about Baptists (white and African-American) and the civil rights era. See " 'Dying from the Neck Up': Southern Baptist Resistance to the Civil Rights Movement," *BHH* 34 (Winter 1999): 33-48; *Southern Civil Religions in Conflict: Civil Rights and the Culture Wars* (MUP, 2002); and his extensive analysis of Birmingham's civil rights leader: *A Fire You Can't Put Out: The Civil Rights Life of Birmingham's Reverend Fred Shuttlesworth* (UAP, 1999). See also Wilson Fallin, Jr., "Black Baptist Women and the Birmingham Civil Rights Movement, 1956–1963," *BHH* 40 (Summer/Fall 2005): 40-48.

The leader of the civil rights movement, Martin Luther King, Jr., is the subject of extensive research in religious studies. His "essential" writings and speeches are collected in James M. Washington, ed., *A Testament of Hope; The Essential Writings of Martin Luther King, Jr.* (San Francisco: Harper & Row, 1986). One prominent expert in King studies is Lewis Baldwin. For example, see To *Make the Wounded Whole: The Cultural Legacy of Martin Luther King, Jr.* (Minneapolis: Fortress, 1992). See also the work of Clayborne Carson: "Martin Luther King, Jr. and the African-American Social Gospel," in *African-American Christianity*, ed. Paul Johnson (Berkeley: University of California Press, 1994) 159-77. A popular biography is Stephen B. Oates's *Let the Trumpet Sound: The Life of Martin Luther King, Jr.* (New York: Harper & Row, 1982). To understand King's career and involvement in the Civil Rights Movement as spiritually motivated, see C. Douglas Weaver, "The Spirituality of Martin Luther King, Jr.," *PRS* (Spring 2004): 55-70.

Chapter 10

Baptists: An International Movement

Literature about English Baptist history is extensive. In addition to general surveys already mentioned, see the following overviews: J. H. Y. Briggs, *The English Baptists of the Nineteenth Century* (Didcot UK: Baptist Historical Society, 1994); Raymond Brown, *The English Baptists of the Eighteenth Century* (London: Baptist Historical Society, 1986); two studies from Ernest Payne, *The Baptist Union: A Short History* (London: Carey Kingsgate Press, 1959); and *The Fellowship of Believers: Baptist Thought and Practice Yesterday and Today* (London: Carey Kingsgate Press, 1952); and H. Wheeler Robinson, *The Life and Faith of the Baptists* (London: Kingsgate Press, 1946). For a broader treatment, not limited to Baptists, see David W. Bebbington, *Evangelicalism in Modern Britain: A History from the 1730s to the 1980s* (London: Routledge, 1995).

Dan Taylor and John Gill were important figures in eighteenth-century English Baptist life. For Taylor's New Connection renewal movement, see: R. W. Ambler, "Church, Place, and Organization: The Development of the New Connexion General Baptists in Lincolnshire, 1770–1891," *BQ* 37 (January 1998): 238-48. For the influential Calvinism of John Gill, see *A Body of Doctrinal Divinity,* 3 vols. (London: printed for Gill, 1769). An analysis of Gill can be found in Timothy George and David Dockery, eds., *Baptist Theologians.* See also Philip Thompson and Anthony Cross, eds., *Recycling the Past or Researching History?* In the "Myth of High Calvinism?," Clive Jarvis questions whether John Gill was responsible for the stagnation of eighteenth-century English Baptist life. Jarvis contends that Particular Baptists actually had a steady growth during the era.

English Baptists took the lead in missionary endeavors at the end of the eighteenth century. The work of William Carey and Andrew Fuller led the way. For a comprehensive overview, see: Brian Stanley, *The History of the Baptist Missionary Society, 1792–1992* (Edinburgh: T.&T. Clark, 1992). Stanley's work has information about Simon Kimbangu who was mentioned in the text. Important primary sources from the era include Joseph Belcher, ed., The *Complete Works of the Rev. Andrew Fuller,* 3 vols. (ABPS, 1845). See especially Fuller's *The Gospel Worthy of All Acceptation.* Additional secondary sources on missions include E. E. Clipsham, "Andrew Fuller and the Baptist Mission," *Foun* 10 (January 1967): 4-18; Timothy George, *Faithful Witness: The Life and Ministry of William Carey* (Birmingham AL: New Hope Publishers, 1991); Roger Hayden, "Kettering 1792 and Philadelphia 1814," *BQ* 21 (January 1965): 3-20; Lisa J. Pruitt, "Possessed of a "Missionary Spirit"? English Baptist Women and Bengali Missions from Dorothy Carey to the Baptist Zenana Missions, 1792–1914," *ABQ* 17 (1998): 285-304; Christopher Smith, "William Ward, Radical Reform, and Missions in the 1790s," *ABQ* 10 (1991): 218-44; and Doyle Young, "Andrew Fuller and the Modern Missions Movement," *BHH* 17 (October 1982): 17-24.

Charles Haddon Spurgeon and John Clifford seemed to dominate the attention of English Baptist life in the second half of the nineteenth century. They clashed in the Downgrade Controversy over alleged liberalism in the British Baptist Union. A sampling of analyses of this era includes: David Duke, "Charles Haddon Spurgeon: Social Concern Exceeding an Individualistic Self-Help Ideology," *BHH* 22 (October 1987): 47-56; William. Estep, "The Making of a Prophet: An Introduction to Charles Haddon Spurgeon," *BHH* 19 (October 1984): 2-15; Willis B. Glover, "English Baptists at the Time of the Downgrade Controversy," *Foun* 1 (1958): 41-51; Mark Hopkins, "The Downgrade Controversy: New Evidence," *BQ* 35 (April 1994): 262-78; and Jack McClelland, "John Clifford and Open Church Membership: The Ecclesiology Behind the Policy," *BHH* 34 (Winter 1999): 69-84. Another figure that often operated outside of Baptist circles was F. B. Meyer. See Ian M. Randall, "Mere Denominationalism: F. B. Meyer and Baptist Life," *BQ* 35/1 (1993): 19-34.

Selected materials about English Baptists in the twentieth century include: Anthony Cross, "Baptists and Baptism—A British Perspective," *BHH* 35 (Winter 2000): 104-21; Michael Goodman, "Numerical Decline Amongst English Baptists, 1930–1939," *BQ* 36 (January 1996): 241-51; and Ian M. Randall, "Arresting People for Christ: Baptists and the Oxford Group in the 1930s," *BQ* 38/1 (1999): 3-18. In *Are We Fundamentalists?* (London: Sword and Trowel, 1995), Peter Masters delineates an independent reformed conservative orthodoxy. For additional information about Peter Masters and Reformed Baptists, see Tim Grass, "Strict Baptists and Reformed Baptists in England, 1955-76," in Philip Thompson and Anthony Cross, eds., *Recycling the Past or Researching History?*

The relationship between Baptists and the Pentecostal movement is explored by Ian M. Randall, in "Days of Pentecostal Overflowing: Baptists and the Shaping of Pentecostalism," in David W. Bebbington, ed., *The Gospel in the World: International Baptist Studies*, Studies in Baptist History and Thought, vol. 1 (Carlisle UK; Waynesboro GA: Paternoster Press, 2002) 80-104. See also Haddon Wilmer, "The Significance of Restorationism," *BQ* 32 (January 1987): 19-27; and Ian M. Randall, "The Myth of the Missing Spirituality: Spirituality among English Baptists in the Twentieth Century," in Philip Thompson and Anthony Cross, eds., *Recycling the Past or Researching History?* In the same volume see the work of Karen Smith on English Baptist women: "Forgotten Sisters: The Contributions of Some Notable but Un-noted British Baptist Women"; and also "The Role of Women in Early Baptist Missions," *RE 89 (1992): 35-48.* For the writings of Anne Dutton, see *Anne Dutton, Eighteenth-Century, British-Baptist, Woman Theologian*, 4 vols., ed. Joann Ford Watson (MUP, 2003–2008). For a sympathetic interpretation of Dutton, see Michael Sciretti, "Anne Dutton, Baptist Mystic" (unpublished Ph.D. seminar paper, Baylor University, 2006).

A standard but older treatment of the history of European Baptists is J. H. Rushbrooke, ed., *The Baptist Movement in the Continent of Europe* (London: Carey Press, 1915). A more recent study is Albert W. Wardin, Jr., "Continental European Baptists in the Twentieth Century," *BHH* 7 (October 1972): 205-10, 234. For a helpful overview of Baptists worldwide, see Albert W. Wardin, Jr., ed., *Baptists Around the World. A Comprehensive Handbook* (BHP, 1995). An important look at European Baptist beliefs is Keith G. Parker, *Baptists in Europe: History & Confessions of Faith* (BP, 1982). See also David W. Bebbington, ed., *The Gospel in the World: International Baptist Studies*, Studies in Baptist History and Thought, vol. 1 (Carlisle UK; Waynesboro GA: Paternoster Press, 2002). See also the writings of Ian Randall, "PIOUS WISHES: Baptists and Wider Renewal Movements in Nineteenth Century Europe," *BQ* 38 (July 2000): 316-31; and "The Blessings of an Enlightened Christianity: North American Involvement in European Baptist Origins," *ABQ* 20 (2001): 5-26. For a specialized older study of the "father" of European Baptists, see: John Hunt Cooke, *Johann Gerhard Oncken: His Life and Work* (London: S. W. Partridge, 1908).

An excellent analysis of Russian Baptists is: Heather Coleman, *Russian Baptists and Spiritual Revolution, 1905–1929* (Bloomington: Indiana Univ. Press, 2005). For additional information about Russia, see: Maurice Dowling, "Baptists in the twentieth Century Tsarist Empire and the Soviet Union," in Bebbington, *The*

Gospel in the World; Vladimir Popov, "Vasilii G. Pavlov and the Baptist World Alliance," *BQ*, 36 (January 1995), 4-20; and J. H. Rushbrooke, "Vasili Pavlov: A Russian Baptist Pioneer," BQ, 6 (October 1933), 361-366. Romanian Baptists are examined in: Ioan Stir, *"Theology of Religious Freedom: The Oncken Paradigm at the Interface of Western and Eastern Cultures,"* (Ph.D. Dissertation. Baylor University, August 2005). Stir also has helpful information about Johann Oncken and his colleagues, Julius Wilhelm Köbner and Gottfried Wilhelm Lehmann. See also R. E. Davies, "Persecution and Growth: A Hundred Years of Baptist Life in Romania," *BQ*, 3 (April 1990), 265-74.

Other helpful articles about Baptists in particular places include: J. D. Bollen, "English-Australian Baptist Relations, 1830–1860," *BQ*, 25 (1974), 290-305; Loston Popo Chambala. "The Development of the Baptist Union of Zambia," *BQ*, 38 (1999), 46-51; Magnus Lindvall, "Anders Wiberg: Swedish Revivalist and Baptist Leader," *BQ*, 32 (October 1987), 172-80; Richard V. Pierard, "Germany and Baptist Expansion in nineteenth Century Europe," in Bebbington, ed., The *Gospel in the World;* and Nils Sundholm, "Baptists in Sweden," *BQ*, 15 (1953), 183-87. For an example of immigrant Baptists in America, see: Chul Tim Chang, "A History of the Korean Immigrant Baptist Church Movement in the United States," *BHH,* 40 (Winter 2005), 58-64.

The history of the Baptist World Alliance has been the subject of several studies. The most recent is Richard V. Pierard, ed., *Baptists Together in Christ 1905–2005: A Hundred-Year History of the Baptist World Alliance* (Falls Church VA: BWA, 2005). An older account is F. Townley Lord, *Baptist World Fellowship: A Short History of the Baptist World Fellowship* (BP, 1955). For an excellent collection of speeches delivered at meetings of the BWA, see Walter B. Shurden, ed., *The Life of the Baptists in the Life of the World: 80 Years of the Baptist World Alliance* (BP, 1985). See also the *BWA Official Reports*. Useful papers are also found in *Baptist Faith and Witness Book 2: The Papers of the Study and Research Division of the Baptist World Alliance 1995–2000*, ed. L. A. Cupit (McLean VA: BWA, 1999). For example, see Richard V. Pierard, "The Globalization of Baptist History"; and Craig Sherouse, "The Formation of the Baptist World Alliance." An insightful look at the BWA meeting in Berlin is W. Loyd Allen, "How Baptists Assessed Hitler," *Christian Century* 99 (1982): 890-91. The role of women is addressed in Karen Smith, "British Women and the Baptist World Alliance: Honoured Partners and Fellow Workers?" *BQ* 41 (January 2005): 25-46.

Selected Websites

Some "official" websites of various "Baptist" organizations, plus some unofficial sites.

American Baptist Churches USA
Baptist General Conference
    <www.bgcworld.org/intro/howwegrew/wegrew.htm>
Baptist Top 1,000
    <www.baptisttop1000.com> "Top 1,000" no longer: as of March 2008 there were listed 7,614 links to "Baptist" websites (of all kinds)!
Conservative Baptist Association
Cooperative Baptist Fellowship
Free Will Baptists, National Association of
General Baptists, General Association of
Lott Carey Foreign Mission Convention
National Baptist Convention, U.S.A., Inc.
National Baptist Convention of America, Inc.
National Missionary Baptist Convention of America
Primitive Baptists
    <www.pb.org>
Progressive National Baptist Convention
Regular Baptist Churches, General Association of
Reformed Baptist Churches of America, Association of
    <http://65.71.233.194/arbca/main.htm>
Seventh Day Baptists
Southern Baptist Convention
Sword of the Lord

Index